Breaking Open God's Word

Breaking Open God's Word

A Three-year Cycle of Reflections on the Sunday
Readings of the Liturgical Year

Steve,
Listen to God's
word in your
heart.
Celine
7-19-16

Celine Goessl, SCSC

BREAKING OPEN GOD'S WORD
A THREE-YEAR CYCLE OF REFLECTIONS ON THE SUNDAY READINGS OF THE LITURGICAL YEAR

iUniverse books may be ordered through booksellers or by contacting:

iUniverse
1663 Liberty Drive
Bloomington, IN 47403
www.iuniverse.com
1-800-Authors (1-800-288-4677)

ISBN: 978-1-4917-7159-4 (sc)
ISBN: 978-1-4917-7160-0 (e)

Library of Congress Control Number: 2015911601

Print information available on the last page.

iUniverse rev. date: 07/22/2015

Contents

Introduction

I grew up at a time when the Catholic Church used *The Baltimore Catechism* as the primary book for educating Catholics on spiritual life. We were considered knowledgeable if we could recite, verbatim, the answers to the questions contained in the catechism. That method faded when Pope St. John XXIII decided in 1962 to symbolically open the windows of church life to let in fresh air. Up until that time, Catholics had known only the basics of the Bible, as we'd neither read nor memorized pertinent passages that would have an effect on our spiritual lives.

Today we yearn to read the Bible so we can pattern our faith on what we find to be an authentic way to follow Jesus Christ. Our Sunday readings contain an Old Testament reading, one of the Epistles, and a Gospel passage. We gather as a community to celebrate the joys, hopes, sorrows, and struggles that we have experienced throughout the week. Two important segments help us to celebrate life as we listen to the word of God and then participate in the Eucharistic prayer, remembering what Jesus asked us to do at the Last Supper when he said, "Do this in memory of me."

I needed to make the Mass more meaningful by preparing myself to study the word of God. That is why I now read the scripture passages during the week and reflect on how they have a significant effect on my daily life. The Bible has become the most meaningful book in my life. After I continued my formal adult education with a master's degree in theology from St. John's University in Collegeville, Minnesota, I went on to receive a doctor of ministry degree in parish pastoral ministry from St. Mary's Seminary and University in Baltimore, Maryland. I also did postgraduate work in liturgy at the Liturgical Institute in Trier, Germany. All of these degrees contained courses in scripture. My educational background gave me the ability to connect the words I read in scripture to the experiences of everyday life.

For several years I have prepared myself to celebrate the Liturgy of the Catholic Church each weekend by "breaking open God's word," assigned as a three-year cycle. During the week I slowly read the scripture passages and then sit quietly, asking the Holy Spirit to enter my heart to help me discern how this word of God can enrich my personal faith life. This exercise enables me to bring a gift with me to church each Sunday to offer fitting praise to God during the presentation of the gifts.

The contents of *Breaking Open God's Word* are my personal reflections representing my own point of view. I sense that Jesus often lived and ministered outside the box of tradition, and as his follower, I try to live my spiritual life authentically. This sometimes calls me to live outside the box. My reflections may shock some, but that is not my purpose. I only want readers to use a creative approach, and I pray that the reflections in this book might spark some personal insights in your hearts and enable you to bring your personal gifts to God each weekend. May the following poem touch your hearts and inspire you to enter into contemplation on scripture.

Celine Goessl, SCSC

Strains of Music in My Heart

The light of the Spirit of God
Awakens me to a new beginning
In which I respond
As I break open God's word
And search for meaning in the scripture
That lies before me each Sunday.

I beg for divine presence
In the depths of my heart
As I discover anew
What you are saying to me today.

My heart beats to the rhythm
Of life enlightened by your word
When I become aware of my heart-breath
That connects with the ancient words
That the Spirit has placed in the minds
Of writers who have given us this word.

I ask that my heart be drawn to your heart
As I reflect on words so ancient and yet so new,
Called to share that word
From my heart and through my eyes,
A gift to be passed on to my readers.

Spirit of God,
How mysterious
To carry you
Into the lives of others as I break open your word:
Your priceless gift to the world.

Acknowledgments

I am deeply grateful to my congregation, the Sisters of Mercy of the Holy Cross, as well as to our associates who have supported me with their prayers, encouragement, and financial aid.

I also wish to thank Jane Weber, S. Kathy Lange, and other friends who read the first draft of the manuscript and gave me precious feedback by correcting many errors that would have gone unchecked. They have been the eyes and heart that helped me look at this manuscript anew as I prepared to send it for a final review by editors of iUniverse.

Finally, I am indebted to my family members and former parishioners in parishes where I have ministered for their financial aid, encouragement, and promise of prayerful support to sustain me during the writing of reflections for *Breaking Open God's Word*. It is from all these persons that I gained insight into what was stored in my own heart as I walked the journey with them and with hundreds of others who have touched my life with their faith.

The Season
of
Advent

Cycle A

First Sunday of Advent

Matthew 24:37–44

A new liturgical year calls us to embrace the message of the religious aspect of Christmas. While society's message centers on gift giving and decorations, it is important to remember the true meaning of this season. When our thoughts and energy follow the pattern of materialism in order to "get ready for Christmas," we easily forget the purpose of this wonder-filled season of Advent. We are called to follow a very different path from that to which society beckons us. The world believes it is not enough to merely lead us in a different direction at this time of the year by filling stores with much that is not "the reason for the season." In fact, they even invade our living rooms with their countless advertisements on television and in our papers and magazines.

The scriptural readings turn us in a completely different direction. The first image we encounter in the Gospel of Matthew today is the story of Noah and the flood. Noah called his friends and neighbors to come with him on a journey of faith, but they only laughed at him and turned away. The flood came with great destruction because people were not attentive to the real needs around them. They were unaware that they had taken the wrong direction in life. We are warned not to make the same mistake but to heed God's invitation to change our lives.

The second image shows us how people disappear from their families and workplaces. It makes us wonder why some people were left behind while others were taken up into the presence of God. Was it because some were more prepared for eternity by their motive to live according to their faith? God tells us to look into our hearts and prepare for our final call. We can do this by reaching out to others as Moses reached out to the people of his day.

The final image is one of a burglar picking his way into the security of a happy household. As we listen to these words during Mass this weekend, let us ask ourselves what robs us of the security

Celine Goessl, SCSC

of reaching our final destiny. Such an account reminds me of an experience I once had in a small country parish. Going into my office one morning, I found the door broken down, all files ransacked, and papers strewn all over the floor. I felt that not only my space but my entire being had been violated.

The primary message in Matthew's Gospel calls us to wake up and watch and to do something constructive as we wait for God to come. We know that Jesus will come again at the end of our earthly lives; the scary reality is that we don't know when this will happen. It is easy to be distracted by the noise of our world, telling us all about a commercial Christmas. This message is so loud that we fail to hear the rumbling of an approaching flood. Perhaps we are so comfortable with our upper-middle-class lifestyle that we do not even hear the thief breaking in upon our shallow, secular, seemingly peaceful space until we have been robbed.

Our liturgical season of Advent gives us time to wait and hope for the peace that comes with the birth of Jesus. It is time to clothe ourselves again with the robe of our baptism and to use it as a shield, much like the way Noah used the building of his ark. The word of God is in our midst like something knocking at the door of our hearts. Let us open up to let God be with us so he can restore our human dignity to its original baptismal innocence.

Take the secular Christmas away, and give us only yourself.

Second Sunday of Advent

Isaiah 11:1–10
Matthew 3:1–12

Today we are called to think about stumps, dead trees, and possibly new growth. Two prophets inspire us: Isaiah and John the Baptist, who envisions our world at peace once again. Isaiah talks about a shoot that grows out of a dead stump, which eventually becomes a fruitful branch and then produces the fruit of justice. I have a bumper sticker on my car that reads, "'If you want peace, work for justice.'—John Paul VI." I believe this is a great way to live life during the Advent season.

John not only raises his voice, but he insists on a path for us to follow. When he baptized Jesus in the Jordan, the Holy Spirit came down to earth and gave us a new vision for a new time. In our own sacrament of baptism, we were given gifts to live out our convictions. Those gifts were poured upon us once more as we received the sacrament of confirmation. We were filled with wisdom, understanding, counsel, fortitude, knowledge, piety, and fear of God. I would add one more gift, that of delight, for it is through our joyful presence to one another that all these gifts shine for others to see and emulate. These gifts might help us to drop the concepts of Isaiah and John from our minds as intellectual ideas and let them move down about eighteen inches—from the head to the heart—to give deeper meaning to our lives.

We are challenged by the voice of John the Baptist, a first-century hippie, unshaven, with rough clothing and open sandals. His call is an urgent invitation for us to come and work beside him and Isaiah, sharing food and life with the poor, working so that war will be no more, and striving to erase the word and concept of killing from our vocabulary. We must no longer allow treating other human beings as slaves and living with domestic violence, drugs, and guns in our society. This can happen if we make positive efforts to straighten out our daily lives and religious practices, along with endeavoring to

Celine Goessl, SCSC

reform our political and economic systems. Then, instead of having to listen to prophets' shouting, we will hear the gentle whispers of peace all around us, coming from our loving God.

We are called today to sort out our lives, clear up our own values, and reassess the values by which we live in our broken society. God has given us all the tools needed to effect a new Advent. Let us stop terrorizing one another and create peace in our own hearts. By listening to the whispers of God, together we will be able to create a new world at peace.

If you want peace, work for justice.
—Pope Paul VI

Third Sunday of Advent

Matthew 11:2–11

Last Sunday, John announced God's wrath, putting fear into the hearts of sinners and calling down fire and brimstone. Now, however, he is imprisoned in a dark dungeon because of his preaching. Such a change of events! And now he hears that Jesus has come with gentleness and joy, eating and drinking with the very sinners whom John was trying to reform. We surmise that John must be having doubts, because the eternity that he envisioned was not anything like the dream that Jesus has. Jesus wants us to stop the injustice, violence, and inhumanity, which was rampant in the world in his time as much as it is today. No wonder John sent his followers to ask, "Are you the one who is to come?"

Today we experience great rejoicing in a paradigm shift that has taken place right before our eyes. John shouted about power and judgment to a faithless crowd, and then a child entered the scene who grew up to become a gentle man of courage and hope. He came humbly, as a baby in a feeding trough for animals. His message is of peace and justice, and he reaches out to the poor and marginalized, walking with the ordinary people of his day. Jesus sends a report to John about his lifestyle of gentleness, compassion, and mercy, and he preaches a lifestyle of forgiveness.

We cannot forget that John had been living a rough life in the desert, dressed in animal skins, eating insects, and drinking contaminated water. He was accustomed to being away from other people and spending day and night in prayer and solitude. He must have expected the Messiah to come preaching repentance and stressing prayer, going to the synagogue, and teaching a new understanding of what life is all about. Without knowing it, John ushered out the old way of life so that Jesus could bring in a new way.

Jesus then turned to the crowd and asked them what they expected of John, someone who lived a rich life of leisure, dressed in fine clothes, and perhaps even was a prophet. What Jesus said

Celine Goessl, SCSC

was shocking and comforting at the same time—that John was a man above par. He immediately went on to say that if we live so as to attain heaven, we will be even greater.

How is this so? Such words do not come without a great price. Our churches may be full this Christmas, but will peace and justice reign in our world? We are asked to have a daily routine of prayer, but will our life decisions help the blind to see, the lame to walk, and the dead to rise? Will you and I be the good news that the poor will hear today?

God has been intense about such a message during this Advent. We are called to help create peace and justice, but it won't happen until we turn our minds and our hearts to the values that reflect what Jesus calls us to do. Let us ask God to help us become instruments of peace by touching our hearts as we go out to help change the world.

We rejoice when we know where we are going.

Fourth Sunday of Advent

Matthew 1:18–24

The spirituality of Advent comes to a high point in the readings today through the hope and faithfulness of a man who is little known in scripture. We finally meet this humble man, Joseph, someone of true honor, even as he stands in embarrassment because he has cut a deal with his future father-in-law, sealing the covenant with a handshake. Joseph discovers that his intended bride is pregnant, though still a child herself. He reflects on what would happen to an unwed mother in his day—a sure stoning by the mob!

Next we meet Joseph the dreamer, whose life has been stressed to the max by an angel's message in a dream. Joseph has been living on visions and dreams for the better part of his life, but this latest dream seemed impossible! The most striking thing about Joseph is the way he accepts this message with complete confidence in God. He gives us an example of the type of faith for which we should strive. He had to be accustomed to giving everything to God. We admire his great patience and humility as he accepts the burdens God places on him. The way in which he deals with what God gives him reminds me of the actions of our holy father, Pope Francis. Francis once said, "Worshiping the Lord means stating, believing, not only by our words, that he truly guides our lives. ... It means that he is the God of our lives, the God of our history." Such a history reaches all the way from Joseph the dreamer to Francis the believer.

God's will was made known to Joseph, not in words but simply in a dream. His heart must have burst with anguish that triggered very difficult decisions for him. So too with Pope Francis, who faces unbelievable decisions in his pontificate. The examples of these men give us the courage to face problems with deeper faith, even when life brings us difficulties that make us feel hopeless and alone. Joseph, the quiet, strong, unwavering man, shows up in this Gospel to teach us how we are to walk the faith journey, no matter what is placed in our path. And Francis, outgoing, vivacious, and just as strong in his

Celine Goessl, SCSC

convictions, shows up today to teach us how to return to a simple, courageous renewal in the church where we, once again, journey together as a Christian community along the path of our Christian journey.

Did God provide dreams and situations of hope, peace, and justice so that we could discern God's will in the hardships of our lives? The lesson today might be that we are called to live with uncertainties, to grasp what our faith teaches us, so that God can dwell in our hearts in a new way on Christmas Day. God wants us to "come home" this Christmas, to open the door and let God in. This is a call to recognize the tremendous shift on our Advent journey.

We have only a brief time remaining in our days of waiting. Let us go to Joseph and Mary with our needs and ask them to be with us and to show us how to make the final preparation for Christ's Mass. Watch for messages from Pope Francis that also will guide us to live into the future.

Jesus, we ask you for the gifts of peace and joy.

The Season
of
Christmas

Cycle A

Feast of the Holy Family

Matthew 2:13–15, 19–23

Christmas was a beautiful celebration set apart from the Sunday scriptures. We will find a personal reflection in the final section of special feast days. Here, we continue our journey from the perspective of Joseph. Jesus had barely arrived on earth before the holy family escaped as refugees, fleeing from violence. Our world situation has not really changed since that time because we have similar violence and problems with immigrants, even today.

Joseph continues to live under the oppression of civic leaders as he experiences real life through dreams. In the Hebrew scriptures, dreams were considered a forgotten language of God until they came alive at crucial moments in Israel's history. Joseph sometimes dreamed when Jesus was in danger. We find him relying on the presence of God in dreams. Are we, perhaps, being called to pay more attention to our dreams as we become attuned to how God slips into our lives through the poor, the oppressed, and the marginalized, who seem to recognize Jesus to a greater degree than we do? It is now time for us, as a family, to stand in solidarity with those in need as we face the struggles and hopes that exist in our own lives.

Ever since that first Christmas, it is impossible to separate our faith from human history, even though our government seeks to keep God out of our lives. Where do we discover Jesus right now? We all dream every night, even though we may not be fully aware of what our dreams tell us. Years ago I took a dreams course in which we were encouraged to write down our dreams as soon as we awakened. I began doing that and discovered all kinds of interesting (and some not so interesting) things about myself. Dreams can be consoling as well as frightening. What would each of us discover if we were more cognizant of our dreams?

Matthew ends his story by accepting the call and the challenge to journey, as God asked him. God knows the reality of our fears, joys, and sorrows. I think particularly of troops coming home from battle to a very different reality because they may be maimed for life. The Gospel today tells us about God's love and friendship that can bring with it peace and justice when we follow God's dream and not our own. As we spend time reflecting on family life, let us become more keenly aware of the possibility of God's dream unfolding in us as God sends messages that we can hear only when we are attentive to the God within us.

We are at a fork in the journey of history, as we are challenged to take the proper direction for our future and our families' future. Trust God's path for us as we dream of a positive, loving, and caring concern for our future and the prospect of a bright dawning for our families in our Christian pilgrimage this year.

I have a dream!
—M. L. King Jr.

Feast of the Epiphany

Matthew 2:1–12

We are still in darkness despite the fact that daylight is slowly getting longer. The stars shine with such brilliance on these cold winter nights that they make me wonder if one of them might have been the star that led the Magi to Jesus. Very much like wise persons, we too seek our Savior, but instead of looking up into the night sky, we are called to look down deep into our hearts as we seek him.

As I read this week's scripture, I became aware of three groups of people who came to visit Jesus. I was astounded by their responses. The first group included the political people—power-hungry folks whose only religion was their own egos and advancement. They remind me of the actions of Herod, a violent person who used others for his benefit. Some of our politicians today do not seem to have changed much in these thousands of years. Some of them still show us how power might be used without the wisdom of light. We can see too many of our citizens, especially our troops, who come to a violent end because of the lack of a Jesus light.

The second group of people included the religious leaders of their day. They seemed to have hidden their noses in books of the law, living in a world of theory and ignoring the love of God, who reaches out with compassion to all people. Unfortunately, some of this group are still with us; for example, leaders who have little concern about the trafficking of human beings or the poor and the marginalized. We might have thought that slavery is dead, only to have it raise its ugly head in our time.

The third group consisted of the wise women and men who had the courage to leave their safe homes and step out into the darkness, where they could see the star that would lead them to Christ. These are the true magi! We only need to open the pages of some of our best Catholic newspapers to find men and women who continue to bring gifts of gold, frankincense, and myrrh to the abused, the poor, the mistreated immigrants, and the mentally and emotionally ill. A

Celine Goessl, SCSC

wise person's gift of gold is a commitment to peace and justice that makes Jesus more visible in our world. The gift of frankincense helps them to be true priestly people as they authentically carry out their priestly duties in response to their baptismal commitment. Finally, myrrh is a gift that shows how we live our trust in Jesus, who has conquered death and given us the gifts that we celebrate at Eucharist. This is a gift that we freely give back to Jesus every time we gather at Mass.

Take time this week to think and pray about which category of people you fit into most faithfully and what gifts you can bring to Jesus in this New Year.

Epiphany—a manifestation of God among us.

The Baptism of the Lord

Matthew 3:13–17

Today, Jesus walks out of his private life in Nazareth into the crowd, where he immediately gets involved with them. Up until now, he had been safe and secure and no one, perhaps not even Jesus himself, was clear about *who* he was. Jesus did not wait on the bank of the River Jordan until all who had come for baptism by John had completed their baptismal covenant. No, he walked with them, among them, into the water to face John and ask for the same ritual.

Matthew, who was the last evangelist to write his Gospel, knows that this day was a turning point not only for Jesus but for all of us. Whereas the other writers definitely state that when Jesus came out of the Jordan, he heard the voice of God, Matthew tells us that God shouted out for all to hear that this beloved Son was now entering upon a life of ministry that we all need to emulate. What was said of Jesus on that day took place with each of us at our baptism. God also tells us we are now God's beloved, upon whom great favor rests; we now have the spirit of God's own life.

The focus is now on Jesus at the threshold of his public life. As we return to ordinary time in the liturgical year, what we see Jesus do is what we are called to do by reason of the relationship that began at the baptismal font. Jesus got involved with all of us. He stayed with people in their joys and in their sorrows. You and I are called today to get more involved so we can deepen our own relationships with one another. This is definitely our vocation—to be involved with anyone who has a claim on us: our children, those entrusted to our care, those dependent on us, our neighbors, certainly our extended family, and the people we will meet on our journey this week.

Jesus was no longer safe and secure as he began walking in solidarity with us. The waters that poured over him at the Jordan were most probably waters of violence that eventually would lead him to a turbulent death. By our own experiences of baptism, even though we were not aware of the repercussions at the time, God has

Celine Goessl, SCSC

called us to walk daily into a tumultuous world in order to do our part to bring about peace and happiness. The violence of our time, the wars and natural disasters, can serve as a reminder that we are called to let the waters of our baptism purify our motives, our thoughts, and our lived experiences as we follow Jesus' example.

Our role this week is to announce Jesus to the world through our actions in our families, our neighborhoods, our workplaces or schools, our churches and, indeed, our entire world. As we begin anew this week, God says to us and about us: "This is my beloved with whom I am well pleased."

How privileged we are to be the hands and feet and heart of Jesus.

The Season
of
Ordinary Time

Cycle A

Second Sunday in Ordinary Time

John 1:29–34

When we were baptized, God planted a special seed of faith in our hearts and from then on, God called us to follow Jesus. Little by little we came to know who Jesus was and that we have a purpose in our lives to let that seed sprout, grow, and blossom. Let us return to the message we were given last week when we accompanied Jesus to the Jordan to be baptized by John. It was the voice of God who announced that we must listen, learn, and live from that nourishment of faith. Then we are able to leap up and shout for everyone to look at the Lamb of God, to see the special person of Jesus with the strength that only God can give us.

Once we know Jesus the Lamb, we are ready to tell others about him. So this week, as we leave church in his name, what will we do to change the world around us so we can bring about peace and help to eradicate hatred, racism, poverty, violence, greed, and lust, just as Jesus did thousands of years ago?

These same terrible crimes that Jesus met with so long ago will continue to surface often in our lifetimes. This need calls us to be the "Lamb of God" with the same call that our Savior had. Before we receive the Eucharist today, we will hear, "Behold the Lamb of God; behold him who takes away the sins of the world. How blessed are we who are called to the supper of the Lamb." This invitation to come forward to receive him should make us want to stand up and shout with conviction that we are ready to carry out the mission to which we were called by our baptism.

At the end of Mass, when Father bids us to go forth to love and serve the Lord, I ask you to remember that we are that very "Lamb" whom we have just received in order to be strengthened for our missions. God's spirit has also come down upon us, and so we courageously go forth to open our hearts and share the richness of our faith that has sprouted, grown, and produced fruit. Let us

Celine Goessl, SCSC

be conscious that we may be the only presence of Christ that some people will encounter in their lifetimes.

God sends us to those who have lost their dignity through lack of faith, through poverty, and through sin that has weighed them down. We have God's gift of the Spirit so we can go and preach, not by words but by the way we live our lives, according to the norm of St. Francis of Assisi, letting that seed of faith grow. Francis sent his followers out to "preach and, only if necessary, to use words." Be the Lamb of God to those in your family first of all, then in your workplace and in your neighborhood, and then in your world. In this way you will take the fruits of today's Eucharist out to others.

Let the seed of our baptism grow and produce fruit.

Third Sunday in Ordinary Time

Matthew 4:12–23

Today we hear Jesus calling us to help create a better world. This is not a new call; it has been heard since the time of Jesus, when he set down a definite plan for his followers after he heard that John the Baptist had been arrested. Jesus then did three significant things: (1) he left Nazareth forever and chose a new home in Capernaum; (2) he began to preach about the reign of God; and (3) he decided that he would not walk his journey on earth alone.

I would like to center on the third point today. Jesus releases the power of the Holy Spirit upon ordinary women and men in various walks of life. Your name and mine are included in the people he calls. As a community of believers, we no longer need to be alone, complaining and criticizing the miserable world in which we live. We are called not only to pray and worship together but to leave our place of worship each weekend and go out to heal, cure, and carry the reign of God into our world.

Matthew makes it clear that Jesus' work is to set up the reign of God in our midst. He announces that this reign is at hand, and from there he immediately lights a beacon on a hill, where he preaches the charter of life through the beatitudes. As he does this, Jesus selects disciples and empowers them with knowledge and courage so they can help spread the good news that the reign of God is at hand. Notice that Jesus does not call priests, Levites, or leaders in the temple but common folk who were fishing, mending their nets, or doing housework. Next, Jesus speaks to us in parables so that whoever wants to listen can truly understand God's word. Then he organizes followers and teaches them at great length. Finally, he speaks to them about the future of the kingdom, where he will return in glory. This is truly a clear blueprint of his mission.

Like his first followers, our minds will have to turn full circle and face the values and standards in our lives because Jesus is about to change our perspective. The rich people of the kingdom will be those who have the greatest emptiness, so there is room for God in their hearts. It will not be the loudest voice that receives attention but the whisper of those who go into their rooms and pray to God in private. In God's kingdom, the first will be last, and the last will be first.

The powerful lesson we learn from today's Gospel is that ordinary people—you and I—are called to an extraordinary ministry and greatness by the grace of God. Our legacy is to take care and educate, to develop peacemaking, to beautify and uplift the poor and marginalized, to nurse and protect the innocent, and to strive for justice by challenging the mores of our culture. Let us take a deep breath and then lace up our shoes for the long journey. We can set our faces toward the east and go out together to make the world a better place for the future. May God go with us!

Don't walk the journey alone.

Fourth Sunday in Ordinary Time

Matthew 5:1–12a

We are all familiar with the story of Moses on Mount Sinai, where he received laws to live a good and faithful life. Today we listen to the Sermon on the Mount, which differs greatly from the Moses experience. He was given laws in an atmosphere of terror and awe, with the command to live honorably. The sermon today comes to us with compassion, gentleness, and peace. It teaches everything we need to know about life and is framed in a very positive attitude. Read the Gospel, and take note that the first and last beatitudes are given in the present tense, whereas the ones in between point to our future reward.

The values of our American dream are at odds with beatitude thinking. We consider the wealthy to be blessed and those who are rich to have great influence and power. On the other hand, the poor are looked upon as a drain on society, and the meek and marginalized may be treated with disdain. We think of the pure of heart as naïve; we encourage those who mourn to seek therapy; and if we are insulted, slandered, or persecuted, lawyers step up to help us file a lawsuit.

Jesus enters this picture with tremendous wisdom, showing us guidelines for a Christian, Catholic lifestyle. He speaks of a new vision with a set of opposite values. We hear how important it is to be poor in spirit, not that we must live without the basics of life but that we have a sense of our own inadequacy and our dependence on God. It is then that we can come to God with empty hearts so God can fill us with grace. Let us live without fear, as though we have nothing to lose. We can surely stand with those whom society ignores.

St. Francis of Assisi shows us an attitude of gentleness with his deep respect for the earth and all of creation, especially of other humans. As a follower of St. Francis, we are called to perform works of mercy and forgiveness without dominating anything or anyone. To mourn helps us to express sorrow for our failings and for the evils

Celine Goessl, SCSC

of our culture. Each day we become aware of our country's evils as we deal with some greedy government figures, with war, and with the death penalty and other injustices we encounter. God asks us to develop an attitude for helping our world, to do what we can to help bring an end to war and misery caused by unworthy motives. Hunger for justice will inspire us and help bring about action for peace.

As we look at the beatitudes and try to carry out their virtues, we realize the message today calls for the most revolutionary social policies that have ever been produced. How are you and I going to be more in tune with poverty of spirit, with gentleness, and with all human rights that call us to be peacemakers? Let us go up to the mountain (to a place of peace and quiet where we can be alone) and invite Jesus to tell us more about his plan for us. In this way, each of us can begin with a few small steps to carry out this vision that Jesus has for us so that we will be counted among the blessed.

We open our hearts to you today as we
listen to your life plan for us.

Fifth Sunday in Ordinary Time

Matthew 5:13–16

Today's message is short and to the point. From our birth, God has called us to a specific vocation, as married people, single people, or people consecrated by vows of poverty, celibacy, and obedience. This is a day to celebrate a lifestyle that conforms to the Gospel on salt and light. I would like to share with you the life that I know best because I have lived it for more years than I want to admit.

I have vowed my life to God as a woman religious. The salt of the world is power, prestige, and possessions. I am to be poor in spirit, as the first beatitude tells me, to live simply and be ready to put others' needs before my own. I am not to seek power over anyone but to share my gifts and possessions in the service of others and to stand in solidarity with the poor and marginalized. I am also to be celibate—to keep my heart open and empty so God can fill it with love to be dispensed to those whom Jesus called blessed in the Sermon on the Mount. I am to strive to reach out to people as Jesus reached out to them. God called me to take a vow of obedience, which tells me to live each hour every day carrying out not my will but the will of the One who sent me to be a minister to the Gospel. My life is to become better by being light to the world and salt for the earth.

But the message in today's reading is not only for women and men religious. Each of you is called to a similar lifestyle. In years past when someone was baptized, the priest put a little salt on the person's tongue and then asked the godparents to light a candle to give to the family. The message of salt and light was there for each of us, so you see, we are all called through the Gospel words today.

We are nearing the time of Lent. It is not an accident that this scripture message is given to us as we prepare ourselves for a forty-day journey in the desert with Jesus. We have responsibilities as practicing Catholics. These responsibilities are brought home to us through the image of being a bright light to the world. How do we keep our lights lit? This happens very well through prayer, self-discipline, and reflection on the scriptures as they are presented to us each Sunday. Each year the church calls us to a Lenten practice of prayer, fasting, and almsgiving. That helps us to light the path for ourselves as well as for those in other walks of life. If we carry out this practice from now until Easter Sunday, no one will be sitting in darkness.

We are all called to be salt for the earth; that is, to keep in touch with essentials by living our common, ordinary lives in a way that gives praise and honor to God so that by Easter, all of those around us can be lifted up to a new level for the glory of God.

Those called to a consecrated life cannot carry on this mission alone. We need everyone who is called through baptism to be salt for the earth and light to the world. Let us go out and set the world on fire with the gifts that God gave us. We can be a support to one another; we can and will make the world a safer, more peaceful, and holier place because we will walk together on our journey in service of others.

Can you hear God's call to be salt and light?

Sixth Sunday in Ordinary Time

Matthew 5:17–37

We need to remind ourselves that Matthew wrote his Gospel primarily for the Jewish community. For this reason, he often includes concepts from the Hebrew scripture. Today he is comparing the message of the Jewish law to the teaching of Jesus. Matthew also knows there are Christians in his audience who, although they are followers of Jesus, continue to worship in the Jewish temple, so with this mixed group of followers Matthew points to some new concepts and asks the people to make a paradigm shift in their thinking. They are called not only to keep the Jewish law but also to go to a deeper level, where they will live a new way through mutual love that Jesus gives them as gift.

The scribes and Pharisees were very careful in observing the law to the tiniest detail, but they were not as observant in showing the spirit of how to love God and neighbor as oneself. They were models of keeping the laws taken from the book of Leviticus, but Jesus told them that they could not separate those laws from the commandments. Jesus gave us another law on how to observe the greatest commandment, love of God and love of neighbor. Loving relationships in the New Testament are a completely new way of life.

The lesson we are to take from today's Gospel is the way in which we are to look at our understanding of the law. We still have laws that have been placed on us in our century. Let us look deeply into our hearts and see what laws control our lives. Perhaps a good measure is in the way that we receive the sacrament of reconciliation. What basic attitudes and values do we have when, for example, we think of the commandments mentioned in the Gospel: not to kill, not to commit adultery, and not to lie? As we think about these laws given to Moses by God, do we examine our consciences in relationship to how our actions affect the people with whom we live and work?

"Do not kill" has a broader concept that includes not getting angry, disrespecting others who are the temples of the Holy Spirit, or

Celine Goessl, SCSC

harboring unkind thoughts of other people, who are unconditionally loved by God. Jewish law had very serious consequences for those who did not observe chastity. But around the world, thousands of people use other persons simply as objects to give themselves pleasure. Think of the exploitation of people who are trafficked for sexual pleasure or to exploit them in the labor trade. It was common in Jesus' time for people to take an oath to guarantee that what they were saying was the truth. In our own day, we often feel that politicians are not the honest people that we expect them to be, and this causes us to be distrustful of them. On the other hand, it is a great gift to deal with people who are transparent and show that they have nothing to hide. If we are truly Christian, we will not ask if something is legal or illegal, but we will judge how the love of God affects our relationships. So it is not simply a question of what is the law but of how we live it by loving God and loving our neighbors as ourselves. This is what we pray every time we recite the Lord's Prayer.

*Today we want to go beyond the law by
doing more than the law asks of us.*

Seventh Sunday in Ordinary Time

Matthew 5:38–48

Matthew continues to weave a lesson for us by using the Jewish scriptures and comparing them to Jesus' message in this new way of life to which we are called. "You have heard that it was said ..." is a phrase that we meet several times, which is followed by "But I say to you ..." When we listen to the message today, we learn so much about who Jesus is for us. It is not primarily what Jesus says but who he is. The example Matthew uses has great significance to his listeners. An eye for an eye, for example, has deep meaning for people who have lived their entire lives by that law. This was the way justice was shown, but Jesus put a new law in its place when he said, "But I say to you." Equality and fairness take on a completely new face.

That does not necessarily mean that we are free of those old concepts. Old ways are still alive in us today. Children argue when they perceive that something is not fair. Adults go further by resorting to suing others when they think they are being maligned. This seems to be a strong motive for many of our present attitudes. What a narrow way of living our law of love!

When we are tempted to retaliate, we eventually will discover that such an action is not life-giving, either for ourselves or for others. Revenge does not promote joy and peace but only tears apart the relationships that we build. True godliness goes far beyond such narrow-minded actions. Jesus tells us of true godliness in the example of someone's striking another person on the cheek. His story also had meaning to the people to whom he spoke. Historically, interpreters tell us when one person struck another person on the cheek, it was considered a serious insult. The godly person was encouraged to turn her/his other cheek and take another insult. This showed that the instigator had no power or control over his opponent.

Another example Jesus talks about is taking someone to court because perhaps that person wants to exercise control over her/

Celine Goessl, SCSC

his opponent. Here is where the new lifestyle comes into play. For example, if a Roman soldier demands that we carry something one mile for him, we should surprise him by offering to go two miles. When we freely choose to go beyond what is demanded for the love of God and neighbor, we show that our obedience is God-centered.

Lastly, Jesus tells us to be generous in whatever we do. Life is not always fair. People are sometimes retaliatory, and we might not be happy with the demands that others place upon us, but we can say, "Let go and let God." When this happens, we will be given even greater gifts than we can imagine. God will show us such lavish love and grace as we move into this new life that we will not fall back into former ways of sin. What a great way to live and to be at peace with God and with others—but even more so with ourselves.

Link the two lifestyles: you have heard it said ... but I say to you.

Eighth Sunday in Ordinary Time

Matthew 6:24–34

Jesus asks us a serious question today: "Why are you anxious?" As we look into our hearts, we see a variety of concerns that cause us to worry about things that we often cannot change. St. Francis of Assisi would most probably tell us to look at nature and learn a lesson from the birds of the air and the flowers in the field. Our response can so easily be to say, "But, but, but ..." Such an illustration from nature brings us face-to-face with the love of God. Our society does not help us do what Jesus asks, so we have to become countercultural in order to become less concerned with material possessions that push God out of our hearts.

Let us look at some ways to remove anxiety or to acknowledge that we might be passionate for more of the world's goods than we need. Again, St. Francis can be a role model for us; he lived simply, sharing even his meager belongings with those who were in greater need. He would tell us two things: that God will give us what we need and that life is too short to put stress on our hearts with anxiety and worry. Look at material things and decide whether they help or hinder your call to holiness, or whether they get in the way of carrying out the mission that Christ has entrusted to you. If having possessions fills your heart as well as your home and causes undue worry, where is there room for God to come to you with greater gifts that bring you peace, happiness, and eternal life?

Each day we pray, *give us this day our daily bread.* We humbly ask God to share with us what we really need to live and grow. Our faith tells us that we should trust that God hears our prayers and will grant whatever is good for us. We also pray, *lead us not into temptation.* Anxiety and mistrust of God is what we might call mammon. When our minds and hearts are fighting with mammon (i.e., material riches), we cannot serve both mammon and God.

God knows our needs even before we ask, but do we know the difference between our needs and our wants? We really cannot serve

God with our minds, hearts, and souls when we are entangled in such things as worldly goods and prestige to the degree that they occupy our time and energy.

As we approach the season of Lent, look at your excess in clothing and food. If you look in your closet and think you have nothing to wear, but your racks are bulging with enough to clothe three or four people, consider packing up everything you haven't worn in a year and take it to the St. Vincent de Paul store. If you open your refrigerator door and say you have nothing to eat—meaning nothing appeals to you—it may be time to look at a way of living more simply. If you give away half of your food and clothing, it might surprise you to discover that you are not wanting in anything. It also would be a good time to empty your heart and invite Jesus into that empty space.

Let us return to the opening question: "Why are you so anxious?"

Seek first God's reign.

The Season
of
Lent

Cycle A

First Sunday of Lent

Matthew 4:1–11

Lent is a time for us to begin a new life in Christ. We make ourselves ready to join Jesus in the desert of our hearts so that we can pay attention to the things in life that really matter. This is not so much a time for denying ourselves as it is an opportunity for returning to good Catholic practices that we have neglected since last Lent—prayer, fasting, and almsgiving.

Jesus had to deal with three temptations. The first had to do more with trust than with food. In our affluent lives today, where is the food when a child dies every two seconds from starvation? God gives food but people sometimes selfishly refuse to share their overabundance. I have been involved in "Feed My Starving Children," an international program that asks people who have plenty to share food with starving children in third-world countries, and I was privileged to help package meals. Families pick up the food at locations near them to keep their children from starving. My concern with this charitable work, however, is that the food not be intercepted by a greedy government and sold at a high rate of interest.

The second temptation has to do with putting God to the test. We want signs from God, but a great temptation might be to want nothing to do with the hardships and failures that come with living in this imperfect world. It might have a lot to do with wanting to experience moments of resurrection. God is with us even when we are struggling with failure and are being treated poorly by those who hate us.

The third temptation talks about the unique place of God in our everyday lives, especially in our prayer lives. Are we remaining faithful to God when we give up our values by lying, allowing injustices, and cutting corners when it comes to prayer and giving time to God on a daily basis? I ask myself if I use as much time to deepen my relationship with God as I do sitting in front of the television or going out to to local bars or places of ill repute or even getting into the human trafficking scene. What lessons can we learn from these three temptations? The first lesson is about trust. Bread is symbolic of what we need for a healthy life—no more, no less. There is a great concern about obesity in our country today. Can we seek to balance the appetites of our bodies with the call of God to a deeper prayer life? The second lesson makes us look at whether we are sensationalizing our faith in God. I believe we have heard bogus evangelizers on television or on the Internet and through others who tempt us to live our faith more superficially. I was struck by an advertisement in one of our local theaters that was shown before the main movie began. It was a fundamentalist evangelizer who wanted us to come to his church because they have "lots of fun"—funky music, games for all ages, and a variety of activities—but he made no mention of a solid worship of God in prayer. The third lesson encourages us to strip away our blindness and peel off the layers of disguise that tell us to eat, drink, and be merry for tomorrow we may die. It is not in our own best interests to settle for a kingdom in this world and not look to an unknown future.

This week we are given a distinct call to return to God through prayer, fasting and almsgiving. We can choose to take the forty days in the desert of our hearts in order to return to a faith-filled focus on God, or we can continue to put our God to the test. However, let's seriously think about returning to a deeper relationship with God and with family, friends, and community and not journeying toward a future that holds only empty and fleeting promises.

Take the road less traveled.

Second Sunday of Lent

Matthew 17:1–9

Jesus asks us this week to leave behind our everyday concerns, our old habits, and our meaningless patterns of life and to walk with him up the mountain. The reason he goes up a high mountain is to seek God's guidance in quiet prayer. Today, let us take time to find a place of peace and serenity, a place where we will be open to the voice of God as God calls us to listen. Lent, for me, is about taking time and space to be with Jesus in prayer.

Let us go back to the three things the church asks us to do as we observe the season of Lent: fasting, almsgiving, and prayer. Fasting is not only giving up food; perhaps we also can fast from noise this Lent. Turn off the television or radio, and set your mind at ease by being attentive to the sound of silence. Have you gone outside lately and listened to the sound of birds singing God's praises? They seem to think that spring already has arrived. This can be an environmental experience that calls you to fast from your noisy environment or at least an opportunity to give your ears a well-deserved rest.

To practice alms, we can use our ears to be attentive to people, especially those we might have neglected lately. When someone demands your attention this week, give wholehearted attention to that person as though nothing else at the moment is important. Perhaps God is asking us to spend more time at home with our families, to avoid watching television during meals, or to sit with the elderly who suffer from dementia. The best form of almsgiving may be taking time to listen attentively without being bored.

Fasting from the noise around us and learning how to listen attentively to others is a wonderful preparation for the third Lenten practice, that of engaging in a deeper form of prayer. One practice that I find rewarding is picking up my Bible sometime during the week and reading the scripture for the following Sunday. Then I begin breaking open God's word by mulling over a passage or sentence and quietly waiting for God to speak to me.

Celine Goessl, SCSC

These forms of Lenten practices are not ends in themselves but ways of preparing us for the moment when we will see God face-to-face, just as the three disciples were given a split second to see the real Jesus on the mountain. Think of what we might miss if we don't take the opportunity to climb the mountain of the Lord and spend some quality time with Jesus every day this week.

We have been to the mountain.

Third Sunday of Lent

John 4:5–42

This is a lengthy story but full of rich ideas about the journey upon which we have embarked. If you have the *Rite of Christian Initiation of Adults*, referred to as the RCIA process, in your parish, you will notice that catechumens will celebrate a ritual for the next three weeks called the Scrutinies. In solidarity with them, we can place ourselves at the well where the lonely Samaritan woman comes to draw water each day. Below is a different kind of reflection and can be used as a monologue to teach the lesson that Jesus has in store for us. I have done this in a parish by creating an action homily.

"I am an outcast, coming to the well in the heat of noontime because the women in this town will have no use for such a sinful woman. I meet an extraordinary man sitting at the well. I have no fear of men because I have been married more than a few times. Some of them I have married and others—well, they were not worth engaging in a serious commitment. I am anxious to strike up a conversation with this man.

"As I approach the well, I recognize that he is a Jew, and Jews and Samaritans are not fond of each other. The Jew asks me for a drink, and I answer him with scorn written on my face and the sound of arrogance in my voice. We talk for a short while, until I realize that this man is getting under my skin. I make an effort to change the subject by telling him that I know he is a Jew, but he still calmly turns my questions into questions of his own. I finally give up and sit down to listen to him.

"I am beginning to think that this man is different from those with whom I have lived in my past. Although I do not want this to happen, he is causing a stir in the depths of my heart. Suddenly, I have no time to draw water because I need to run back to Samaria and tell the people about this incredible man! I beckon them to drop their own buckets of stagnant water and come to hear how he speaks of living water. The townspeople do not think I have any worth but,

Celine Goessl, SCSC

strangely enough, they follow me back to the well. I think all of us should spend the rest of our lives carrying out the message we heard from him today.

"We have spent far too much time gossiping about others, putting others down, looking out only for our own profits, cheating, and lying. We may have been too apathetic to use the time God has given us this Lent, but we still have four weeks to turn our lives around. It is not too late—come! Jesus is waiting for you and me."

Let us live each day as though it were the last day of our lives.

Fourth Sunday of Lent

John 9:1–41

Blindness is one of the most traumatic experiences in life. My mother was blind during the last ten years of her life. From her experience, she taught all her children very profound lessons, not only physical but spiritual, that would carry us through our journey with great appreciation for the gift of sight. Restoration of physical sight is shown in today's story as merely the outer shell of a miracle. My mother's life did not have that kind of miracle. Her miracle was an inner vision that came to her because of her blindness, which took away some of the trauma in her life and made her a more compassionate and loving person.

She taught us to look into our hearts and open them to God's light. Her lack of sight brought other gifts to her, as we realized her other senses had become more keenly aware of walking in the light of Christ and did not depend on light from the outside. Because of her acceptance, she taught us to look at the blind spots in our lives in order to let the light of Christ shine through us as beacons of light to others.

Jesus spit on the ground and made a salve to rub on the eyes of the blind man. This reminds me of the story of God creating human life from the dust of the earth. It is also a reminder of what happens when we are touched by the waters of baptism. The blind man did not see immediately. Jesus told him to go and wash in the pool of Siloam—a word that means "sent." The story today is linked to the story of the woman at the well, another baptismal story denoting a conversion of the heart. It is the same lesson with this man, but he had to let his newfound sight develop slowly. When neighbors asked who had cured him, bit by bit he referred to Jesus as a prophet and finally as the Lord.

Like my mother, what this blind man lacked in sight he eventually gained, little by little, in insight. All he wanted in the beginning was his physical sight, and once God granted his plea, he began to build a new relationship with Jesus. With this wonderful gift came a clearer vision of realizing the deeper realities of life, coupled with faith to see what God intended him to do with his life

We have now passed the mid-mark of Lent. Today God calls us to cast off our darkness and walk in the light of Christ; to become beacons to a world that lives in the darkness of sin. Do you and I have the twenty-twenty vision that enables us to be the light of Christ by letting a spark of light break into our hearts as we journey toward the resurrection of Easter? Jesus offers us a new vision so we may see well enough to help others come into his light.

Let us put on new glasses and walk in the light of Christ.

Fifth Sunday of Lent

John 11:1–45

Most of us, at some time, have stood at the grave of a beloved one, and so we know the pain and anguish of Martha and Mary. I remember standing at the grave of my younger brother and pronouncing the final words of blessing as I wept over the loss of his young life. It was an opportunity to bring things into perspective and to have a chance to reflect on the truly important things in life.

What happened to Lazarus also happens to us every day of our lives in so many ways. Jesus calls us forth from our tombs, but we might be tempted to refuse to come out and experience freedom. Why is it that sometimes we prefer to remain bound, helpless, frustrated, blind, and deaf to the grace of God? It is at such times that we need the Christian community to roll away the stone and take the bandages from our arms and legs, remove the stones that have covered our eyes, take the cotton out of our ears, and bring us to life once more to live in the midst of our families and neighbors so that we can continue to grow in love with their help.

A few times in this story about Lazarus, we sense that Jesus truly loved his family, that they definitely were part of an intimate circle. Jesus wept—a human result of the sadness of a heart full of pain and sorrow. Somewhere I read that this shows what happens when a "head cohabitates with a distressed heart." Most of us have been in that situation, and this feeling causes us to wonder why Jesus arrived only after four days even though he knew of Mary's and Martha's sorrow. We could stop here and have a theological discussion about death and grief, loss and mourning, but perhaps there is a deeper question we need to contemplate. Do we believe that Jesus loves us as much as he loved Lazarus, Martha, and Mary? If so, why are we so frightened of the possibility of having our "tombs" opened so that the rot of our sinful lives will be exposed? The voice of God is calling each one of us to help others he calls forth from tombs of violence or unnecessary pain and sorrow. That same voice is calling us to

Celine Goessl, SCSC

live compassionate lives by following the ideal of "love, not war." We are called to pray for our government so our legislators will live the Golden Rule of doing to others what they would want done to themselves.

God still weeps today because there is sin and violence of all kinds present that destroys human life. Each day our newscasters speak of physical death and killing, of economic injustice, of continued oppression of the poor. We stand at the tomb of the living, and when we see all the destruction that we have caused, we call one another forth by breaking open God's word. Now is the time to encourage ourselves and others to live the life of resurrection to which God is constantly calling us.

There is not a more powerful story in the Gospel than what we have heard today. We know that Jesus put his own human life on the line by journeying toward Jerusalem when he knew the leaders were looking for a chance to kill him. Let us put our lives on the line this week and do something to confront evil, violence, injustice, and inequality so that we will be ready to walk the last few miles to Calvary with Jesus.

The road to Calvary is steep and narrow.

Holy Week
and
the Season of Easter

Cycle A

Palm Sunday of the Lord's Passion

Matthew 21:1–11 (*The Gospel read at the blessing of the palms*)

The following reflection uses the Gospel for the blessing of palms because it sets the stage for the entire week. Jesus is not fooled by the shouts of the crowd who hail him as a great king. He knows that the palm branches they wave will soon become the cross, and the shouts of triumph will soon be overshadowed by the jeers of a mob calling for his death. Without being entirely aware of what is about to happen, we turn our own faces toward Jerusalem. We see Jesus give up his life for us; he beckons from the cross that we do the same for others.

We are called today to reflect on this final lesson of Jesus as he prepares for his own death. Imagine yourself to be the beast of burden carrying Jesus through the streets of Jerusalem. Gratefully carry this burden because it will be up to you to be the body of Christ when he is no longer with us on earth.

Or imagine yourself standing among the people at the side of the road as Jesus passes by. What kind of cloak will you put on this beast of burden to make the ride more comfortable? As I reflect on my Franciscan heritage, I would choose compassion, hospitality, peace of heart, and simplicity and give it all to Jesus as I continue my Holy Week journey.

We also will need branches from a tree to lay on the ground to make a fitting path for him. Reflect on our branches of prayer, fasting, and almsgiving during Lent, and offer this to Jesus as a final gift as he dismounts and lays down his life for us.

The time of his glorious entry into Jerusalem has been short-lived. As we listen to the reading of the Passion today, it helps us to realize that circumstances in life can quickly change. We need to be ready to make such a paradigm shift when surprises or burdens enter our personal lives.

Let us lay down our proud hearts and take up whatever crosses await us. The palms we bring home today will be symbolic of glory and a sign of our conversion. Let us keep those palms someplace visible in our homes because this week will be a long week, and we will need reminders that the burdens of this life are nothing compared to what awaits us on Easter morning!

"Hosanna," followed by "Crucify him," burns
in our ears and saddens our hearts.

Feast of the Easter

John 20:1–9

The Gospels of Matthew, Mark, and Luke talk about another Mary who accompanied Magdalene, but only John tells us that Mary came to the tomb alone. There were no angels, no gardener around, but only Mary was chosen for this early morning encounter. I wonder why Mary, a woman, was sent to tell the leaders of the church that Christ had risen. Only later would Mary Magdalene return and find the gardener, whom she begged to help her and who would call her name and open her eyes as she received the gift of recognizing him for whom she was yearning. How awesome!

We do not usually talk about cemeteries on Easter Sunday, but we realize that our faith did not begin at the stable in Bethlehem, or at Jesus' baptism in the Jordan, or even on Calvary; it was at the empty tomb in a cemetery. Have you ever thought of a cemetery as a fitting place to announce the Easter mystery? When I go back home, I often stop at our parish cemetery to renew my memories and reminders of resurrection as I stand at family graves and remember each of those I dearly love and keep tucked in the recesses of my heart.

We also can return to Mary Magdalene to renew our faith and grow in strength by viewing the graves of those who led holy lives and are now laid to rest until their bodies will rise on the last day. Our faith tells us that these persons are alive and are celebrating Easter in heaven. Easter tells us that our graves also will be empty and that death is only for an instant of passage from this world to the next.

Let us take time this week to walk with Mary Magdalene or with Peter or John. Drive out to the local cemetery and feel the excitement in your heart at the faith that has grown in you during Lent because you believe in the resurrection. It is easy enough to be faith-filled during such experiences in life, but there also will be times of emptiness. Ask any saint how he dealt with the emptiness he felt at the sight of this empty tomb. This week, also take time to write a personal Easter story, and outline the ups and downs of daily life and how to deal with them in a positive way. It is a good time to look at your faith and realize how strong it has become as you reflect on your life as a Christian.

Next week, we will have something to bring to the liturgy to show Jesus how deep our faith has become. As Jesus looks into our hearts, he will give us the same message he gave to Thomas as he looked into his heart when the two met shortly after Jesus rose from the dead.

Blessed are those who have not seen and yet have believed.

Second Sunday of Easter

John 20:19–31

The joy of the Easter encounter continues to warm our hearts each time we recall the experiences of the past week. Perhaps you are still locked up in your world, as were the apostles, but I hope you are out and about, living and discussing the encounters our risen Jesus had with Mary Magdalene, the couple on the road to Emmaus, and even Thomas. It amazes me that Jesus would appear to Mary Magdalene and to the couple on the road before he went back to his own chosen group. These "outsiders" already experienced the gift of the Holy Spirit and the peace that Jesus brings. I think perhaps it was because their hearts were more ready to understand Jesus' message. Thomas was also a courageous person who left the locked upper room. Did he do this because he wanted to assure himself of the good things going on outside the room, while the rest remained too frightened to venture out?

Unfortunately, Thomas was not present when Jesus came to breathe the peace of the Holy Spirit on those in the upper room. So much happens in our scripture today that we need to take it apart and look at the pieces of such good news. Jesus comes to bring peace to those who had run away and had forsaken him such a short time ago. His gift goes even further than our imagination can stretch. He is about to send them out on a mission; he adds the gift of a mission that releases them from fear and catapults them back into the world with renewed courage to do that which remains before them. Jesus' love for them shows itself to be so profound that words just cannot explain what was happening. We hear Jesus express his deep love for them simply by a sigh or a breath. He breathes his Spirit on them, and new life explodes within their hearts.

The second half of our story today takes place a week later—it is too much to take in at one sitting, both for the disciples and for us. He comes again with the same greeting of peace, and this time he calls Thomas to profess his faith. Thomas can be held up as a

Celine Goessl, SCSC

model for what we need in the Christian community these days. He teaches us how to act when everyday difficulties or questions about happenings in certain corners of the church body are brought to light (e.g., the clergy-abuse situation and the struggle Pope Francis has with trying to get everyone on board regarding our ecumenical outreach to all people). Thomas could very likely be the patron for our bishops as they face the problems that plague them in their office as servant leaders.

Once the facts were laid out for Thomas, he humbled himself and made a profound act of faith on which he would continue to live. Let us pray for our local bishops this week, that they too will respond with the humility and courage that we see in Thomas.

Make us poor and humble of heart.

Third Sunday of Easter

Luke 24:13–35

This story has a profound depth that can renew our faith. It is the story of our journey through life and how we can make that pilgrimage profitable by using the graces we receive at Eucharist, our personal prayer, and breaking open God's word in the scriptures. Once we reflect on this story, we come to realize that we can walk our journey without the physical presence of Jesus because, as we break open God's word, our eyes will be able to see, with faith, all that we need to accompany our life journeys.

The climactic story is set on the eve of Easter. Cleopas and most likely his wife are disappointed that the Messiah did not free them from their life of slavery. It appears they had asked for the weekend off from work in order to go to Jerusalem to celebrate the Passover. Some scripture scholars believe that Emmaus was a group of barracks for the Roman soldiers, of which this couple were slaves—they did the work no one else wanted to do. They had hoped there would be an end to their struggle for justice and that Israel might be returned to its original glory. What a heartbreak to return home with seemingly nothing changed in their lives! That was what saddened their hearts as they walked home—that is, until a stranger caught up with them and engaged in a heartwarming conversation with them.

They finally arrived back at their humble home and offered hospitality to the stranger for the night. In the dark of the night, they were willing to share their meager worldly goods with him. Their hospitality paid off when they sat down to a simple meal. After the meal, the stranger left their physical presence, but their hearts were on fire and their eyes were opened, so much so that they rushed the entire seven miles back to Jerusalem to share the good news with the disciples.

This story has several levels of meaning. I want to share with you this good news as it relates to the Eucharist. One place we are assured of encountering Jesus is at Eucharist. On that road to Emmaus, let us

Celine Goessl, SCSC

share three elements of the Eucharist: (1) the people of God walking together; (2) God's word broken open so our eyes of faith can see; and (3) the sharing of a meal.

Cleopas and his wife probed a deeper reality of their experience. They remembered that they felt overwhelmed because of the recent events. They had lost hope in Jesus, but by the time the stranger fell in step with them, they were ready to be led to a deeper reality, to hear the word that made their hearts burn. We also need such a word to take away the dimness of our faith.

Next, bread was broken and shared, and as Jesus handed it to Cleopas and his wife, their eyes were opened, and they recognized him. Ordinary food changes into energy for our bodies, but Eucharistic food changes us into Christ's energy. They no longer were tired and downtrodden but had the courage and energy to rush back to share their experience.

So when our Eucharist ends this weekend, I hope you will leave church with the fire of the word of God in your heart and energy surging through your body, as you are sent out to "love and serve the Lord." Each Eucharist places in our hearts a tremendous gift that tells us we must go out and share what we were so freely given.

Happy sharing this week.

Fourth Sunday of Easter

John 10:1–10

Jesus gives us a lovely pastoral picture in today's Gospel. He speaks of a shepherd who gathers the sheep every night into an area surrounded by a fence or a wall without a gate. After the shepherd examines each sheep, calling them by name, he soothes any wounds with a healing touch of oil and then gives each one a drink of cool water. Then he lies across the opening to keep the herd safe from any type of animal or human. Such a procedure is what any faithful shepherd would do.

During this Easter journey, I also feel my life being examined each evening as I say an Act of Contrition before retiring. I ask Jesus to look at my bruises and scratches so he can heal them. Then I am offered a drink from his overflowing cup of grace. The next morning I am called again to be a leader in the Catholic community by reason of my vocation and chosen profession. This Sunday is called Vocation Sunday, and we hear each of us called by name and given a place in the reign of the risen Lord. Jesus' flock will always be in need of a strong and compassionate leader, but does this leader necessarily have to be a celibate male who is ordained? Perhaps there is a reason why there is a crisis in the number of people who choose priesthood or sisterhood today. Could this be a wakeup call to all of us to become more aware of our baptismal commitment as servant leaders in the church?

We are living in the age of the laity! It has been many years since the Second Vatican Council, which called us to look at vocation, or a call from God, in an entirely new way. Why are we so slow to heed that call, as we keep insisting that leadership is for priests and sisters? In my many years as a pastoral minister, the best years were those in which the laity in the parish were called forth to use their God-given gifts to build up the body of Christ. In parishes where this happens, the love of Christ is alive and well, and people come to know, personally, the risen Jesus. When the ordinary person in the pew is encouraged to come forward to share his/her gifts with the community, ownership happens. The flock, under the guidance of the Holy Spirit, grows into a wonderful group of committed Catholics who know they are loved and valued, just as a shepherd loves and values individual sheep for whom he/she is a leader.

Today the untapped reservoir of all the baptized is being called upon to become active in the church. We can no longer overemphasize the clerical model of church because we know this has caused a poor legacy of neglect in the past. The charisms of the baptized and confirmed have been left sorely untapped. We are living at a crossroads in the history of our church, and the time has come when we can no longer step backward. The forward road is to truly believe that the body of Christ is a community of equal partners. You are gifted by the Good Shepherd, and that same shepherd, Jesus, is calling you by name. This is a voice that none of us can ignore.

We open our hearts and let in the voice of God.

Fifth Sunday of Easter

John 14:1–12

"In my Father's house ..." I've often thought of this as a mansion in heaven that Jesus is preparing for us. But why do we need mansions when we will be free spirits with no bodies? The Father's house is not really a physical building but perhaps a symbol of Jesus. We can imagine that Jesus is the Father's "house," the dwelling place, the divine presence, the sacred meeting place with God. In that sense it depicts room for a great diversity, where people dwell with their gifts, talents, and ministries. We are the baptized living stones through which divine energy flows, making each of us a sacred dwelling of God's presence in our world.

If Jesus is that mansion and we are his presence, the power that comes from on high enters in and flows through the community of all of us as we share divine life and are freed from our sins, cleansed of guilt, bandaged up, and healed. Several years ago I participated in a healing service where we prayed for the gift of the Holy Spirit to come to us but not for us only. That Spirit was to pass through each of us into another and for anyone for whom we prayed to be healed. It made me truly feel that I was dwelling in the Father's house and that Jesus was there in the presence of the Holy Spirit, working through him and the Father. The power of Jesus, which is the Holy Spirit, permeated all the rooms of the mansion of that gathered community.

Jesus shows us that we are the temples of God or, in other words, the presence of God on earth. We will soon celebrate the Ascension, in which that "house of God" goes back to the Godhead and leaves us to be the rooms that God has given to us and to others for their habitation.

To Thomas's question about how the rest of the world can know the way, James Thurber, in an American fable, has some very good advice for us. He says that before we die, all of us should learn where we are going and why. If we can answer these questions, we can be assured of the symbolic mansion that Jesus goes to prepare for us; we go to the heart of God, where we will find shelter from the darkness of a sinful world in which we now live, a world that needs to be sheltered. We are presently walking our faith journey with the Christian community so that together, we may live forever in the mansion of God who is Christ. We are the living stones, the building that those who come after us will recognize when they witness the testimony of our lives.

We are built upon the foundation of Jesus Christ.

Sixth Sunday of Easter

John 14:15–21

We begin most of our prayers with the sign of the cross. The Gospel today talks about all three persons of the Blessed Trinity, so I will share a reflection with you that is more of a personal journey because of my great devotion to God as the Holy Spirit. As a child and a young sister, the Father was very important to me. Later on, as my spiritual life shifted and deepened, it was Jesus who took on great meaning in my Christian upbringing, but for many years now, the Holy Spirit is the person who resonates most deeply in my heart. Perhaps it is because I see more feminine qualities in this third person.

I look around at the situation in our church, where its history seems to lack a feminine aspect. We see only male hierarchy surrounding the pope. I often sit in the chapel and ask Jesus to peel my heart open and empty it so that this life-giving fullness of the Spirit can come in and make a home within me and to teach me the depths of love that I have to offer as a woman.

Why has the Holy Spirit become so important in my spiritual life? I think it is because I recognize the great need we have for an advocate, a feminine presence, to bring the world and the church to its knees. We have strayed from the beauty of the presence of true love in our daily lives. The church, which is the people of God, suffers from the scandal of sin. It needs the fire of the Spirit to bring us back to the ideals that Jesus laid out for us. Our civic society also needs the fire of that Spirit for the same reasons. Jesus sends us love through the Spirit so that we will carry on God's work in both our spiritual and civic lives.

The Holy Spirit does not force entry into any person's heart, but she will touch our lives and form our hearts if we ask. "I will not leave you orphans; I will come to you ..." Let us ask the Holy Spirit to come and live within us, to know us intimately, to work through us so we may be the presence of God. We are not alone because we trust that together, we will be able to keep the two greatest commandments

Celine Goessl, SCSC

of love. This week is a good time to make a more conscious effort to love ourselves and others so that the Spirit will come and take root in our lives. It will help us celebrate the upcoming Feast of Pentecost.

John tells us in the Gospel that God will be revealed in the fullness of the Trinity when we are well prepared to receive such a mysterious gift. If we are willing to place our lives into God's hands, God will love and bless us and share his mission with us. We can accomplish so much through God that will help us reach beyond our greatest joys and expectations. Pray to the Holy Spirit this week that she will be with us and with the leaders of our church and our world.

Come, Holy Spirit, enkindle in us your love.

Ascension Day

Matthew 28:16–20

While I was working as the pastoral administrator in a local parish, I conducted a funeral that I will never forget. A woman had died rather suddenly, and her spouse of fifty years asked whether he could get up at the service and give a special message to his children. He was well known as a man of deep faith, so it was not surprising when he told his children not to sit around moping and encouraged them to have faith. He asked if they knew why he was at peace with this sudden death. He said that although he would miss his wife, he was to journey alone, just as she had to make her final journey to God alone. He was not going to sit around, as the disciples seemed to have done after Jesus ascended into heaven. No, he was going to be out and about, doing what Jesus told the disciples to do—to be his witnesses to the ends of the earth. If only those men would have had the faith that this man exhibited. After all, Jesus had given his farewell discourse, yet all they could do was ask him if he was going to restore the kingdom to Israel. They became sky gazers on that day, and we know what kind of people have their heads in the clouds! It is easier to sky gaze than to get out and become witnesses for Jesus.

Saying good-bye is not easy, but life must go on. With Jesus' disappearance from our sight, we realize that he remains with us and asks us not to lock ourselves up and do nothing; he wants us to move into the future with courage. We are raised up in hope, and as we hold up our heads, Christ expects us to keep our feet planted firmly on the earth. There are people who know how to come to God if they set off down the road into the future and travel wherever the call of Jesus leads them. The Holy Spirit will be with us as we carry out the mission that he began on earth. We can do much for a church in pain today by going out and letting our lives become a book for others to read; then they will know that God will never abandon us or leave us orphaned.

Celine Goessl, SCSC

We become aware by reading today's scripture that there are times when Jesus must depart so that he can gift us with even greater blessings. We know that he is with us all of our days, even to the end of time. His great gift to us will be the indwelling of the Holy Spirit. We will never have to say good-bye to our God, for God always leads us when we walk in the footsteps of the one who loves us unconditionally. By the way, the man I spoke of above is still reaching out to others in their times of need and pain. Let us learn from such an example by taking some time each day, between now and next Sunday, to empty our hearts of all that is not of God and to prepare for the gift of the Holy Spirit at Pentecost. Then we too can spend time doing what Jesus asks of us: to be God's witnesses to the ends of the earth.

Reach out in faith to a lonely person this week.

Feast of Pentecost

Acts 2:1–11

It has been seven weeks since Easter. We come to the conclusion of another segment of our liturgical year with the celebration today. We do not celebrate the gift of the Holy Spirit often enough, so this feast is significant for us.

The beautiful gift of the Holy Spirit came into the world at the time of the Jewish Feast of Pentecost, one of the three major feasts celebrated in the space following Passover. It seems to have been some kind of a harvest celebration, but also on this day the Jews commemorated the gift of the commandments given to Moses on Mount Sinai. It indicates the time that the followers of Jesus used to Christianize their own feast days, patterning them off those of Jewish history.

This is an extraordinary time in the church year, when the apostles, along with Jesus' family, stayed in the upper room and from there had a transforming experience of wind and fire. Set in the midst of the present feast, we find a great number of Jews gathered who now experienced how bold the apostles were in coming forth to proclaim the reign of God in new and exciting ways. Peter's preaching was given a universal flavor as he proclaimed the Gospel to all nations, both Jews and Gentiles.

What does all of this mean for us as we celebrate Eucharist today? It reminds us that this is the day when the Holy Spirit is given to believers of all denominations. There is now an inner unity through that Spirit, even in the midst of a struggling church that must celebrate its unity surrounded by the culturally divergent expressions of many faiths that are visible in the world and, indeed, in our towns and cities.

The same wind and fire still blow through our own hearts. The fire may have gone out, but if we reach down deeply into our hearts, we know its heat still warms us. Sit down in some quiet space, close your eyes, and become aware of the breath and the fire within your being. Inhale deeply and let the presence of the Spirit set your heart on fire once again. Continue this breathing exercise for a couple of minutes so that there is an experience of what the apostles felt. The effect will be comparable to that first Pentecost.

It is so wonderful to be living in our time, when we know the need that God has for us to continue the work of Jesus on earth. While Jesus was alive, the *breath of God* remained in his body. When he ascended back to God, that Spirit was released to us. Consequently, you and I are being sent on a very strong mission—to go out into the world around us with the enthusiasm, passion, and energy given to us by that same *breath of God,* bringing good news to all those we meet this week. We will not have the fanfare that accompanied the birth of the church, but we do have faith, hope, and love and the unique gifts of wisdom, understanding, fortitude, knowledge, piety, counsel, and fear of God that we initially received at baptism and were strengthened at confirmation. All this remains in our hearts so that we have something to pass on to those whom God sends us.

Let us be among those who fly on the wind of the Spirit with fire in our hearts. Let us soar together into the dawn of the reign of God as our future destination.

Fire and wind—two strong elements of energy within us.

Feast of the Holy Trinity

John 3:16–18

This feast day is so profound and yet so simple that it is difficult to reflect on the fact that we cannot fully understand who God is. There is a tension between who we know God to be for us and our trying to articulate what we do not know. We realize this is one of the greatest mysteries of faith and words that defy reality.

I think of the familiar quote "Two's company, and three's a crowd." Somehow the feast today does not fall into that category. Three with the Trinity symbolizes completeness, a relationship that shows us such a fullness that we cannot explain it. Does the number three have anything to do with our beliefs? We can begin with the holy family, where three figures create the family of Jesus. Among the first visitors were the three Magi. As Jesus entered the desert just prior to his public ministry, he was tempted three times. Finally, as Jesus came to the end of his early life, the man he called "rock" denied him three times. On Calvary, Jesus was crucified between two thieves, and we are reminded that three crosses outlined the horizon on that day. Finally, Jesus spent three days in the tomb.

Let us take some quiet time this week and meditate on the presence of "three" in our lives so we can discover new insights into our relationship to the Trinity. We begin most of our prayers with the Sign of the Cross prayer as we name God as Father and Creator of all that is; Son as Redeemer and someone to imitate in our everyday actions; and Spirit as one who sanctifies us with grace and is the source of a love for which we long.

We have here a humble attempt to make some sense out of this profound mystery of the Trinity. The relationship that each of us individually experiences is beyond what we can say in words, but it leaves a great openness to experience God in our own way and rejoice at the wondrous opportunity to imitate ways of knowing God more intimately as we deepen our love for the Trinity.

Celine Goessl, SCSC

This is a very brief reflection today, but space is left on this page so that each of us can fill in our own relationship to each of the persons of the Blessed Trinity. Take time to sit quietly in a place where you can be alone and feel the presence of this divine reality.

In the Name of the Father and of the Son and of the Holy Spirit …

Feast of the Body and Blood of Jesus

1 Corinthians 10:16–17

When we look around us in the world, we see people suffering a number of hungers, but perhaps the greatest of these is the hunger that makes us yearn to be one body. We need to have meaningful relationships so we can function in the best way that is humanly possible. For this reason, the reflection today is based on our second reading, which is brief and full of food for thought.

The Eucharist is important for us in our daily lives, yet it is evident in our church that many people are deprived of this Eucharistic food because they lack male, celibate priests to pastor the many parishes that have closed, especially in poor areas, where the people have no means of transportation to attend Sunday Eucharist. Added to this is the actuality of attending Eucharist in mega-churches, where it is impossible to have the kind of intimate relationships that we have experienced, where people come together to celebrate the life they lived during the week. There is a serious crisis in our church. What are we to do?

If sharing the Eucharist is to mean more than going to Mass, we need to find new ways of nourishing the deep yearning that makes our hearts restless until they rest in Christ. This seems to be the reason why adoration of the Blessed Sacrament is becoming a meaningful devotion once again. In my own spiritual life, I need time each day to sit quietly in the chapel and open my heart to the presence of Jesus in the Blessed Sacrament. I need that environment, where I can spend a greater length of time beyond the Mass to develop energy from God that will send me out to be Jesus' heart, hands, eyes, and feet. I need that meeting place where I can be with Jesus in a very personal, intimate way and savor that time I spend in the chapel.

Receiving Communion or taking time for adoration lacks something if it doesn't lead us to action—going out to serve the needy, the poor, the marginalized, and those who suffer. St. Augustine once said, when holding up the consecrated elements, "Receive what you are, and be what you receive." Today's feast is a covenant we make with God to go out to serve others. We open the doors of our hearts and our homes to accept people as they are, whether they are family members, friends, neighbors, or enemies. This covenant could also mean that we join peace and justice groups to make a difference in bringing about the reign of God here in our own little world; or it could mean reaching out farther to care for the needs of those in other areas or countries who are walking the journey of life but who need to know that we care.

Let us be Eucharist for someone this week.

The Season
of
Ordinary Time

Cycle A

Ninth Sunday in Ordinary Time

Matthew 7:21–27

We most likely have never experienced as many natural disasters as we have lately. That is why the challenge that Jesus gives us today in the Gospel has a deeper meaning than ever. We are to build our houses (our faith) on solid rock so that when the wind, rain, and hurricanes come, our houses will not be swept away. Global warming is becoming very dangerous and makes us beg one another to stop polluting our environment and become serious about how we pattern our everyday lives, which should not be on consumerism but on reverence for the earth.

We enjoy nature and the gifts God so freely gives us, but at the same time we demand a certain use of material goods that erode our natural resources. We use things that are made to last only a short time, and then we yearn for something new and different. It is like the rain and wind and floods that buffet us and cause our houses (ideals) to collapse and fall into ruin.

Jesus tells us to build our homes carefully, starting with a solid foundation. If the foundation is not part of our lives in Jesus, then we can't expect to make that house a home. We know that if we build a solid spirituality on Christ, then the worst natural disasters cannot damage it. Our spiritual life is always under construction. Jesus describes two distinct realities: a house built on rock and one built on sand. Most of us take our foundations completely for granted. Foundations are often hidden, and we don't think our lives have much to do with them. Yet we rely so much on the foundation that when it crumbles, we are surprised because we haven't been conscious of the comfortable way in which we have lived our lives. That is why Jesus tells us to build on rock—the rock of his word.

Let us take time today to examine our spiritual lives, whether our houses are built on mere religious observance or on a genuine faith in God. Many people today do not attend church regularly, and the blocks on which they are expected to build are in steep decline.

Celine Goessl, SCSC

We might wonder if lack of church attendance will be a trend that is irreversible. Statistics indicate that Christianity is waning, while those with no religious affiliation are gaining momentum.

However, if we observe more carefully, we sense a high level of concern regarding the crumbling of our society, particularly among the younger generation. Don't be fooled by outward appearances. God looks into our hearts, which tell more of the story about how we build than about some of the things we do for others to see. Build on rock and not on sand. Be aware of your motives and the depth of your foundation, and you will know whether or not your house will withstand the passage of time.

We want to build a lasting foundation.

Tenth Sunday in Ordinary Time

Matthew 9:9–13

The Gospel today has a two-pronged message for us. The first is Jesus' invitation to Matthew. Jesus gazes on each of us and calls us to follow him. The second prong is of greater importance in our daily lives: the invitation to sit at table with Jesus. Matthew leaves the tax collector's table and accompanies his Master immediately, without hesitating. From there he moves to the family table, where food and conversation is shared.

At a time when our daily lives consist of fast-food meals and too much activity to allow families to sit down at table, much of the meaning of sharing a meal as the center of family life is lost. When I still lived at home, our family sat down to three meals a day, and if we were not there, we not only felt the loss of sharing food but even more, the participation in conversation.

For Jesus, table sharing was of great importance, and it was here that he gave us insight and excitement about the reign of God—a message to saint and sinner alike. When we celebrated the Feast of *Corpus Christi,* we reflected on the Eucharist, the participation at the table of the body and blood of Jesus. Each week at our liturgy we experience the great sign of oneness and sharing. How sad that the table of the Eucharist has now become a sign of division in Christianity. It seems that Christ wants the table enlarged enough to seat all of us, but we have built walls that remove compassion, mercy, and the invitation that Jesus desires. At his table with Matthew, we do not experience any boundaries, but our Catholic communities seem to have problems with, for example, divorced and remarried Christians, persons with sexual orientations not to our liking, or people with AIDS. Jesus tells us today that he has come to call sinners, not those who are righteous.

I can readily see Jesus going into any bar in our country; or standing on a street corner, talking with the un-churched; or having lunch with a lonely person who is already on his/her third marriage.

Celine Goessl, SCSC

Can we imagine such a Jesus who is ready to call us out of darkness into the light of his presence and even to his table of love and concern? "Follow me" is the message I need to hear this week, so my response can be as immediate as Matthew's if I seek out the underdog and invite her/him into my home and to my table, where we can nourish each other with food and conversation.

Another very fine practice is to gather our families to have one meal together each day, now that schoolchildren will be home for the summer. When we are once again comfortable about gathering and sharing at our dining room table, the Eucharist at church on Sunday will become more comfortable and meaningful because it will be accompanied by a sense of belonging at the table of the Lord, where saints and sinners alike gather.

To dine means more than a ten-minute stop at our family table.

Eleventh Sunday in Ordinary Time

Matthew 9:36–10:8

After Jesus taught the people on the mount, he walked into the countryside to minister to the large crowd. He looked at the people and sensed a great need in their hearts. Most probably, knowing human limits, he knew it was time to look among the disciples to gather a small community of followers whom he wished to send out to continue ministering to the needs of the people. He began to unfold his plan by building up a prayer community that would make justice, peace, forgiveness, and love available to those who were ready to become Christians.

Although Jesus called Peter the "rock," he wanted to build a society in which there were no masters and no servants but only those who would freely share the gifts that had been given to them, so this first small community began as equals. They were called not to *rule* the world but to *serve* it. He had given a perfect example and now, as he was preparing for his own return to the Father, he would commission the twelve to continue the ministry he had begun.

From that time to the present, every baptized Christian in the world has become a disciple and has made visible the compassionate love of Jesus. As then, we still struggle with the effects of sin, disease, scandal among leaders, lack of creative love for others, the weakening of marriage and religious commitment, corruption in the government, the effect of greed that cause wars, and many more sinful acts. Now is the time for us to develop discipleship; that is, learn to listen, and learn to follow Jesus and be his example to the world. Remember, Jesus sends you and me to do this today. Yes, we know that we have limitations, but that is so the power of the Holy Spirit will be more evident in the actions we perform for the honor and glory of God.

Jesus' strategy is, first of all, to teach us to pray, because without prayer our lives can become hollow and haughty. Second, he sent us out to bring peace and justice, forgiveness and love to all who need

---

Celine Goessl, SCSC

God's grace. We are the only body of Christ that is visible in our broken world, and that is why we are called to make the good news visible—because the reign of God is truly at hand. We do not know the hour or the day, but you and I are called not only to sow but also to reap.

Let us go forth in the peace and love of our God and to give to others what we have so freely been given.

May we follow in the footprints of Jesus.

Twelfth Sunday in Ordinary Time

Matthew 10:26–33

We continue to hear of criticism and bad publicity about the church, and so it is consoling to hear how Jesus prepares us as we face rebellion against organized religion. Three times in today's Gospel, Jesus tells us not to be afraid. In fact, we are told this throughout the New Testament, almost as many times as there are days in a year. We are also reminded that fear is one of the emotions to which we must not succumb. It will cripple us and keep us from being what God calls us to be as disciples of Jesus.

I am reminded of one of our founders' sayings: "Let us be courageous and strong." Anyone who has experienced criticism or opposition knows how difficult it is to follow this view. Jesus says three times, "Do not be afraid." This can be interpreted as a warning against three sources of opposition that we encounter in our daily lives—first from within, then from others, and finally from the prince of darkness. When we look within, we can readily feel a sense of fear or dread when we measure the cost of discipleship. Are we ready to put our complete trust in God and "let go and let God," as those in Alcoholics Anonymous are constantly reminded to do? Once we have conquered fear within ourselves, let us turn to a fear that is caused by others, especially by those who fear light and remain in darkness. The Christophers also give us a wonderful phrase: "Rather to light a candle than to curse the darkness." In dealing with this concept of fear, it takes courage and discipline to stand up for what we know is right, even if it means standing alone.

Finally, Jesus tells us once more not to be afraid of the prince of darkness. When we attempt to break away from sin and addiction in our daily lives, it can mean a struggle against the forces of evil that are physically stronger than we are and, but for the grace of God, we will not be able to withstand that kind of fear that takes control of our hearts.

Celine Goessl, SCSC

We are not alone in this struggle because all of us belong to a family, a community, a group, or an institution that will supply, support, and strengthen us, even in these days of uncertainty and rebellion against God. Use "I am not afraid" as a mantra for your daily prayer this week, and God will reward you with courage and strength for your Christian witness of being a modern-day prophet for God.

For further inspiration, read Jeremiah 20:10–13, and learn how one of the Old Testament prophets survived.

Be not afraid, for God is with you.

Thirteenth Sunday in Ordinary Time

2 Kings 4:8–11, 14–16

Ordinary time appears to be a misnomer for this season of the year. Our readings are anything but ordinary as we continue to break open God's word and hear the call to discipleship. If we pattern our lives on the readings for each Sunday, it will be a busy time. Jesus leaves no wiggle room when it comes to doing his work.

This week I am using the Hebrew scripture 2 Kings 4:8-11, 12-16 for our liturgical reflection. It centers on the call to be hospitable. Some time ago, I stayed at the home of a friend, and what a wonderful example of hospitality she gave me. St. Francis of Assisi also practiced the strong virtue of hospitality, and as I embrace the Franciscan rule of life, I am proud to have inherited the charism of hospitality, simplicity, and humility from the Franciscan rule—although I don't always measure up to the ideals that Francis left us as a legacy.

When we reflect on hospitality as shown in this passage from the Jewish scriptures, let us think about receiving the word of God, personified as a visitor in our daily lives. Think about breaking open the word in a welcoming manner in the same way as the couple in our story today welcomed Elisha. A necessary quality for such a welcoming is humility. I have to admit that I am ignorant of many deep meanings that are presented to us in this reading. My eyes are blind in much the same way that the eyes of the couple on the road to Emmaus were blinded when Jesus walked with them and explained the scriptures.

Another quality in dealing with the word of God is the faith required to understand the challenges that are before us when we read the Bible. It is a good practice to take a moment to pray to the Holy Spirit before we pick up our Bibles to break open the word. This is a living word that asks for a welcoming hospitality that God wishes to have us practice. Our hearts need an attitude of both hospitality and welcoming. The last quality that I think of relates to time—an extended period of coming back again and again, as Elisha returned

Celine Goessl, SCSC

over and over to the woman of influence. It was only when he had visited a number of times that this woman asked her husband to make a special room in their home for him to stay when he passed through their region.

The special room, the welcoming attitude of hospitality, can be built in our hearts this week. Take some time to build that room and then invite others to share the space that you have built. Listen attentively to the voice of God through persons that God sends into your life. Then invite them in to share the gifts that you have been given. Remember, just as in the story, we will be rewarded for the hospitality that we show to others, especially to those most in need of our care and concern.

Jesus calls us, through his example, to be master builders.

Fourteenth Sunday in Ordinary Time

Matthew 11:25–30

This is one of my favorite Gospels. I was delighted to be able to retire from full-time ministry in 2004, but in 2006, God called me back to a very strenuous ministry when my sisters elected me as the leader of the USA province of the Sisters of Mercy of the Holy Cross. I was frightened, but Jesus helped me to delight in what he said to me at the time: "Come to me, all you who labor and are heavily burdened, and I will give you rest." Jesus' words soothed my heart and gave me a strong sense of peace and quiet.

When we look around at the misery and burdens that many people have to bear, we realize that our encumbrances are light, and Jesus has given us an easy yoke. The word "yoke" comes to mind from my early childhood experiences, when I saw our Amish neighbors do all their farm work with horses. Usually two horses worked together, yoked with a wooden harness that was put on them so that they could do heavier work without too great a burden on either horse, since they were obliged to help and support each other.

Jesus speaks about the church leaders of his time having put unnecessary and burdensome yokes on their people's shoulders. So often in the Hebrew scripture, we read about the burden of the law. We know that Jesus came to lighten our burdens, but we know that at times, we still experience heavy burdens put on us by man-made laws. Or is it because we have placed heavy expectations upon our own shoulders? We labor under the illusion of a grand future and people looking up to us because of the wonderful things we accomplish. The heaviest load we sometimes carry is the burden of our own unfulfilled ambitions, not only as individuals but more especially as a nation.

I believe Jesus is calling us to lay down our arrogance, our material wealth, and our attempts to dominate as we view war as the one way to be the domineering nation that our ego tempts us to be. If we want to experience the easy burden of our way of life,

Celine Goessl, SCSC

then it is important that we reach out to those who are weary and burdened, especially our troops in war-torn countries. It is not only our families who are weary and burdened under the weight of war but also the families where war is being fought.

What can we do in the midst of a burdensome and weary life in which so many, especially the poor, fare so poorly on a daily basis? The Gospel shows us the gentle and humble Jesus who invites us to serve Gospel ideals and to shoulder a new burden—that of truth, love, and peace. Let me return to the image of my Amish neighbors, working with their yoked horses. It becomes a strong image for me to sit up and be attentive to Jesus' reassuring and comforting words: "Come to me, all you who labor and are heavily burdened, and I will give you rest."

Let us ask Jesus to place one part of the yoke around our shoulders, knowing that he will place the other half on his shoulders. Then our yoke indeed will be easy and our burden light.

Spouses, take on the yoke of your marriage commitment today.

Fifteenth Sunday in Ordinary Time

Matthew 13:1–23

Today we have a picturesque story of Jesus stepping into a boat and going out from the shore because the crowd was so great. As he gazes upon the hillside above the shore, he calls attention to a farmer who is spreading seed in his field by hand. The farmer's gestures are exaggerated so as to produce ridicule and laughter from among the crowd. They readily see that this Palestinian peasant really does not know how to farm because three of every four seeds are thrown out where they cannot possibly produce a harvest. A true farmer would find himself in the poorhouse in one season. Besides, he would be the laughing stock of his neighbors. Jesus' listeners were most likely making fun of this poor man.

As in stories that are parables, this story had just enough of an everyday experience to grab the people's attention until Jesus, as he is often wont to do, gives a shocking twist to what he is saying. God becomes the stupid farmer and wastes three-fourths of the seed of his word on the soil of their hearts. The laughter quickly subsides, and the people begin to realize that Jesus is talking about the soil in their own hearts. It must have had the same effect as the time when Jesus bent down and began writing something in the sand when a group of men had brought a woman to him because they caught her in adultery. Jesus' response to them was "Let the one without sin cast the first stone." Jesus tells this story from another simple everyday experience so these men can get behind what is seen by the eye and look at what is present in their hearts.

Today we place ourselves in that audience because Jesus is talking to us about how we might plow, cultivate, and seed the word of God in our personal lives. The allegorical interpretation shifts the point of the parable away from the farmer to our responsibilities. As in ancient times, the seed is planted before the soil is plowed. Our hearts might need a thorough plowing and cultivating before we can break open God's word and reap a harvest. In some people, there

Celine Goessl, SCSC

may be a stone that blocks growth, representing a hard lump of an unforgiving heart. The word cannot take root if we hold grudges under the guise of self-justification. Dig up the rocks so that next time the seeds will find the fertile ground of a receptive heart. Apply a little water of daily prayer to help the growth.

There might also be thorns that choke the word—thorns of worry about the evils of the world and the lure of wealth. There might be a sign hung on our hearts that reads "This house is full." There is no room because we are preoccupied with worldly concerns. Happily, for most of us, we have hearts that are prepared to receive whatever God has ready for us.

Jesus challenges us to let our hearts be plowed, tilled, watered, and seeded. Take plenty of time for prayer so this message will become more important than any other concerns you might have. Give Jesus your best, rich soil so his seed will produce a fine harvest that you can share with others and have enough left over to store up some eternal riches for yourself.

Become a sower of good seed.

Sixteenth Sunday in Ordinary Time

Matthew 13:24–43

What is heaven like? Have you seen the movie *Heaven Is for Real*? We all have a curiosity about what lies ahead for us when we die. Jesus does not give us a clear image of heaven, but he uses three parables to give us a bird's-eye glimpse of what we might expect. First, he tells us that heaven is "like a person who sowed good seed in a field ..." Second, heaven is "like a mustard see that a person took and sowed in a field ..." Last, heaven is "like yeast that a woman took and mixed in three measures of wheat flour ..."

Take time to think about what we can learn from these examples. They might well say that God has a sense of humor and acts in a surprising manner in order to catch our attention to show us something new and powerful. It makes us sit up and take notice; it calls us to be awake and alert, to value and understand what has already happened, but it does not let our experiences inhibit us or become a binding force for our future. Within each of our hearts, we come to realize that we have both wheat and weeds. God gently and compassionately lets us grow at our own rate until the harvest, when we will have to be separated into the good and the not-so-good as we stand before God to give an account of our lives. God lets a mustard seed grow perhaps where it ought not to be, but it grows tall and strong. When one drives through the countryside, one often sees beautiful fields of golden-colored mustard where hay was planted. Farmers watch that nasty weed grow in their fields; when the cows eat the mustard plant, it taints their milk, which cannot be sold at the factory. If only our faith, which was planted as a very small seed at our baptism, could yield such a harvest, not for destruction but for good. This is a story that depicts the trials and tribulations that make us undesirable if we let such setbacks annoy us and allow us to become negative.

Then Jesus gives us a loving and caring image of yeast that is mixed in flour so it becomes a leaven. This parable provides

Celine Goessl, SCSC

another strong message that our hearts need—the yeast of God's word, followed by the love given to us from Jesus and strengthened by the Holy Spirit, so we are ready to go out to share God's gift in a new and powerful way. This image has meaning for me because I remember when I tried my hand at making bread from scratch for the first time. I was proud that I measured everything and kneaded the dough, which I placed in a pan to raise. After a very long period, it didn't rise at all, and then I noticed the small package of yeast still on the kitchen counter. The next day I tried it again, and this time it became a delicious loaf of bread.

Jesus is not delivering a treatise on agriculture, nor is he pulling weeds from our hearts. He knows that the path we walk toward eternity will always have weeds and surprises. We make bread to feed the world, and this reality gives us courage and strength to be a leaven for others.

Let us go back to the beginning of this reflection and the question about what heaven is like. It is a season of harvest, and at the gate we can root out any weeds still left in our hearts. We can be good bread that will feed the spiritual lives of those around us this week and then, when the time of final judgment arrives for each of us it will be a celebration of great joy, where we can reap the fruit of God's humor as we are ushered into God's presence.

We will savor the bread we eat this week.

Seventeenth Sunday in Ordinary Time

Matthew 13:44–52

We continue this week with more parables about the reign of God. Last week we asked the question, "What is heaven like?" Today we have a related question: "Where is heaven?" Jesus gives us three more fascinating parables to which we need to listen carefully and hold in our hearts this week.

We live in a world full of seeds and weeds; yeast that can be good or bad; and dredges from the ocean that can bring up valuable and worthless material, as well as buried treasures. We are told that the time of separating the good from the bad has not yet arrived, so we still have time to look for the reign of God. There are treasures in everyday life, but where do we find them? God asks us to search for heaven in bits and pieces of life. The treasure of the Gospel is our faith, and we are called to make the search for heaven a priority.

We all have different and varied values. Some people search for possessions, prestige, and power. The worldly push is for material goods, the chance to control others, and boost our egos to look and feel important. In the long run, these things do not bring security but only cause illusions that keep us from being our real selves. It is only love and the deep conviction in our hearts that will help us find treasures. We also find the real pearls of our faith journey by selling what we have and leaving things behind. The tragedy is that when we find beautiful spiritual treasures, we are hesitant to pay the price for them. We might be tempted to act like the rich man who wanted to follow Jesus but had so many worldly possessions that his heart became heavy when he was asked to give up everything in order to become Jesus' disciple.

Let us look again at each of the parables in today's Gospel. The kingdom is depicted as a field that is bought with lots of money. Realize that in Jesus' time, farmers did not sell their property but kept it in the family. Moreover, Jewish law would consider this sale illegal because in an agricultural world, family interests would have

Celine Goessl, SCSC

priority. As for the merchant, he could be considered a thief because he would buy something for a low price and then sell it for a higher price. The large net cast into the sea hauls in both good and bad fish, and only after the fisherman has everything on shore does he divide up his catch. Jesus appears to be giving us more shockingly new and different ways of behaving.

So going back to the opening question, where is the kingdom of which Jesus speaks so eloquently? A story is told that God gave the angels a secret treasure and then sent them to bring it to earth. They asked God if they might hide it in the highest mountain, but God said no because only the healthy could climb the mountain. They then asked if they might bury it in the farthest shores of the ocean. Again, God said no, because only the rich could afford to travel that far. The angels were perplexed and had no idea where to put this secret treasure until God told them to put it within reach of everyone—rich and poor, healthy and sick, young and old alike. God told them to plant the secret treasure in the hearts of all God's children. If we discover that beautiful treasure within our hearts, the price will never be too great, because that is where we will find heaven.

Seek first God's reign and all else will fall in place.

Eighteenth Sunday in Ordinary Time

Matthew 14:13–21

We have been nourished by God's word for the past few weeks in order to be ready for the ministry to which Jesus is calling us today. Let us place ourselves in the crowd that is following the Lord to the place where he had withdrawn to be by himself. The crowd is still large, although it may have a different configuration. Maybe those who gather today will be the great number of unemployed, the frightened immigrants, the people with addictions, those who are homeless and without family ties, and those who are disenchanted with our church. This crowd still has a hunger for God but does not know where to turn.

Jesus had just heard of the death of his cousin John. He went out alone to pray and to mourn, but the crowd followed him and brought the sick and helpless and lonely to him to be healed. Jesus' response was to have compassion on the crowd. The entire crowd had a great hunger for his message, just as this contemporary crowd today has similar hungers and needs. We would all be intent on listening to Jesus, and in being so intent on listening to him, we would completely forget about the passing of time until the sun was setting. The disciples, Jesus' intimate followers, did not understand him because of their lack of faith, so when Jesus told them to feed the crowd, they did not understand what he was asking of them. We need to stop and wonder what our answers would be if we were told the same thing. We might have a multitude of lame excuses—I am tired of giving, or I have already done my fair share, or I don't even have enough money for my own needs.

I believe the miracle that we witness from Jesus today is called "compassion." Jesus takes the simple food offered by a young boy, and the disciples then portion it as they begin passing out the food. There seem to be others in the crowd who are touched by Jesus' compassion, so they bring out things they had tucked away for themselves in the folds of their garments. Suddenly, many in the

Celine Goessl, SCSC

crowd pass out their provisions, and the food multiplies to such a degree that a great amount is left over. That very afternoon, God broke into their hearts so that everyone was able to go home well fed, bodily and spiritually.

Let us apply this message to our own situation today. God calls us to be sacraments of God's presence every time we come together to celebrate the Eucharist. This is an ideal picture of what the church is called to be. Jesus gives himself to everyone, not caring who is Jew or Gentile, woman or man, rich or poor. We all come as equals and as members of our church to be fed and to feed others. As a Eucharistic minister at liturgy, can you see yourself as "the body of Christ, giving the body of Christ to the body of Christ"? What a privilege to be the one to share the bread of life and the cup of salvation.

Our ministry is not over when we leave the church building today. We are sent out, remembering that five loaves and two fishes are symbols of the power for goodness, which we all have in our hearts—a sign of the true compassion of Christ.

Look for a real miracle in life this week.

Nineteenth Sunday in Ordinary Time

Matthew 14:22–33

This is another heartwarming story of Jesus' relationship with his people. He sent the disciples to a boat and dismissed the rest so they could go home. He then climbed up the mountain, where he could have quiet time to pray. This is very probably the breather that he needed after hearing of the death of his cousin John the Baptist.

The boat into which the disciples climb is symbolic of the church, which today is caught in the violent storm of scandal, the cover-up by church leaders, and funds to pay expensive court cases, along with the continued lifestyle of some of those in authority. We are surely in the turmoil of a violent storm in which the people in the church-boat are tossed about unmercifully. We might ask ourselves if it is safer to be inside the boat with the security it provides, battered by the waves, in Jesus' absence. Is it possible that there is greater security being outside the boat, walking on the huge waves, and choosing a very different kind of security, knowing that Jesus is there and will reach out a helping hand if we ask? Other questions surface: "Where is Jesus? Where do we want him to be? And where do we feel safer?"

We have the example of Peter, who steps outside the boat. He is not faulted for this action, but his deficiency lies in his lack of courage and trust. In the first reading from the book of 1 Kings 19:9, 11–13, Elijah is also asked to step outside the cave and listen carefully for the message of God. He finds the message not in the storm but in a gentle breeze. That breeze can pass us by if we do not take time to listen carefully and be attentive to God through quiet times and places for prayer. This week, take time to be attentive to God's speaking to you. Find your own cave or mountain, and let God whisper to your heart.

It will soon be time for children and adults to go back to school. A wonderful way to begin the new school year (or a new job) is by taking time to be with God and asking for the courage of Peter or Elijah before beginning your new duties for the year. Jesus will be

Celine Goessl, SCSC

there to reach out to us if we ask. For those of us tossed about by the waves of violence, if we choose to stay in the boat (the church), we need to invite Jesus to come in and guide us to safer waters, where we can step out of the chaos of life and into the divine presence of God, who loves and cares for us. A few minutes spent each day in quiet prayer will keep the waters of life calm. It is when we take the kind of risk that Peter took that Jesus then can take us by the hand and lead us to safety.

As you walk up to receive Communion today, know that this is your invitation from Jesus to step out into the deep and walk on the water of life so that you can courageously live your faith. Remember, Jesus tells us not to be afraid because his love is stronger than fear, and he promises to be with us forever.

Sometimes it is okay to rock the boat.

Twentieth Sunday in Ordinary Time

Matthew 15:21–28

As we become more familiar with the scriptures, we realize there are a number of women who assume important roles within the stories of the Bible. Today's story is especially meaningful for me because, as a woman who has ministered within the church for over half a century, I can relate to the incident of being challenged in an attempt to put me into a box that does not give women what they can justly expect. This Canaanite woman is a true role model for women in the church today. She displays qualities that show the magnitude of her faithful prayer life and her persistence on what is rightly hers, refusing to take no for an answer.

In this story, the miracle for which she begs appears to take a backseat to the conversation that she has with Jesus. First, notice that Jesus ignores her. He then draws a wall around his ministry. Finally, he tells her in coarse words that he cannot throw his food to the dogs. But she does not go away. Her comeback must have surprised Jesus, as she appears to change his perspective on his mission. The reception she got does not discourage her. When Jesus does not answer her, even the disciples beg him to give her what she wants. She continues to demonstrate a strong persistence, and then Jesus recognizes the signs of the times. Look back at the story, and notice there are three characters: Jesus, the persistent woman, and the frightened disciples.

Let us take a closer look at the persistent woman and understand how she shows the qualities of greatness: her persistence, her humility, and a bit of humor. Her persistence is remarkable. She has to break through the barriers of prejudice toward Canaanites and, in particular, women Canaanites. Her daughter is terribly ill, and she is so charged up with energy to find a cure that she refuses to be diverted. Her eyes see the power of God in Jesus as she watches him carry out his ministry. The second quality is her humility. Her prayer displays this virtue because she kneels and does not use well-chosen words or beg on behalf of her own merits. She lets no insult distract her from the purpose of securing a cure for her daughter. Finally, humor enters into this story. We need holy humor when we relate to the God we see as a God of surprises. The conclusion to this story has a wonderful surprise for us. Her positive thinking turned an unpleasant situation into a delightful ending. She did what we might call a rewiring of her brain.

I have been amazed at my own spiritual journey lately. I think I found the reason for the progress I have made in deepening my relationship with God—by wiring my brain with positive thoughts and energies. Each morning I thank God ahead of time for the wonderful day that lies before me. I try to hem in my entire day with a prayerful, scientific thrust called positive redirecting of brain impulses, which will give me God experiences. I might never have thought of such a move if I had not read the books *What the Bleep Do We Know!?*, by William Arntz and Betsy Chasse, and *The True Power of Water: Healing and Discovering Ourselves*, by Masaru Emoto. You might want to read these two books and let the information in them help you to become a brave, persistent, humble, and happy person that the Gospel woman portrays for us.

Never underestimate the power of a woman.

Twenty-First Sunday in Ordinary Time

Matthew 16:13–20

A good teacher often approaches a new topic by asking a question. Jesus, the masterful instructor, is walking along with his group of followers. As they come to the edge of the Jewish territory and are about to cross into the Gentile district, Jesus suddenly stops and asks them two questions. The first is in reference to who other people say he is. They seem to have no problem parroting answers of others because such responses do not carry with them any type of commitment on their part. We too can reply with answers we have heard from others. Some say he is their personal Savior, while others will simply call him a good man and perhaps somewhat of a prophet. They cannot give a deeper explanation because they might not have developed a personal relationship with this mysterious man, whom we Christians have come to know on a deeper level.

Jesus lets them banter back and forth with broad answers, but at one point he stops them with another question that we too must answer if we are authentic followers of Jesus. Our answers will not be as profound as Peter's response, but they are just as important to Jesus as that rough, uneducated fisherman's answer was. Who do we say that Jesus is? Some answers might be that we can call him our brother, our best friend, our beloved, the light of our lives, or the companion with whom we walk daily. Whatever names we give to Jesus, each comes with a commitment that we make, not only to him but to ourselves.

After going through such an exercise, another question is important. It is a question that we put to Jesus: "Who do you say that I am?" This answer takes some serious quiet time of reflection and contemplation so that we will hear what Jesus has to say to us personally. This could be a very good examination of conscience at the end of the day. Just quietly ask Jesus the question, and then sit or lie back and listen to what he can tell you about how you have lived

Celine Goessl, SCSC

your day for him. Jesus wants to be present in each minute of the day as he seeks an intimate relationship with us.

Take time each day this week to ponder these three significant challenges, and let this Gospel message come alive for you. Take time to walk into new territory, like Jesus and the apostles were doing as they left their familiar country and crossed over into a foreign land. Become Peter in the story and live your life accordingly, but do not get vainglorious, as Peter did. If you read the passage in Matthew:16:22–23, which follows today's reading, you will understand the pitfall of becoming overconfident to the response that Jesus gives you as he singles you out as the special person in his life. Listen with a humble heart and show love for Jesus by reaching out to others in love and simplicity.

Jesus, who do you say that I am?

Twenty-Second Sunday in Ordinary Time

Matthew 16:21–27

As Jesus' journey draws him closer to the time of death, he becomes more and more insistent on the proper behavior of his disciples, and especially today, he centers on the "leader" of his small company. We cannot make sense of this Gospel unless we reread last Sunday's message. Peter was highly praised for his answer of who he thought Jesus was. Within six short verses of today's Gospel, Jesus was calling Peter a devil.

Personally, I need to use this message as a mirror from which I pattern my own behavior. Each morning I slip a cross on a chain around my neck, a symbol of my commitment to the crucified Christ. Many of us wear crosses, and sometimes I wonder if those who do so have ever reflected on the significance of that symbol that proclaims to the world that they also are followers of the crucified Jesus. We do not always live by what the cross symbolizes—that the cross is a burden that we carry on our shoulders daily and not just a pretty piece of jewelry that we wear around our necks.

With the pattern of life in our society today, we seem to have little tolerance for suffering and pain. Just look at the numerous pain-relief medicines found at our pharmacies. Perhaps our medicine cabinets bear that out too. We seem to want a trouble-free life, happiness without tears, roses without the thorns. When we are bombarded by all the commercials on television, we come face-to-face with the great myth of modern American thought—that life can and should be perfect health and inimitable happiness. That is certainly not the ideal of the Gospel message, nor was it the ideal life that our parents and the older population experienced in their lifetimes. We sometimes scoff at the thought of accepting suffering as the will of God. That sounds like a pessimistic attitude, but it might also be closer to the ideal of what it is that we are attempting to live with, using pain medicine, drugs, and alcohol in an attempt to make us pain-free. Can suffering be a magnet that draws us closer to God?

Celine Goessl, SCSC

Jesus addressed his followers with the words, "Whoever wishes to come after me must deny self, take up the cross and begin to follow in the footsteps of the Master." This is our call with all of its demands. If we want to be Christians and journey with our Master, we will voluntarily become gentle and humble of heart as we take up our small crosses of everyday life. Our lifestyle will not be burdensome if we realize what a privilege it is to follow Jesus. Then the crosses around our necks will become symbolic of what is in our hearts and on our minds. There is always something positive about carrying our burdens.

If we wear crosses, let them indicate to the world that we are happy, humble disciples of Jesus who willingly take up our crosses because we know that Jesus' yoke is easy and his burden is light. Pain and suffering are transitory moments that we endure with God's help, for our reward will come to us in ways that we could never imagine. We do not have to wait for eternity to be rewarded. Jesus is with us each day, and he walks with us, even when we are not aware of his presence. May Jesus be with each of us this week as we experience the peace and joy of walking with the one who hung on the cross so that we would have an example and model for our lifestyles.

If you wear a symbol of the cross or have it tattooed on your body, know the commitment you have made.

Twenty-Third Sunday in Ordinary Time

Matthew 18:15–20

The Gospel speaks of a process to follow when we deal with forgiveness and restoration and shows how important are the concepts of power and peace. Matthew 18 focuses on life inside the church, specifically how we should deal with sin and evil. Several years ago, our religious community gathered a set of protocols to help us learn how to deal with the difficulty of reconciliation. When any family or Christian community faces the problem of reconciliation, the following protocols can help. We all know of people who have damaged the moral fiber of their lives by leading lives of sin. Some of us may need to forgive and others may need to be forgiven.

Here are six guidelines that will help with the reconciliation process:

1. Create value for yourself.
2. Be open to feedback and help from others.
3. Act with compassion toward yourself and others.
4. Be patient with yourself and others.
5. If you have a problem with someone, deal with that person directly and honestly.
6. Stay current and seek the reconciliation you need within twenty-four hours, and certainly do not let more than seven days pass when either you or someone else needs the reconciliation process.

Forgiveness takes a lot of work from both parties. Any alienation from another person is serious and cannot be shoved off or glossed over. Most of us are very uncomfortable with confrontation, but if we listen to Jesus today, he gives us a pattern that is an expansion of the above protocols. The first step is confrontation alone with another person. If this fails, take someone with you, and if this is unsuccessful, prayerfully ask for assistance from the Christian community. Remember that when we seek reconciliation for ourselves or others, we do it because of a desire to heal and not to hurt.

There are many examples of the need for healing in our society today. Perhaps problems have been overlooked for years without addressing them because of fear. At some time in each of our lives, we may have encountered problems such as drinking, drug addiction, sexual abuse, marital infidelity, or neglect of family responsibilities or social accountability that take away the peace and happiness to which God calls us. Jesus reminds us in this Gospel that we are called to follow the difficulty of confronting the person with whom we have a problem. One gross example that we have in our church today is the reaction of bishops and those in authority who have not followed the call of Jesus to address sexual abuse of children. It is our duty to confront them because of their lack of following through on their duties.

Matthew 18:19–20 offers the final reminder of the critical importance of prayer in any reconciliation procedure. The maxim that a chain is as strong as its weakest link is not new to us. Prayer is the bolster we need to strengthen such a chain so we can carry out our duties as Christians. The keys to bind and loose were not only given to Peter thousands of years ago but to each one of us.

What needs to be reconciled in your everyday life?

Twenty-Fourth Sunday in Ordinary Time

Matthew 18:21–35

Let us continue our understanding of the need for reconciliation as we listen to the brief exchange between Jesus and Peter and the vivid parable of a master who forgives a servant. We might have to sit a long time with this parable before things come into focus because it can have deep meaning that brings up profound hurts in our own lives. Have you ever gone to someone who wronged you and asked to sit down and talk honestly about it? How would you deal with someone who would say to you, "I forgive you, but I will never forget"?

The lesson from Matthew talks about what is happening inside the church and also what is happening inside us. It will often take time to come to grips with a reflection on the difficulty of genuine forgiveness. Read the passage again, not only with your eyes but more with your heart. It will become obvious that there is a gap in this parable. The servant, on having been forgiven, doesn't rush home to his family to rejoice and show gratitude. He doesn't celebrate the fact that he and his entire family have been spared, because he really did not "feel" God's mercy and compassion. Otherwise, he would not have gone out and almost immediately used the same situation on another worker as a power play to squeeze out a much smaller debt that was owed to him.

In the Lord's Prayer, each day we pray that God will forgive us to the degree that we forgive others. This sentence in the prayer that we all know so well hits us with blinding clarity—that our ability to forgive is the measure of the depth of our faith in Jesus. Forgiving means the kind of forgiving that never ends because we come to appreciate the goodness and mercy of God. It is not about justice but about mercy. In the Lord's Prayer, we need to pray for that profound experience of mercy in our own lives so that we can pass on that beautiful gift, especially to those who have offended us. If we harbor

Celine Goessl, SCSC

any anger, we need to let go of it before we can move on with the forgiveness process.

Forgiveness, like love, is a mystery. It cannot be measured or counted. We need to sit and reflect on what we are saying in our daily prayers so that we can appreciate our merciful God's forgiveness. Jesus tells us that God forgives unconditionally again and again and again, so that our hearts can be encircled with that mercy that helps us to reach out to others in a gesture of love.

Whom do you need to forgive this week?

Twenty-Fifth Sunday in Ordinary Time

Matthew 20:1–16

I noticed that from last Sunday to this Sunday, we completely skipped Matthew 19 in our liturgical year. I wondered why, so I sat down and read the entire chapter, and there I found the story of the Pharisees trying to trap Jesus by asking a question about divorce. There is a small section on Jesus blessing children, but the greatest amount of space has to do with the rich young man who wanted to be a disciple but turned away, sadly, because he must have felt that Jesus' demand of discipleship was too great. We are never told what he eventually did, whether he thought about it and then returned to be Jesus' follower or whether he removed himself from those who were following Jesus. After this story, Peter, who is wont to put his foot in his mouth, pipes up and reminds Jesus that he and the rest of the apostles have given up everything, so what will they receive for this great sacrifice? Jesus promises them a hundredfold and eternal life. For the next three Sundays we will be treated to stories about vineyards and promises of life for all eternity.

Judging from human standards, there is a real lack of equality in what the parable asks of us. We are to concentrate on God's generosity and largess and not on human standards. If we get too uptight about how unjust this situation is, we will miss the lesson of the parable. Those who worked all day will get the same reward as those who came an hour before quitting time. We have to remember that God does not put value on the heads of people because of the riches or work that they have done while they lived here on earth. God loves us unconditionally because we are made in God's image and therefore have value beyond our finite understanding of who we are. The holy person and the sinner who repents will stand side by side in heaven.

God's ways are certainly not our ways, and God's thoughts are not our thoughts. The problem here is not the way God treats people when God acts in a favorable manner for each person, but in the way that we perceive what God should do in response to the smallness of our thinking. The primary idea of the parable is in the landowner's words as he asks if we are envious because he is generous. Somewhere I read that if we want to reach heaven some day, we must be ready for surprises. This is it! Stop and think about all the amazing and unexpected things God strews in our paths every day. I feel sorry for people who do not like surprises because they miss so much happiness in life that can lift them up and renew their spirits.

This week, let us walk the journey with Jesus and be ready for surprises and even shocks that will call us to change our perspectives on life. Strive to be poor, simple, and humble, and by the end of the week you will begin to realize how rich, loved, and precious you are to God. After we experience God in this new way, we can pass on God's surprises to those with whom we live and work.

God, please surprise us today.

Twenty-Sixth Sunday in Ordinary Time

Matthew 21:28–32

Jesus has now entered Jerusalem, and the events that will take place provide a background for the next few Sundays. He continues to make clear to us what it means to be his followers. Jesus is simply saying, "Actions speak louder than words." Living with someone who is constantly changing his/her mind is not pleasant. Most of the time, the consequences of changing one's mind are not significant, but for the two sons in today's Gospel, it was crucial.

The father is in a place where his neighbors can listen to what is going on in the conversation between him and his two sons. The father gives a task to the first son, who refuses to do what he is told, a shameful behavior. The neighbors who were listening probably did not realize that the son finally changed his mind and went out to do what his father had asked. Then we listen to the conversation with the other son, and I surmise the neighbors also heard him tell his father that he would do the task. However, did the neighbors realize that he did not carry out his promise? Both sons said one thing and then did the direct opposite. Changing their minds was crucial, but let us trust that in the end, someone eventually finished the work in the vineyard.

The story is for young and old alike. When children walk away with broken promises, what are the parents to do? And when parents verbally promise something to family members but then do not carry out their word, what do children think? Jesus asks a pertinent question at this point: "What is your opinion?" This sets up a challenge for all of us. No matter what we say, the real issue is what we do in the long run.

God looks into our hearts and wants an honest answer. Our excuses for not going out to do the work we promised to do can range from waiting for our pastor or bishop to give more detailed directions, to not being sure whether we can take on certain responsibilities, to convincing ourselves that we cannot stick out our necks to do something prophetic because it might set a dangerous precedent—and then what would we do? No matter what we say, the question is what we believe in the depths of our hearts and how we act on that belief.

All of us have some traits of both sons in our personalities. Sometimes we respond to what we hear with enthusiasm, but at other times we do not feel like doing what is asked of us. It is such a consolation to know that God continues to call us to accountability whether we say yes or no. By looking into our hearts to see what God sees, we know that we must face the needs of our time and stand up to live the values and lifestyle that we profess to live.

We know that many today are making their way to the reign of God, even though they might not belong to any religious denomination, and their actions speak louder than their words—the prostitutes and the tax collectors of our century. On the other hand, there are those in the church who said yes but who are scared to run the risk of doing what they have promised to do. How many leaders of our churches and civic communities are afraid to put their hands and their feet where their mouths are?

To which group do you belong?

Twenty-Seventh Sunday in Ordinary Time

Isaiah 5:1–7
Matthew 21:33–43

Today we have two readings, one from the Hebrew scripture and the other from the Gospel. These readings are closely aligned, as they both ask us to reflect on the story of a vineyard. This is the third Sunday that we are given parables about a vineyard.

Isaiah shares a folk ballad in which he sings of the infidelity of the people of his time. That is why Isaiah is so frustrated and angry, and these emotions come to the forefront as the ballad unfolds. He says the owner of the vineyard plants his field with great care. The quality of his work is his personal expectation, not God's work. That may be why the prophet is not too optimistic about the future. He is not giving his people a second chance. This appears to be his mind-set as he cries out against what has happened in his vineyard.

Matthew, on the other hand, reflects on the first-century problems of the Roman owner who had peasant tenants to do the work, so the owner is free to go on vacation. Now we delve into the story about a kind and generous owner who gave the work to the haughty and evil tenants. Although the owner has planted a wonderful vineyard, he does not seem to check up on his tenants. As the harvest time comes, he sends someone who lives in the area to gather his grapes.

This is a metaphor for the reign of God and obviously, the vineyard belongs to God, where we are invited to labor and produce fruit. The wicked tenants know the law, and so they decide to harm, maim, and even kill those who come to gather the fruit for their master. The law says that if someone dies and leaves land behind, the first one who claims the land can have it. They show how shrewd people of the world can be, not realizing that this vineyard was very different and that they could not lay claim to anything. Not only did they not get the land but in the process, they even lost their lives because of their wicked ways.

Celine Goessl, SCSC

Some of us might have had the same idea of wanting to get ahead. We must remember that God expects us to be good and faithful servants, cooperating with the owner (God) to put our whole energy into producing an abundance of fruit. But the only way to do this is to die to ourselves in order to carry out the will of God. Only then will we inherit the abundance that God has waiting for us. How discouraging it can be to work so hard to be successful, only to have our crops fail. We might throw up our hands in frustration and give up. God is patient and waits for us to come to our senses. God never gives up on us, even if we turn away from him for a time.

The point of this vineyard drama is as obvious to us in our time as it must have been for those who listened to Matthew in his time. We are challenged to make this story more personal in our own faith lives. Take time this week to sit quietly and decide what the outcome will be.

Be still and know that I am God.

Twenty-Eighth Sunday in Ordinary Time

Matthew 22:1–14

As the time of Jesus' death approaches, he very likely wishes to show the leaders why it is important that he identify with sinners and outcasts. The people need to be shaken out of their complacency and of the judgment they place on others. In spite of Matthew's violent position, he is definite in wanting to challenge his listeners. Why else would he act with such rage, interrupt the wedding preparations long enough to destroy the invited guests, and burn their city before he goes back to put finishing touches on the wedding banquet? He then sends his servants out into the highways to invite anyone they can find.

No longer is the party for those who were originally invited, but now everyone, good and evil, is welcome. This reflects the fact that those called by God are made up of very unlikely people. Just look around you in church this weekend. You probably will discover an unusual mixture of people, as we all come into this banquet hall as equals. That is why so many of our modern churches are built in the round. As we approach the altar, no one has the front row alone, while others must remain in the back row. We all come to the table of the Lord without any privilege of prestige, power, or rank. The only requirement we have in approaching the altar to receive the body and blood of Jesus is that we wear our symbolic baptismal robes and are worthy of the trust that has been handed to us through this sacrament.

It might surprise some that having received the sacraments and attending weekly Eucharist is not a sufficient reason to remain at the wedding feast. It would be like coming in without a wedding garment because that garment represents the good deeds that we perform during the week. It has nothing to do with what we are physically wearing but everything to do with how we have dressed up our hearts. God looks into our hearts and is quite demanding of the choices we make and the human actions we perform as a preparation for approaching this holy banquet. God is never stingy with us. We are provided a constant banquet of rich food and royal entertainment and are given a wedding garment in the form of the incredible generosity that God offers us free of charge. Many are invited to the banquet, but only the elect are welcome to stay. Coming into the reign of God in heaven is one thing, but in order to be assured of a place at the table, we also must follow the demands placed on us so that we are properly clothed to follow Christ on his journey to the cross.

Follow up this Gospel with a book on your favorite saint and read about the demands of being clothed with the necessary wedding garment. Then you will have a model to emulate and steps you can take to ensure that you are on the right road to God's reign.

The gathered community on Sunday is made up only of equals.

Twenty-Ninth Sunday in Ordinary Time

Matthew 22:15–21

This is a perfect reflection for us who live in a country that demands separation of church and state. It is also a good time to think about our responsibilities to God in relation to our accountability to our government. One cannot turn on the national news without some question about the moral values of persons in high offices in Washington, DC. Added to that, we are closely following the happenings at the Vatican with Pope Francis. All of this reminds us that we don't have to live in an either/or world; it is best to live both lifestyles. We have serious obligations to both church and state.

Tensions exist between our faithfulness to God, our duty to our country, and our loyalty to Jesus in the church but not necessarily to all of the hierarchical pronouncements that come from persons who are not as honest and forthright as Jesus is in today's Gospel. As good Catholics, we need to keep our sight and thoughts on the things of God while our feet remain firmly planted on the earth. Saints in the past have proven that we can love God, country, and church and be devoted to all facets of our spiritual and physical life, but it may take us a lifetime to give all three what is their due.

If we back up a bit and think about the three previous Sundays with their pertinent messages, it will be very clear what belongs to God. God asks us for faithful service. God also sends messengers to collect the harvest of what was cultivated in the vineyard stories from the past few weeks. This is obviously God's right. Finally, last week God invited the good and the evil to a banquet. It does not take too much imagination to realize what belongs to God in this parable. We know what we owe to God and what we owe to church authority because it is clear in scripture, especially in the Acts of the Apostles and in many of Paul's letters. Is the same true about our accountability to the state? We might find it ironic in today's Gospel that good citizens of Jerusalem are walking around with Roman

Celine Goessl, SCSC

coins in their pockets, in light of the fact of the questioning that is going on about Jesus.

Of course, we cannot be too quick to judge them; all we need to do is reach into our own pockets of life and reflect on the coins we find there. Our coins are the talents, the treasures of faith, and the time given to us to prove our worthiness of the image that we bear, since we are made in the image and likeness of God. Give your rightful respect to our secular government but remember that absolute worship is to be given only to God.

Whose image does your life bear? Is it the likeness of prestige, power, and pleasure of the world, or is it a prayerful, emotionally mature, socially sensitive, and environmentally alert attitude of giving back to God what is God's and being politically responsible in giving to Caesar what is Caesar's?

Where do we find the true image of God?

Thirtieth Sunday in Ordinary Time

Exodus 22:20–26

Today I have chosen to reflect on the Hebrew scripture because it speaks so graphically to the needs of our world today. After reflecting on the Exodus passage, it will be beneficial to turn to Matthew 22:34–40, and read it as a follow-up. We can use it as a strong reason to be compassionate toward those we still oppress. God will demand an account of our actions because God has given us two great commandments that we must obey. Jesus cares deeply about how we treat one another because we are all made in God's image.

To go to church on Sunday and to declare that we love God above all things while we remain indifferent to the needs of those around us—especially the poor, the widowed, the downtrodden, and the marginalized—is a reduction of what we are called to believe and to do. Reaching out to others is a valuable lesson that God commissioned Moses to pass on to the people of the Exodus. Today, God commissions us to reach out especially to those who have been wronged.

As the people in war-torn countries and in countries overcome by natural disaster cry out, God hears them but needs us to reassure them that we have heard God's voice and have come to their assistance in the name of the Lord. This reminds us to recall all we have done to the people in other countries, even in just the past few years. There are many times when we have turned our faces away when we heard of human atrocities of injustice in third world and European countries. God listens to them and demands that if we are the oppressor, we must correct the wrongs we have done. God calls each of us today and gives us the opportunity to show by prayer and by good deeds, more than by words, how we can reach out and prove that all people are made in God's image and likeness. We have stepped up to the plate numerous times and have done our share but unfortunately, there also have been times when we turned our backs on those who needed our compassion and care.

Celine Goessl, SCSC

We have made many attempts to recognize all people as our sisters and brothers and have put into practice what we have learned about Jesus' compassion. We are a generous nation, but we must constantly be aware of helping where and when we can. Our help, if it is genuine, cannot be given with a condition that places new burdens on the oppressed. Yet how often do we help our neighbor and at the same time hold on to his/her cloak with both of our hands, not letting go until our conditions are met? Let us not go to bed this night without loving enough to embark on a personal plan that will develop patterns of compassionate behavior as we join with our Catholic community to reach out to anyone who needs us.

God is calling you to something new.
What is your heart telling you?

Thirty-First Sunday in Ordinary Time

Matthew 23:1–12

Matthew seems to have a sense of humor. His story today sneaks up on us. We can sit back comfortably and watch Jesus taking the religious leaders to task for their actions. Then suddenly, in verse eight, he jars us out of our apathy by addressing us personally. This story is not aimed at condemnation of the Jewish religious leaders of Jesus' time but directly at us. So often we also do not practice what we preach.

As we are still in the midst of scandal within our church, we wonder how Jesus would treat our leaders who have covered up their own sins behind the Roman collar or the robes worn as a sign of their dignity in the community.

The religious authorities in past centuries make a point of their importance by enlarging their phylacteries (small leather cases worn on their left arms and foreheads, containing important Hebrew texts) and extending the fringes of their prayer shawls, showing that they know and keep the letter of the law. We hear how they yearned for titles and placed heavy burdens on their followers without carrying any burdens on their own shoulders. All the titles they hoarded conveyed a certain superiority that has no place in a community of the church.

Sometimes people still ask sisters why we are not wearing habits or why the priests are not wearing black suits and Roman collars. In the past, such clothing set us apart from the rest of the Christian community and could make us feel very comfortable because we were treated as more special than others. We cannot deny that the collar or the veil was somewhat of a symbol of power and privilege. When we reflect on today's reading, we see that clothing does not make one better than others; we have always known this. It is service that Jesus requires, not any specific garment that we wear. We can be tempted by a variety of "tassels and titles" that people place upon us as symbols of respect, but in the depths of our beings, we know

Celine Goessl, SCSC

that the true measure of who we are is what we hold in our hearts and show by our servant leadership.

The idea of religious leadership as seen in terms of service and avoiding pomp and even ostentation is a true sign of the hallmark of an authentic Christian body of persons. All of us are called to be humble and to show a modest spirit as our way of life. For Christian leadership, this becomes a great responsibility. We all need to resist our culture's pressure and influence and not permit status, titles of honor, or hierarchical structures to obliterate the true sign of who we are as the body of Christ. We are persons of equal importance, called to continue the ministry of Jesus without asking for or even desiring privilege or special deference. We know in the deepest recesses of our hearts that "actions speak louder than words."

The Christian community is a company of equals.

Thirty-Second Sunday in Ordinary Time

Matthew 25:1–13

In our world of uncertainties today, we can be sure of one thing: death! This is an appointment with God that none of us can ignore or cancel, but some of us are unwilling to face the inevitability of death. People just want to live with no thought of being accountable for the journey that they began when they were born and baptized into the Christian community.

This is the first of three parables on which we will reflect for the next few Sundays. They will center on the eschatological fact of eternity. We enter into one of the darkest months of the year after the beautiful colors of autumn have faded and before the white snow arrives. It is a time, when we are called to reflect on the last judgment and the end times.

This first parable is not about the wise virgins being selfish because they are unwilling to share their oil, nor is it about foolish virgins who have fallen asleep, for we know that all ten virgins have become weary and have drifted off. No, it is about being accountable as to how we are living our lives in the day-to-day struggle of being worthy of our baptismal call. The most obvious symbol in this parable is oil. Let us look at oil as the light within us that was placed there at our baptism. With the oil came the exhortation to keep that light burning in order to bring it to God at the end of our lives. The oil that we need to provide throughout our lives must burn so brightly that others will be drawn to God through us.

Discipleship is a lifetime affair with God that needs to be nourished and guarded faithfully. It is not enough to have spurts of faithfulness. We need to continue to keep the oil lit, even to the midnight of our lives. It is difficult to make lasting commitments in the world today. We are not privy to the information about when our life on earth will come to closure. God has put each of us on earth for a specific purpose and when that purpose is satisfied, God will call us back for an eternal reward and say to us, "Well done, good and

Celine Goessl, SCSC

faithful servant." The problem is, we are not absolutely clear about what our specific purpose is; that is, what we need to do for God's honor and glory before we can go back home to eternity. That is why we will not know the day or the hour.

One thing we do know for sure: the message of the wise as well as the foolish virgins cautions us to be ready at all times for the coming of the Lord. This week, we let our light shine from within and do all we need to do to keep the oil in our lamps burning with a constant flame that will be so bright that it will light the way for us and for those around us. Let our motto be "Let my light shine for the entire world to see that I am striving every day to give glory and praise to God."

Light a candle in church and pray for perseverance.

Thirty-Third Sunday in Ordinary Time

Matthew 25:14–30

Whenever we encounter a parable about a master and a servant, we can be sure that it has something to teach us about our relationship to God. Today, we read about talents. A talent in Jesus' time was a large sum of money. Today, however, let us look to a simpler meaning of talent—the gift that God gives us so that we may give it away to others before God comes back to require an account from us.

Anticipating Jesus' return at a time when we are not expecting him can place some fear into our lives when we think of accountability. Each of us has been given many talents that we know are huge shares in God's gifts. We have no other choice than to do something with what God has entrusted to us. Whether it is ten or five or one, we need to use our talents to help us live out the Gospel message. It doesn't matter how many gifts we are given, nor does it show that God has more confidence in some people who are given greater gifts. It is just a way of giving us something to work with as we carry out God's will. These talents are not our personal possessions; they are ways in which we use our unique personalities in reaching out to others to share with them what we have freely received. Some of us have a genuine knack for working with special-needs people, while others are called to spend their energy with the mentally gifted ones. Still others are more adept with their hands or are especially talented in the arts.

I believe that the talents we are given, whether great or small, will be the measure with which we will give an account when we meet God face-to-face. As we approach the Advent season, this is a good time to look at the gifts that are ours. Perhaps ordinary deeds we have amassed this past year do not seem to matter that much, but they are important in God's eyes. Ordinary work, when done with enthusiasm and energy, helps to take away shadows in our lives that can blur the good that we do or the temptation that we have to make

Celine Goessl, SCSC

little of the goodness within ourselves. Gifts used for the benefit of others will double our initial number of talents.

Possessiveness is a vice in our society today. It is an attitude that stems from our minds and hearts and centers on our security, our comfort, and our well-being as the important things in life. It tells us to bury our treasures so they will not be stolen. When we analyze such conduct, we realize that we are the third person in this parable. Our culture rewards such people. We know how privilege protects the rich, how self-thinking and self-acting restrict opportunities, where those who see themselves as poor and have negative images about themselves are victimized. However, this is not what the third person is about; it is the person who lets fear dominate life so that she/he becomes incapable of giving away gifts. This will result in the condemnation of his/her actions.

Let us turn to the idea of virtue in the form of talents that God has invested in each of us so that we can pass them on to others or give others a good example by the way we live out those virtues. What matters in the end is "action" in Gospel terms—a bold, risky action on our part to do what we can with the unique gifts we are given. Give it all away this week in order to get ready for the new church year that will be here in a couple of weeks. The Advent of Jesus is coming to us with the greatest gift of all—him!

Count our talents as special gifts from God.

Feast of Christ the King

Matthew 25:31–46

Our Gospel today pulls all the messages of the past couple of months together. Jesus' message could hardly be more explicit as he clearly maps out the challenge of the reign of God. What we have learned during all these months is that the reign of God is within us. It is time to turn our hearts and our entire lives to Jesus as we realize that God will judge us according to the works of mercy that we do during our time here on earth.

We live in a society with little concern about kingship. History indicates not very much was edifying about earthly kings' lives or their reigns. We are reminded that if we long for a king, for someone to emulate and look to for guidance, the only one who will fit that description is Christ the King. In our daily prayer we say, "Thy kingdom come," and then we get up and go to work for that kingdom that we carry within ourselves. It doesn't surprise us that love for the poor takes precedence in the work we do for the kingdom as we work out our salvation. Redemption is as near as the neighborhood soup kitchen, the shelter for the homeless, the city jail, or even the park bench that the homeless call home.

At the end of our liturgical year, we are reminded of the coming end of time, but we need to live in the interim as we seek out the suffering Christ, who is manifest in the hungry, the thirsty, the stranger, the naked, the sick, and the imprisoned. The reign of God begins when we resolve to serve God in those who live on the edge— the marginalized. We need to enter into ourselves many times each day as we look at the kingdom within, seek guidance and strength to broaden our ministerial territory, and share the kingdom with all those who manifest Jesus to us. The way we live now will determine how we will spend eternity.

Christ the King is present in the kingdom of heaven, a segment of which is right here on earth. He has called us to engage in social ministries of compassion. Winter is upon us in the Midwest, and

---

Celine Goessl, SCSC

it is time for us to seek out the poor, the hungry, and the naked to share the richness of our lives with them. I hope that as a nation, our president, whoever he/she is, will give all Americans the opportunity to change their lives so that they can be one with the people who are treated like second-class citizens and let them know that we care and that they are just as important as anyone in our great American family.

This week, as you reflect on the kingdom of God within yourself, take plenty of time to reach out to others. You may be the only Christ figure that they ever will encounter. As we help others, we are storing up treasures for ourselves and are making the American dream a reality, where all of us, regardless of color or creed, will bring about a better kingdom on earth, one that is more in alignment with the reign of God. Can we make this possible as we strive to change our hearts and reach out to those most in need of a smile or a hello or stop to take time to let others know that we care?

Farewell to the old year and hello to the new one.

The Season
of
Advent

Cycle B

First Sunday of Advent

Mark 13:33–37

Advent opens the church year by beckoning us on a journey toward Jesus, who is coming out to meet us. Although Advent is a period of four weeks, we travel on a road of unknown distance until Jesus comes to each of us individually at the end of our lives. There is not a single day when he does not come knocking at the door of our hearts, asking us to be doorkeepers until his return.

One task of a doorkeeper is to keep out intruders or unwanted folks who seek to harm us. This Advent, we want to keep sin out of our lives by taking extra time to reflect on the meaning of the season. We do not want this to be a time of wearing ourselves to a frazzle by decorating, gift buying, and storing up things for ourselves that we can ill afford. We want to make this the biggest and best Christmas ever for our families and friends. Many parishes have booklets and other prayer aids available to show us how to be watchful doorkeepers.

Another task of a doorkeeper is to let in those who have a right to enter. Let us allow prayer, peace, and quiet reflection into our hearts by being aware of the footprints of Jesus. He comes to help us during this important preparation for his coming at Christmas and also his Second Coming to each of us at the time of our death.

We are pilgrims on a constant journey toward God. It is not that God is absent, but sometimes our experience of God seems so far away that we might feel there is an absence. It is like the sun during these days of winter that feels far from us because we miss the warmth of the hot summer days. Advent is a period when the church so wisely gives us time to take stock of our journey, consult our maps, and walk steadily on the road toward God. We must constantly be on the lookout for God because he/she is a God of surprises and will surely burst into our lives at a time when we least expect divine presence. The days are short, and the journey is long. God has given us many gifts and responsibilities to carry out, but it is up to us to discover what God expects of us.

This is a far cry from what the world demands of us these days. Our culture would have us store up earthly goods, go out and shop until we drop, and then wonder how we are going to pay for all the things we bought and really don't need. Our church asks us to store up treasures for heaven and to walk the journey of faith with hope in our hearts that will help us to confidently walk with Jesus as we come in sight of our true home, where God is waiting for us much longer than we have waited for God.

What will your preparation for Christmas be like this year?

Second Sunday of Advent

Mark 1:1–8

A story is told of a small boy who used to play in the shadow of an old grandfather clock in his home. Each time the clock struck the hour, he would try to sharpen his math skills by counting the number of strikes. Just as the clock began to strike the hour one day, the mechanism jammed, and so after the boy counted twelve, it continued to thirteen, fourteen, fifteen, sixteen, and seventeen. The boy was so excited that he ran to his parents to report that it was later than it had ever been.

That is the message of John the Baptist today. It is time for a shake-up, a paradigm shift; time for a new wave of hope to break into our broken world. It is time, most of all, for us to prepare for the return of God, to set things straight once again as we look forward to the coming of Christ into our hearts and into the world. Preparing a way for God to enter our hearts is a time-consuming and costly business, and we may need more than a twelve-hour period. Our time-clock mechanism, however, may not jam, so we need to take at least the next three weeks of Advent to turn ourselves around and listen to John's message. Let us shift our priorities, return to a more simple life that does not include the consumerist pressure, and stop the hectic round of parties and frantic search for gifts that make even our Sundays a time to turn away from God as we search for the wrong things.

So what does John call us to do and to be? Some time ago, a young journalist founded an award called the Giraffe Project. This award was given to persons who were the courageous John the Baptists of their day. It was primarily for those who stuck their necks out on behalf of others, such as women and men working for justice in our society, for those who demonstrated against the use of unjust warfare and the piling of weapons, for those who called for an end to biased practices in the church, and for those who clamored against the rich becoming richer and the poor being annihilated.

Celine Goessl, SCSC

The list could go on, but it is for us to decide to whom we might give a Giraffe Project award or perhaps to make a list to indicate why we should be given the award.

God looks to us and asks us to prepare the way. That request brings us face-to-face with confrontation of evil around us, both within ourselves and in the neighborhoods where we live. What will each of us do this week as we seek to use the time given us to make our world a place that is fitting for God to return and once more to live in our midst? Our baptism calls us ever more deeply into ongoing relationships with God. We have three weeks to hear John's voice calling us and to make a personal response.

Take quiet time to listen to the call of God.

Third Sunday of Advent

Isaiah 61:1–2, 10–11

Several years ago I participated in a Steven Covey workshop on *The Seven Habits of Highly Effective People. As we* worked with habit number two—"Begin with the end in mind"—we were asked to write a personal mission statement. I chose the Hebrew scriptures instead of the Gospel because it appears to speak loudly about a plan of action for Advent. Today, we light a rose candle on the Advent wreath and proclaim that this is a day of rejoicing. Isaiah gives us a multitude of reasons for such an emotion. The Spirit of God was not only upon him but upon all of us as well. The reason to rejoice is that we are empowered by our baptism and confirmation to help bring an end to oppression, suffering, and humiliation of the poor. We bring the same message that the shepherds will hear from the angels at the birth of Jesus. There are so many poor in our midst today, with unemployment rising, the minimum wage still below the poverty level, and many people who are homeless. There is plenty to do for these people, as well as the healing of the brokenhearted; those who are anxious, discouraged, lonely, and suffering injustice and indignity; and those suffering emotional and psychological trauma. We are called to bring hope and comfort to such people. We don't have to look too far to find them. They may well be in our backyards or in our living rooms.

As we read farther in Isaiah's prophecy, we find another program of reform to which we are called, one that might help bring about a radical modification in our society. God calls us to "proclaim liberty to captives and release to prisoners." Captives are mentioned first and most probably relate to victims of war caught in the line of violence on both sides of warring nations. There are many slaves in bondage to vicious powers, especially children caught in human trafficking. We even have large corporations in the United States who are unjust to their workers, particularly the older population they hire.

Celine Goessl, SCSC

This gives us enough work to minister to the needs around us so that we can see the religious reality of the anawim as we are reminded to announce a year of favor from God. Such a year, especially a jubilee year, is a time to eradicate all debts, to redistribute land equitably, to release anyone bound in slavery, and to allow people to return to their ancestral homes. That is what Advent is really about—a God of justice coming into our world. Clothed with mercy, we will help to make this a time when justice and rejoicing will spring up because we heed the voice of Isaiah. We have two more weeks until Christmas to work faithfully for such a new world order. Even our smallest efforts will bring great joy on Christmas Day. You might want to take time to write a personal mission statement that will enable you to begin working for a renewed idea of what you can do to make the world ready for Christ's return.

The thrust of my life mission statement is to ...

Fourth Sunday of Advent

Luke 1:26–38

The reflection for today is a piece of poetry that I wrote during a
desert retreat in Arizona.

Awesome!
The light of the Spirit
Awakens me to the dawn of life
A daily occurrence
In which I respond
With Marian simplicity
"How can this be?"

Not one final answer
But a daily cry
Into the darkness
Of an unprecedented future.

I beg for another sign
But you only send
Light in darkness

Awesome!
Called to discern
What awaits me each dawn.
I see only your light—
Help me to say "Here I am!"
Let it be done through me.

Called to share light
From my heart
Through my eyes
My life radiates the sight

Celine Goessl, SCSC

That helps me respond

Spirit of God
How awesome
To carry *you*
Into the darkness of this day

Say yes to what God is asking of you this day.

The Season
of
Christmas

Cycle B

Feast of the Holy Family

Since Christmas is seldom celebrated on a Sunday, I encourage you to turn to the back of Breaking Open God's Word *to find the Christmas reflection under the heading "Special Liturgical Celebrations."*

Luke 2:22–40

Today is a special day to think about family life. We have the great example of the holy family to emulate. Mary and Joseph have taught us that parents are the primary teachers of their children because they are the ones who help children develop unique personalities and behavioral skills they will need for their lives. Parents are also the ones who, by their words and example, will pass on their faith to their children. We realize that this holy couple passed on to Jesus the rich traditions of the law by which they lived. They were carrying out the law spoken of in Exodus and Leviticus by taking Jesus to the temple and by introducing him to the rituals of their time.

Luke tells us there were two important people who had spent much of their lives in the temple in anticipation of the coming Messiah. Those people were the first ones that the holy family encountered when they entered the temple. Simeon was a devout man, and because he had led a life of holiness, he immediately recognized Jesus, and joy burst forth from his heart as he proclaimed, "Now, Master, you may let your servant go in peace … for my eyes have seen … a light of revelation to the Gentiles." He went on to prophesy to Mary that there would be sad times ahead in her life and in the life of her son because of powerful political persons who would cause them many sorrows.

The holy family then encountered Anna, another prophetic voice who thanked God for giving her the privilege of seeing her Savior after all her years of prayer and fasting in the temple. Both of these figures tell us who Jesus is and give us a glimpse of what is in store for the future.

Celine Goessl, SCSC

WELCOME TO MY WORLD
OF
"BREAKING OPEN GOD'S WORLD"

I would like to introduce you to my book so you can find the right page each week for the next three years. This is a three-year cycle of reflections on the Sunday scriptures. Might I suggest that you read the introduction on pp. vii-viii before you use this weekly reflection series. Also, the conclusion on page 379 will give you more information and let you know that anyone who uses my book for your personal meditation have a promise that I will be praying for you each week.

Christmas, Ash Wednesday, and All Saints Day will not occur on Sunday each year, so I have written a special section at the end of the book (pp. 370-377) as a way of looking at these feasts as part of our faith journey from our own birth – to reconciliation when we have deviated from the path of faith – to the time when God calls us home and rewards us with the gift of eternal life. I have written some poetry, which you will find on different pages of this book.

The year 2016 is piece of the cycle we call Year C. My reflection for this week (July 23-24) the Seventeenth Sunday in ordinary time, is found on pages 332-333. This is where you begin since you have now heard the readings for this weekend. I did not include the scripture passages but they are included at the upper left-hand of each page. You can use your Bible or missalette to read the passage. It will enable you to remember the Word of God for each week. At the end of each reflection, you will find a thought for the day/week.

Sister Celine

We will hear about the ups and downs of family life as we go through the liturgical year with this family. We will see that there are times of sorrow and joy in their family life, just as there will be in our own lives. Today, let us take time to pray for a spirit of love and faith in our family. Life continues to be a struggle for most of us as we reach out to our children with love and faith and ask God to bless them by touching each member with gentleness and compassion to support family life.

This week, let us center our prayers on the faith that we have lived from our own childhoods and ask Mary and Joseph to teach us, by their example, how to remain faithful to God. Our children will see our examples of service and our attempt to bring the spirit of the holy family into our lives.

May your protection surround your family.

Feast of the Epiphany

Matthew 2:1–12

We are still in darkness despite the fact that the days are very slowly getting longer. The stars shine with such brilliance on these cold winter nights. It makes me wonder if one of them might have been the star that led the Magi to Jesus. As with wise persons, we too seek Jesus. Instead of looking up into the night sky, we are called to look deep down into our hearts to find him.

Reading today's scripture from Matthew, I became aware of three groups of people who were seeking Jesus. I was surprised and saddened by some of their responses. The first group included the political leaders of their day. They were power-hungry folks whose only religion was their own egos and advancement. They reminded me of the action of King Herod, a violent man who used others for his benefit. Some of the politicians of our time show us how power might be used without the wisdom of a star leading them to Jesus. We can see so many of our citizens, especially our troops, who come to a violent end today because of our world leaders' lack of a Jesus light.

The second group of people included the religious leaders of their day. They seemed to have hidden their noses in the books of the law, living in a world of theory and ignoring the love of God, who reaches out with compassion to all people. Unfortunately, some who follow this pattern are with us today. For example, we have leaders with little or no concern regarding crimes of human trafficking, the sins of drug use, and the ever-growing use of guns in our society. We might have thought that slavery died at the time of Abraham Lincoln, but it has raised its ugly presence in our time.

The third group consisted of the wise women and men who had the courage to leave their safe homes in order to step out into the darkness, where they could see the light that led them to Jesus. These are the real magi! We need only to open the pages of some of our best Catholic newspapers to find men and women who continue to bring gifts of gold, frankincense, and myrrh to the abused, the trafficked, the poor, the mistreated immigrants, and the mentally and emotionally ill. A wise person's gift of gold is a commitment to peace and justice that makes Jesus more visible to the world. The gift of frankincense helps them to be true priestly people as they authentically carry out their priestly duties, in response to their baptismal commitment. Finally, myrrh is a gift that shows the way in which we all live our trust in Jesus, who has conquered death and who gives us the transcendent gift that we celebrate each weekend at Eucharist. This is a fitting gift that we freely give back to Jesus every time we are sent out to share what we have received from the altar and from fellow citizens gathered in Christian community.

Take time this week to think and pray about which person you fit into most faithfully. What gifts have you gathered this week so that you have something to give back to Jesus as you live into this new year?

Praise God for the wise people who surround us.

The Baptism of the Lord

Mark 1:4–11

This is the Sunday in which we are told that Jesus has chosen to enter into our human condition, to stand at the Jordan in solidarity with all humankind. Many of us were baptized as infants and knew little of what was happening to us. Just as we read in last Sunday's reflection, it is parents and godparents who are responsible for mentoring the baby, so as to help her/him to begin the life of grace because of the seed of faith planted in the child. Through the pouring on of water and the coming of the Holy Spirit into his/her little life, the baby enters the community of the church. If the adults do not follow through on the promises they make, then the sacrament will remain dormant because grace will not be given without consent of someone.

Those who come to the waters of baptism accept the responsibility along with their godparents, who walk the journey of faith with them. Together they tap into the graces given through anointing and indwelling of the Holy Spirit.

Go back and read the Gospel of Mark and recognize Mark's reference to Old Testament symbols. Isaiah is the first scripture reading for today, and it too has beautiful references to the cleansing and receiving of a new spirit in our hearts that would have remained stony without God's grace. Isaiah also shows how pleased God was with Jesus as he stood in the waters at the Jordan. It was there that Jesus' public ministry was initiated when God's voice was heard: "This is my beloved Son in whom I am well pleased."

Our baptism also initiated us into the ministry that God destined for us from birth to death. This is the in-between time for us to prove our authentic call as we go out to others to bring them the good news of salvation. Jesus, our brother, will support us and will give us the grace to make his mission our own when we follow through with the great commandment of love. But more than that, we must listen to the beatitudes that will help us see beyond race or creed or gender

Celine Goessl, SCSC

or nationality, to welcome others as we would want to be welcomed into the body of Christ.

We read in the Gospel message that the seed that is planted in the ground must die in order to produce fruit. That is the pattern of our lives. We awake each morning and remember to offer all our prayers, works, joys, and sufferings to God. During the day, we try to faithfully follow Jesus along the journey of our own baptismal commitments. God's grace will sustain us on this journey. All we need to do is ask, and we will receive.

Called by God and commissioned to serve

The Season
of
Ordinary Time

Cycle B

Second Sunday in Ordinary Time

1 Samuel 3:3–10, 19

Today I have chosen to reflect upon the Hebrew scripture because it follows a pattern of Jesus' call to us when we received the sacrament of baptism. We would need to read the entire third chapter of Samuel in order to put this reflection into perspective. In fact, we need to know that Samuel was brought to the temple to give service under the tutelage of Eli, the high priest. This took place soon after Samuel was weaned as a child. Eli was getting old, and this seemed to be God's method of replacing him with new blood and refreshing ideas.

Samuel is the figure of all of us, insignificant and of no particular importance in life. We may not be important in the eyes of our culture, but it is exciting to know that in the eyes of God, we are special because God's word is calling us to an intimate relationship. God does not care if we are women or men, black or white, married or single, rich or poor. God just asks us to have the courage to open our hearts and answer God's call to our baptismal commitments. We notice that Samuel tells God to speak because he is listening. That is the same stance we take in order to hear the call because God can only speak when we are quiet enough to hear. This is why it is important to have a peaceful place to sit quietly so that we can listen to God.

We live in a world that bombards us with constant noise and activity. There are false gods everywhere to distract us—primarily power, prestige, and possessions. Recognizing the call of God in the midst of such chaos will not be easy. It can happen that God's call will come as a soft whisper, and we can miss it if we haven't taken time for prayer in the silence of our hearts.

There is a great concern about the crises of religious vocations today. God's call reaches far beyond where we might think it to be. The call can be heard more clearly if we introduce a paradigm shift into our lives by letting go of the old so that new forms of religious life can emerge. The Second Vatican Council started this kind of process;

Celine Goessl, SCSC

we are called to follow up by reading some of those documents, especially *The Decree on the Apostolate of the Laity*. The "Eli's" in our lives must fade so that the "Samuels" can rise with new life, as we turn to ways of deepening our relationship with God. God constantly invites us to come and see what the future holds.

Look at the three characters in this story—Eli, a priest who strengthens his faith when he learns that his life will take on a different journey; a responsive Samuel who is ready to do the will of God; and a persistent God who calls them to love more fully. Who are you in this story? Look around! This week we begin ordinary time, celebrating the memory of Martin Luther King Jr. and praying for Christian unity. It is a new time in life, in which we have been called to renew our relationship with God and with one another at the beginning of a new year of grace.

Let us begin anew.

Third Sunday in Ordinary Time

Mark 1:14–20

We will use the Gospel of Mark for our inspiration during most of the coming year. Mark is a pioneer evangelist and the first to capture the life of Jesus and write it down for posterity. Mark's form of writing is simple but mysterious and challenging. Today, he gives us a glimpse of the beginning of Jesus' public ministry. The very first thing Jesus does is to call people to walk the journey with him and to learn firsthand from the Master how to make the reign of God present here on earth. For the next three Sundays, the story of Jesus' public life begins to unravel, and we are caught up in the story as we personally hear the call to follow him. The Hebrew reading last Sunday showed us how Samuel was called by God. Today we see another prophet, Jonah, having a similar call to continue God's work in his time. As we go through the week, we know that God also has called each of us to do the same thing; namely, to make Jesus' presence real for those with whom we live, work, pray, and play.

It is consoling to know that Jesus called uneducated, smelly, rough fishermen to belong to this first group of "ministers." We can relate to these earthy men and therefore, right from the beginning, we realize that God also calls us, not because we are finely educated, sophisticated people holding high offices but truly because we are simple and humble enough to hear the voice of God. God is pleased with us because we are ready to respond, "Here I am, Lord. I come to do your will."

Casting and mending are two prerequisites for helping to build the reign of God. As God calls us today, God asks us to cast our nets far and wide so that we can mend the broken lives of those who need to have the comfort of belonging to a group that can hold their joys and sorrows, works, and prayers in an organized fashion, which we call "church." Remember, Jesus does not call you to a cozy, private religion—a relationship between God and you only—but to

Celine Goessl, SCSC

be a disciple who can leave all things at a moment's notice when an opportunity to spread the good news of Jesus is offered to you.

Four men woke up one morning as fishermen and by evening, their lives had been turned upside down, and they found themselves as disciples of Jesus. Every morning when we wake up this week, we might think that we are ordinary people, going to ordinary work, but Jesus will call us to discipleship. As we leave our homes, our jobs, or our salaries, our social status is not nearly as meaningful as the call of Jesus to go out and find those *big* fish so we can haul them into the kingdom of God.

Wake up to a new call each day.

Fourth Sunday in Ordinary Time

Mark 1:21–28

For the next two Sundays, we will encounter Jesus as one who speaks with authority and power. We will also experience how people of his time were riveted to his words and amazed at the spirit with which Jesus preached and worked his first miracles. It seems strange that at the very beginning of his ministry, Jesus immediately encountered evil. The culture of that time was filled with destructive evil, which is not so different from the world we live in today.

One of our large urban churches had a mentally ill person attending Mass. He remained in the last pew in church and continued to repeat the prayers of the priest. He began quietly at first, but by the time of the Eucharistic prayer, he became noisy and even added profanity to the responses. People were angry, but no one tried to remove him from the assembly. At the sign of peace, a woman left her pew and walked over to him to wish him peace, and others got up to do the same. The man began to weep openly, and a young child, hearing the sobbing, went back and sat on his lap. The Mass continued, and the person remained quiet for the rest of the liturgy.

I wish such an act of love could happen in my parish church. I have never thought of the sign of peace in such amazing terms. I wonder if I would have had the courage of that first woman who reached out to share what was surely embedded deeply within her heart. Do we consciously think about the power of the sign of peace when we are asked to turn to others at Mass?

We count on modern medicine to help people struggle with their psychic diseases, and in our way of thinking, we do not see these afflictions as devil possessions. However, we do realize that evil can destroy those who are dominated by addictions, such as alcoholism, false values, money, ambition, excessive working, power, and the like. Jesus comes to us as Eucharist to share his power so that we will be healed and freed from these afflictions. When we offer that sign of peace in the coming weeks, let us include a prayer for the

---

Celine Goessl, SCSC

ones we have touched by a handshake or hug, and silently ask that they be healed of anything that keeps them from the love of God. Then, before receiving Communion, let us ask God for the grace to be healed of any evil that might lurk in the recesses of our own hearts.

Let us be more conscious of what we are
doing at the sign of peace.

Fifth Sunday in Ordinary Time

Mark 1:29–39

Mark seems to have developed a habit of working in multiples of three. In today's Gospel, we come upon three distinct scenes. The first is the private miracle that Jesus works on behalf of Peter's mother-in-law. Very little is said in this brief description of the sick woman whom Jesus raises up. It is praiseworthy that she immediately goes out to prepare a meal for her guests. The story of this miracle spreads very quickly, but the day remains calm because people were not allowed to travel on the Sabbath. However, when the sun went down, we see Jesus entangled in the second scene. People began coming from all directions to this man who was full of compassion and who would undoubtedly heal as many as he could handle. These miracles now became a matter of public knowledge because the multitude who gathered was witnesses. Finally, people had to take leave to go home for the night.

It is then that the third scene comes into focus—that of Jesus rising very early the next morning and walking out into the desert to be alone in order to contemplate what God was calling him to be and to do. He knows that his sudden popularity is not the center of his ministry, so Jesus checks in with God in a quiet time and place, where he can be alone to prepare for the day ahead. When his followers discover that he is missing, they hunt him down because great crowds of people already are filling up Peter's yard, demanding to be touched by the miracle worker. I can imagine their joy when they found him and told him to come back because "everyone is looking for you." What a surprise when Jesus curbs their enthusiasm by telling them he will not return but must go to other towns to spread God's kingdom.

It is from this third scene that we learn a great lesson today, as Jesus went aside to converse with God in prayer. It is important to take time every morning to prepare for the day by looking into the mirror of prayer. There, we can experience God in our own image

Celine Goessl, SCSC

of God's reflection as we are given enough light and direction to let God shine through us, so we can see to what we are called and then draw strength for the day. Jesus can correct us, as he corrected his followers, and set us on the right road of making God's reign clearer for those we meet during the day.

Jesus submits his healing ministry to the greater power of proclaiming how God comes to set the world on a new path, a road to lasting peace for which the world yearns. God gives us the power to help create such a world, if only we believe in miracles.

May peace prevail upon earth!

Sixth Sunday in Ordinary Time

Mark 1:40–45

The news of miracles will bring busloads of people to clamor after a moving statue or one that weeps copious tears, to places where people claim to have seen Mary, or to images of the face of Jesus on the side of a wall. Have we reduced Jesus and religion to what we might call the almighty magician? Certainly, this is the kind of ministry that Jesus would wish to avoid. What he wants from us, for example, is the ability to reach out and touch the lepers in our own society.

Such an act reminds me of the great Franciscan saint, Francis of Assisi. As Francis was riding his horse one day, he passed a leper on the road, and because his heart had been so touched by prayer, he had to turn back, dismount, and not only reach out his hand to the leper but kiss him. Actually, Francis embraced three lepers on the road that day. The first leper was the real one, who might not have been real in our sense of the word, because St. Bonaventure tells us that when Francis got back on his horse, he turned around to look at the leper once more and did not see him, although Francis could see for a great distance in all directions. The second leper that Francis encountered was the leprosy of his own sinfulness, the dark side of his personality. Remember that this man was a young, pleasure-loving son of a wealthy statesman. He faced the fact that he felt repulsed by the leper but then changed his ordinary response of turning away. The third leper Francis met was the crucified Jesus himself. It was only just before his death that Francis wrote that it was Jesus who led him to the leper.

Think of what it meant to embrace someone who was considered unclean by society. We are called look at those persons who today work with persons suffering from AIDS, those who reach out to the street people, those who stand in solidarity with people who have declared themselves "gay," terrorists from around the world, or anyone else who threatens our lifestyle and anyone against

Celine Goessl, SCSC

whom people are prejudiced in our society today. As followers of St. Francis of Assisi, the Holy Cross Sisters around the world are called to embrace this kind of ministry.

All societies have their "untouchables," and where they are, we need to be. However, we are not called individually to such a beautiful ministry. God also calls each of us who read this message today. Jesus not only declared "untouchables" clean but also sent them back into their own communities to return to normal life within society. Community is the heart of the matter, and that is also the core of our lives as sisters and brothers who follow St. Francis and Christ. If you want to do something special for God today, contact a priest, brother, or sister with whom you are acquainted. They can give you more information on how you can become a woman or man religious. This is an invitation to be a follower of Christ by walking faithfully in his footsteps as the first disciples did.

Decide to which vocation God calls you—a religious vocation, a married vocation, or a single life.

Seventh Sunday in Ordinary Time

Isaiah 43:18–19, 21–22, 24 *before you read the Gospel*
Mark 2:1–12

It is necessary to read the passage in Isaiah as a backdrop to the double miracle that Jesus is about to perform. In this first reading, God calls us to let go of the old and walk into the future with new hope. God says, "See? I am making something new." But that cannot be seen except through the eyes of our hearts. With this in mind, let us go to the miracle in today's Gospel.

After the direct miracles that we have witnessed in the past couple of weeks, this twist comes as something new. The four men had to concoct a creative method of getting their friend to Jesus. They took the necessary steps, even though it appeared to be a roundabout way. The features in this story are a bridge that will connect the past miracles to the debate stories that will run through the next chapter in the Gospel of Mark. Even the way Jesus performs this miracle is not direct. Knowing his audience, especially the scribes who are following him only to trip him up, he began with a controversial approach: "Your sins are forgiven." Jesus shows that he has come to restore us to full life so we can live a new lifestyle. Paralysis of the body is cumbersome, but paralysis in our hearts is even more of a concern to Jesus. All of us become paralyzed in some way when we turn our hearts away from a gracious God who loves each of us unconditionally. Once we see such a disease and acknowledge it, Jesus can cure us.

Again Mark talks about several groups of people in this miracle story. First, there are the four men who are friends of the sick man. They didn't have to tell Jesus why they had taken such stringent measures to bring their friend to him. He knew of the faith in their hearts. Would that we had friends who were so faithful; better yet, that we would be such faithful friends. Second, there were the men from Jerusalem. A number of them sat quietly and watched the entire scene. They listened intently but were silent, for in their hearts there

Celine Goessl, SCSC

began the decision to get rid of Jesus. They were highly educated men, custodians of orthodoxy but would keep the crowd in the old way of living and would not even show interest or listen to God who came to make all things new. Finally, there was the paralyzed man himself, who lay silent and who did not let us know what was going on in his heart—or even if he knew how crippled his personality had become.

Where do you find yourself in this crowded room? To which group do you belong? Take time today or during the week to think about how to bring someone to Jesus to be healed. Are we bruised leaders who can no long trust anyone because of negativity, unable to rise from our sinful ways, or are we in any way paralyzed? Are we willing to ask Jesus to heal us? Each of us is in charge of our own lives. Let us look into our hearts and let Jesus come in so that God can do something new to lift us, either physically or spiritually, from our sinful ways.

What keeps us paralyzed in our spiritual lives?

Eighth Sunday in Ordinary Time

Mark 2:18–22

Jesus hardly has time to catch his breath after healing the paralytic, teaching by the sea, and calling fishermen to follow him. He has begun his public ministry but is almost immediately in conflict with the Pharisees. Today, even some of John's followers question Jesus about why he fails to observe the custom of fasting. As usual, Jesus has a ready answer. He gives them three images:

> One does not fast when it is time for a wedding feast.
> One does not sew new cloth on an old piece of clothing.
> One does not pour new wine into old wineskins.

Our lesson this week is to realize that something new is happening and that we cannot continue to live according to our old ways. What was proper for a situation in the past is not necessarily suitable for our time. Jesus calls us to create a new attitude in our minds. He says that the old form of religion needs to be replaced by a relationship that comes from the heart. Is this not just as true for us today? Our hearts are different from what they were a year ago because we have grown and are at a different place in our spiritual lives. We are being called to renew our Catholic faith in such a way that we are faithful to the past but equally open to the present, as we reach out in hope to the future. Such newness can pose a threat because it calls us to take a risk, to give up our sense of security with the old and move beyond our present human experience to a new vision of life that Jesus offers to us.

Change is definitely challenging, but it is a grand alternative to standing still and not growing in our relationship with God. In our world today, change might well be the greatest challenge with which we must cope. Too often, people come to church to seek the certainties of the past, to go back to the pre-Vatican lifestyle. If we yearn for such a return to the old, it is truly putting the new wine of our lives into the old wineskins of time or sewing a new piece of cloth onto the garment that we were clothed with during our youth. Jesus calls us to rejoice as though we were celebrating a wedding. He calls us to enter into a new way of life and to inspire others to become witnesses in seeking this new clothing or new wine, because they come to see how happy we are that we have chosen this new way of life. We are constantly called to follow Jesus by living differently from the people of the world and by showing the joy that comes from living God's new lifestyle.

We have been called to something new for the past few weeks through the actions and words of Jesus in the Gospel. Look back to the message of the fourth, sixth, and seventh Sundays in ordinary time and realize how much of the old simply cannot accommodate the new to which God calls us today. If we have difficulty recalling those situations, we can return to those Sundays to break open God's message and see with new eyes and hearts.

We are called to bring our hearts into line with
our past, our present, and our future.

The Season
of
Lent

Cycle B

First Sunday of Lent

Mark 1:12–15

This is certainly a brief message today, but the insistence that we radically alter our lives is strikingly present. It calls to mind the hope that we have for the future. The Hebrew scripture for today is Genesis 9:8–15, which gives us a marvelous image of hope—the covenant expression shown as a rainbow.

Our Gospel passage is filled with the challenge of a journey toward hope as we are invited to go into the wilderness of our hearts. Let us link our lives and take that journey together as we walk through the next forty days, following our dreams and the reassurance of the good things that are to come at the end of our pilgrimage. If we prepare in this way, we will step into a resurrected life on Easter Sunday. With this in mind, it will be a journey of coming home to the mission Jesus has entrusted to us to be the good news for the salvation of the world. We need not fear because we remember the steps of many who have gone before us, walking that same path into the desert and then on to the sea, following the ordinary roads of everyday life. It is our way of the cross—the long ascent to the peak of Golgotha and an awareness of the proverbial tombs and the signposts along the road until we reach our destiny.

During these days we will walk with one another, knowing that we are never alone. But we need to choose some special times for prayer where we enter our own desert. We can use it as a place of transition from our sinful past into a future that promises a wonderful land of our dreams, a period of letting go of what held us back in the past so we can enter into the land of hope prepared for us in eternity. I believe God wants our journey this Lent to be an adventure into the experience that our brother Jesus had in the desert. In Mark's brief account, three points will help us become aware of the direction that we are to journey. First, there is the role of the Holy Spirit. Jesus had been baptized in the Jordan, and the Spirit immediately led him into the desert. Here in the wilderness, there is the opportunity to leave

Celine Goessl, SCSC

distractions behind and walk through an arid wasteland, where we can reflect on our commitment to life, be in touch with our roots, and learn once again what we need to sustain our spiritual lives. Second, there is the temptation by Satan. Temptation here means that life will not be cozy and nice, but it can be a testing ground for us to choose life in a new way, walking a different path from the one we walked during the past year. The third message is that the reign of God is at hand. Our future is to be in this realm and not along the path of greed, destruction, or violence.

Joy and peace are the guideposts awaiting us as we venture along the journey of God's dream and hope for us. Which is more important: to get somewhere or to be attentive to the trip along the way; to travel alone or with others; where we are right now or where we want to be forty days from now; and what we want to let go of or take with us? Remember, we have a rainbow of promises from God, a hope of arriving at springtime, both on this earth and in our hearts, and facing a new creation in which our desert will bloom!

Have a safe and wonder-filled journey!

Second Sunday of Lent

Mark 9:2–10

The second Sunday of Lent always presents us with the story of the transfiguration of Jesus. Again, Mark is brief, giving just enough information for us to look at and apply it to our daily lives. Three questions come to mind when I read this account: (1) Where did Jesus go? (2) Who did he take with him? (3) What message is God giving us?

1. Jesus often went away or up a mountain at peak moments in his life. Our Lenten journey also takes us to out-of-the-way places, high up so that we can see life from a different perspective. It takes us to a place where we can see greater things that are in store for us, a place of unlimited horizons so that we can dream about how we might be able to make Jesus better known in our world and in our church but most of all in our own hearts.

2. Jesus certainly did not take his most faithful followers. If he had, at least one woman would have been present; for example, his mother or Mary Magdalene. It makes me ask myself who I would take with me on my journey. Am I particular about persons with whom I share my vision and my dreams? Are they always the best people to choose? Are they people who have similar dreams, or can I profit from someone who sees reality differently?

3. Of all the things that happened at the transfiguration, what message stands out to help me make Lent more meaningful? God comes in a cloud to overshadow those present. I am reminded of a similar experience of driving across the Mackinac Bridge in heavy fog. I have experienced this, and so I realize how I am engulfed in blocking out distractions and setting my vision on getting where I need to go. It is in such an environment that I can hear the call of God more clearly. The message on the mountain was "listen to him."

Celine Goessl, SCSC

These questions can give us direction between now and Easter. Jesus is about midway on his journey to Jerusalem, where he will experience death and resurrection. Like him, I need to take time to go to a special place to refresh my spiritual life. Who can I ask to spend time in prayer with me so we can experience this refreshment together? God may be calling me to include a most unlikely person. Finally, I feel called to spend more time in quiet contemplation so I can really listen to God. Such a program calls for a serious resolution to take the next several weeks to embark on this journey and think about these questions. I challenge all of us to take time during the next four weeks to keep these points before us so we can be transformed with Christ on Easter Sunday.

What vision do you have for your life this Lent?

Third Sunday of Lent

John 2:13–25 *If your parish has an RCIA process, you might be using John 4:5–42, found in cycle A.*

Actions speak louder than words! Ever since Jesus was in the temple when he was twelve years old, he knew that he must be about his Father's business. I believe he saw many things that were not God's will, even in those early days. Coming once more to the temple before his death, he knew he must do something about this place of worship that was intended to be a place where people could express their prayers and where God could show his presence to the chosen people once again.

What was wrong at the temple? First of all, the entrance was too crowded with nonessentials because the businesses set up there had grown enormously. Foreign currency was not allowed in the temple, lest the image of a pagan ruler profane the temple precincts, so there had to be money changers available for those who came from other countries. Can you imagine the noise and the shuffling of people and activity not conducive to prayer?

The tender, loving Jesus, who had just cured so many people and had walked among his chosen ones as a gentle shepherd, now came into the temple with quite a different personality. The situation had become so terrible that he needed to alert the people to what they had done to his Father's house. This beautiful area that had been a place of sacred worship, a focal point for a pilgrim's journey, and a sanctuary removed from the pressures of life had become so corrupt that it had to be radically replaced by something that would return it to its original purpose. What Jesus did in his Father's house reminds us of what really matters.

Looking at the situation in our own hearts, we must ask ourselves whether Jesus would need to come storming in to whip us back to a holiness that may have been covered up by the clutter that clings to our hearts. It is time to ask Jesus to clear away the junk in our lives and free us to come to God as a human made in God's image and

---

Celine Goessl, SCSC

likeness. Let us ask Jesus this week to clear out from the temple of our bodies all that obliterates true worship and deeper communion with God. Let our bodies become beautiful and living temples of the Holy Spirit once more so we will show to others by our actions that we are Catholic Christians.

Remember, actions speak louder than words.

Fourth Sunday in Lent

John 3:14–21 *If your parish has an RCIA process, you might be using John 9:1–45 found in cycle A.*

In order to see a more complete picture of today's message, we need to go back to read Numbers 21:4–9, and then turn to John and read the whole story of Nicodemus from John 1:3. Jesus spoke to Nicodemus about the need to be born in the light that he was to bring into the world. When Nicodemus asked how this could happen, Jesus gave him a summary of salvation in three actions:

1. He presented a picture of Jesus being lifted up, first on the cross and then at his Resurrection. When Moses held up the bronze serpent, people were healed. John used this image to show how Jesus lifts up and helps a sick world darkened by sin.

2. The power behind Jesus' healing ministry was to show us God's love for the world. It is such love that reaches down to our sick, bruised, and hurting world, where we are entangled in wars, heinous crimes, and terrorism. These are only a few acts of darkness. Only love can bring light into our lives as God invites us to rise up with Jesus and share divine life.

3. The last action calls us to step out of our sinful lives of darkness into the light of Christ. If we continue to avoid the light because it hurts our eyes, we will truly remain in darkness. Our Lenten Gospels constantly call us to leave the ways of darkness behind and walk toward the light so that we can experience newness of life at Easter.

If your parish observes the Scrutinies from the RCIA process today and next Sunday, let us kneel in spirit with the elect and acknowledge the dark spaces in our lives. Let Christ reach down and pull us into his light. All of us gravitate toward darkness at times. Sometimes when we look at the "rooms of our lives," we wonder if some of them have not even been wired for electricity. Oh yes, we are

Celine Goessl, SCSC

happy to show off the rooms of our religious involvement, our work situation that is above reproach, or the love in our family lives that brings joy to our hearts! But what about those other rooms that have shady dealings and can only be seen by lighting one little candle or by flicking the button of a flashlight so that the light can scrutinize the dark corners of our lives? Then too, we all have places where we keep our skeletons, but that is such a dark room that we just want to move on because we are too frightened to even go into that space.

Jesus came into the world to be our light. Light always insists on truth about who we are, what we are doing, what our story is, and with whom we share life. We might not want to see too clearly, but the presence of Jesus beckons us to look more deeply into the rooms of our hearts these next few weeks as we journey toward the light of the new paschal candle. Jesus challenges us to keep that light with us so that our future will be well lit, showing us where we are going. Be the light of Christ this week in preparation for Easter.

We are asked to light up our world with peace and joy.

Fifth Sunday of Lent

John 12:20–26 *If you have the RCIA in your parish, you will be using John 11:1–45 from cycle A.*

As winter is chased out by the demands of spring weather, it is fascinating to see the beginnings of flowers and plants pushing up through the earth where they have been dormant since last fall. It reminds me of the grain of wheat that must be planted and die before it can be transformed into new life. Farmers surely know the meaning of this scripture because it is exactly what they will be doing in the next several weeks.

To be buried in the earth has new meaning for us as we think about what it entails to accept death in order to live. In the course of a lifespan, each of us must face many deaths. A teenager must die to immature ways in order to become an adult; a single person will feel the stretch of death from centering only on oneself to preparing for an upcoming wedding. We all need to die to former selves and advance in age and grace as we reach retirement status. Some of us will die to the beauty of retirement, if and when God calls us back into active work and ministry. We cannot go forward into new life unless we are prepared to die to the old.

Today we become aware that we are God's "grains of wheat" as God calls us to an eternal harvest of immortality. Before that can happen, we need to be planted deep down where we would not necessarily choose to go. Dying to selfishness and sin and anything that turns us away from God is a necessary process before we can experience the springtime of new life. Lent has been a germinating period, where our dying helps us to live a richer life as we reach out to others in prayer, almsgiving, and fasting. Jesus calls us to prepare ourselves to burst forth with new life. That can happen in just two weeks, when we will celebrate the Feast of Easter. It is then that we can look back and realize how the seeds of our good deeds, our generosity, and our efforts to place others' needs before our own will bring forth growth in abundance. When this happens, we will

Celine Goessl, SCSC

be able to hear the words of scripture, "Well done, good and faithful servant ..."

We still have the Good Friday pain and disappointment and the silent waiting of Holy Saturday before we reach Easter joy. Some of us may be prepared to bring forth abundant fruit already today! Perhaps some of us will need the next two weeks to do a little more dying so that we can master the transitional period from death to new life. Let us look at how our lives resemble the process of the grain of wheat that is planted in the ground. It dies so new life can grow in a transformation of hope that follows the dullness of winter. The excitement of summer is before us as we enjoy the growth of new life that Jesus will produce in us.

Enjoy the fruits of life each season of the year.

Holy Week
and
the Season of Easter

Cycle B

Passion (Palm) Sunday

Mark 14:1–15:47

We are entering Holy Week, which leads to the high point of our liturgical celebrations. God gives us this entire week to look at our lives, accept responsibility for our sins, and decide who we are in the drama of Christ's passion, so we will continue to take steps to prepare for Easter resurrection.

Mark unfolds the drama of the week in four acts:

1. *The conspiracy to kill Jesus.* Mark talks about the humble servant Jesus, in contrast to the haughty people who continue to hang their hopes on prestige and power. Even the apostles, who have been with Jesus for so long, could not recognize what will happen to him. Let us place the spotlight on Jesus as he prepares for the Passover supper. One curious point in this story is the mention of a man who is carrying a water jar. That is a job usually done by a woman. I wonder what significance this has in our society today.

2. *Jesus is deserted.* Mark emphasizes how much Jesus is misunderstood, especially by his own followers. He must feel totally abandoned because Judas has gone off, Peter will deny him, and the rest will hide. Even as he goes to the garden with three disciples, they sleep until there is the sound of footsteps on the gravel and flickering lights shining through the olive trees. The arrest is about to take place, with Judas leading the soldiers.

3. *The trials.* Mark now presents an interlude concerning Peter. This is the last time we will encounter Peter in Mark's Gospel. Mark continues to show, with brutal honesty, the hearts of the other postles. He is sparing in his description of the actual trial.

4. *The Crucifixion.* The clock has ticked away and Mark's sparse words are quick to place Jesus on his journey to Golgotha. In addition to Jesus' physical pain, there is the constant

Celine Goessl, SCSC

mockery of the crowd. Then Jesus cries out, the day becomes darkened, and all is silent. *Stop!* End of story—or is it?

We come to the conclusion, but not before Mark makes one more pertinent point. At the end of the story, an outsider comes up as the only person who is strong enough to proclaim out loud who Jesus really is. As Jesus is taken down from the cross and buried, we are left to ponder as we stand before the bare cross. The rest of the drama is left for outsiders and some women, who have nothing to lose, as they put the final touch on the Crucifixion scene.

Who are we in this story? What have these events to do with us? I look back at the drama and wonder what I would have done in Peter's shoes, or Judas's, or the shoes of the other ten. Do the priests, in their self-righteousness and eagerness to reform others while ignoring themselves, tell me anything about myself and some of the leaders in our church today? I see in Pilate the abuse of authority and in the crowd a thirst for excitement and blood. And Judas? A bit of him is in all of us.

It is important for us to find a place of solitude where we can look over the events of Holy Week, placing ourselves in the position of each of the players, looking at both the good and the bad qualities in each of them and then deciding what we will do as we silently walk the way of the cross this week.

Finally, let us place our attention on Jesus and spend time with him in each of the above acts. The Judas, Peter, and Pilate pockets of our hearts need cleaning out. This week, we need to take more time to look into our hearts and do the "spring cleaning" that needs to happen before we celebrate the Easter joy of resurrection.

Walk with Jesus this week.

Easter Sunday

Mark 16:1–7

Jesus had lain in the tomb over the Sabbath. Early in the morning, just as the sun was rising, the call of life came down from God. Jesus lives! The resurrection of Easter cannot be achieved by any human or by an evolution of any sort. It is very difficult to wrap our minds around this feast day. Three women come back to the tomb in order to give a more fitting burial to Jesus by wrapping his body. Since the Sabbath was coming soon after Jesus died, they didn't have time to wrap the body properly. The preparation had to be done in such a hurry on Good Friday. They had no concern about how to roll the stone away from the entrance. They only knew that they had to finish what was begun in such haste.

What a surprise when they approached and found the tomb open. Inside, they found a young man who told them that Jesus had been raised. As I return to what happened such a short time ago when Jesus was being nailed to the cross, I wonder if this was the same man who was seen running away, naked, from the scene of Crucifixion. Had he been a follower of Jesus, or might he have been the author of this Gospel, who had been so fearful and didn't want the authorities to know that he was even connected with Jesus? Since this young man was a witness just before the Crucifixion, could he also have been a witness to Jesus' resurrection? Whoever he was, he had a message for the women to go and tell Peter and the other disciples to go to Galilee, where they would be given further instructions after seeing Jesus once again in human flesh.

It appears that this young man certainly knew details that others may not have recognized, so he could have been the author himself. After a brief pause to contemplate who this was, we continue the journey as one of the women who received the message of resurrection. It might be profitable to go out to the local cemetery and walk among the tombs of our beloved dead to contemplate his/her experience of this special day. It seems rather odd to use a

Celine Goessl, SCSC

cemetery as a focal point on such a high holy day, but it could bring us a deep connection with our loved ones. That might fill our hearts with joy and excitement to think about what those bodies, dead in the grave, might be experiencing this very day, for their spirits are with God in eternity.

After such a cemetery experience, let us think about writing our own Easter story. Take a good look at the sight of where we might rest in peace some day. This thought can strengthen our faith and help us look more deeply into our hearts to see how our faith has carried us on our journey up until this glorious day of celebration. If we take time to write our personal stories, we will have a great gift to bring to the liturgy next weekend. We can share this gift at Mass in thanksgiving for our connection to Jesus and for belonging to the body of Christ that gathers in our parish church each week.

Continue to reflect today on the young man who gave the women such a beautiful message.

The Second Sunday of Easter

John 20:19–31

All four Gospel writers open the miracle of the resurrection by indicating that the tomb was empty. There are some other similarities, such as Jesus' appearance, even though the doors where the disciples were gathered in fear were locked. The greeting of peace was a shared inclusion, but here they depart from the main focus and go on to give a variety of details. John is the only one who gives a lot of attention to Thomas, who was not there when Jesus appeared to his disciples the first time.

Jesus came not only with the gift of peace, but he also opened their hearts to implant the life of the Holy Spirit within each of them so that they could go out and proclaim what they had seen. With the sight of Jesus and the gifts he brought them, their lives would be forever changed, and their hearts would burn with the fire of divine love from the Holy Spirit, even before that same Spirit would surround them on the Feast of Pentecost.

"I won't believe it unless I see it with my own eyes!" Have you ever said that when someone tried to give you incredible news? I can readily feel how Thomas must have felt when his fellow men told him they had seen the Lord. Thomas really wasn't a "doubting" man, but he wanted to be sure about such an unexplainable phenomenon. Look at Jesus coming back a week later and offering Thomas the convincing proof. Then realize what a faith-filled man Thomas really was. "My Lord and my God!" It seemed to be an immediate response to the appearance of Jesus once more in their midst, bringing them the same greeting of peace. Because we believe, even though we have not seen with our human eyes, Jesus has called us "blest." Let us pray for an increase in our faith, especially when we have moments of doubt, as Thomas did.

Thomas challenges us today. His courage and witness call us to stand up and let his reflection shine through us. John uses the figure of Thomas to carry one of the main threads of truth that we see in this entire Gospel, that of a deep faith in all that we have come to know in the life of Jesus and the lives of his followers. It is a message we cling to as we go out to work for the reconciliation of all people in every age.

The final passage in today's scripture is a type of conclusion in which he gives us the purpose of writing his Gospel. He continues to invite us to a deeper faith life as we take time for breaking open God's word.

Lord, we do believe. Help us to believe as Thomas did.

Third Sunday of Easter

Luke 24:35–48

The Gospels for cycle B are ordinarily taken from the words of Mark. However, last week and today we take our inspiration from two other evangelists because Mark's Gospel does not contain resurrection stories. He ends his Gospel abruptly. No portrait of Jesus can be complete unless his resurrection story is told with enough details to have his disciples go out and continue the work that Jesus began.

Luke continues the account of the resurrection in three segments:

1. Beginning with the experiences of those who were his close friends, Jesus' familiar greeting is now stamped in their hearts. "Peace be with you." Jesus asks them to free themselves of fear and the anxiety, a natural reaction for anyone whose world is suddenly turned upside down by unexpected events. Fear tended to block the hearts of the disciples, and this kept them from believing what was happening. Jesus knew this, so he asked them to give him something to eat. Jesus often sat down at table to eat with his friends. This was an action that was familiar to all of them. Meals were important for Jesus to continue the relationships that he had begun with each of them.

2. Jesus spent his human life teaching. That is a wonderful way of opening the hearts of others and encouraging them to understand what their future might hold. Jesus showed them that he came to bring something new, to cause a shift in their lives by declaring a new era that he was inaugurating. They had to learn much more about their faith because they were now called to be the hands, feet, and mouth of Jesus, passing on all that he had instructed them concerning God.

3. We have the call to continue the work that he showed them during the three years that they were with him. As he called down the Holy Spirit upon them, he opened their eyes, hearts, and minds to understand what their future was to

Celine Goessl, SCSC

become when he ascended into heaven. The Eucharist that we celebrate each Sunday is the center of the life of the church. We gather in a similar fashion as the disciples did so that we can also proclaim the mysteries that God has now entrusted to us. Jesus says to each of us today, "You are witnesses," and now that we have been given faith and a mandate to spread that faith, we must be ready to be what God calls us to be and to do.

We are a resurrection people, sent out to spread the good news.

Fourth Sunday of Easter

John 10:11–18

The story of the Good Shepherd gives us a threefold meditation about where we can go and what we can do so we may be Christ in the world today, carrying on his ministry.

1. In the first meditation, the Gospel talks about Jesus as the Good Shepherd, in contrast to a hired hand. Sheep always need a leader, and Jesus shows us how to care enough to search out those who have strayed from the church. We are also called to take care of those who have been bruised or hurt, especially the children who have been traumatized by religious leaders acting like hired hands, with little concern for what they have done to the tender lives of those they have hurt. We are called to be leaders and healers as we seek out those who need the loving care of Jesus.

2. The second meditation is about Jesus, who tells us, "I know mine, and mine know me." This describes the fact that there are no strangers in our church. Each person is known to be a friend of Jesus and is important in our Catholic community as one who has equal rights and responsibilities. This does not mean that we all fit into the same mold but that Jesus knows us individually and cares for us to the degree that he will not leave us out of his sight. Each of us is loved as though we were the only important one of the flock. If our families, our churches, our communities, or our schools would have such an attitude, we could live in such a wonderful world!

3. The third meditation in today's Gospel has a lot to do with vocation. Vocation describes women and men religious, priests, deacons and associates but in addition, each of us has been invited through baptism and confirmation to use our hands to help others, our feet to go to the poor and the needy, our eyes to see misery that we can relieve, and our ears to hear the message of the Gospel that we are called to pass

Celine Goessl, SCSC

on to others. This is what it means to be a good shepherd. Since Vatican II, there has been a growing awareness of the gifts of the Holy Spirit that are given to all persons, without distinction of color, race, or sex.

The crisis of vocations in the church today is that we have not recognized or encouraged the tremendous potential given to each member of the body of Christ. We may not be called to make a commitment to religious life, but we are all called to build up the body of Christ in our families, our parishes, and our communities.

This is the wonderful time of spring, when farmers are out in the fields tilling the soil so that crops can be planted. It is also planting time in our hearts, so we will have good pastures in which we can graze as we grow in our faith. This happens when we listen to the call of God and are willing to reach out to others with the need to pass on the word and sacrament that we receive at Mass today. If we imitate the Good Shepherd, we will receive an immense reward.

We are good shepherds of God's love.

Fifth Sunday of Easter

John 15:1–8

Our lives seem to be so dull. Activities and people demand our attention, day and night. These things keep calling us away from our primary purpose in life. During this time of Easter joy, we need to think about becoming more fruitful. Today's mention of the vine and the branches gives us the opportunity to think about the important things in life. John tells us that in order to bear more fruit, we sometimes need to be pruned, much like the vines on a branch that are cut away so new vines can sprout forth. Pruning can be a painful experience, but the life that sprouts from our hearts is something that God promises us.

Like the vine and the branches in all of the Gospel writings, the grapevine can become unyielding and produce only sour grapes if it is left to grow wild. The growth of grapes is meant for our nourishment. A grapevine grows rapidly and must be pruned often if it is to produce good fruit. Sometimes the process of pruning means the radical cutting away of tendrils that will not produce fruit. So it is with us. Are we humble enough to let God do the necessary pruning in our lives so we can become all that God wants us to be? I remember a parishioner who talked about how this pruning is necessary, but he said that he told God, "Go ahead and prune, but please don't make it hurt." Sometimes the hurt must accompany the pruning because we might not be firmly rooted and grounded in God unless God cuts away unnecessary things in our hearts that need a deeper cutting than we are ready to bear.

When we think about the call of God to carry on Jesus' mission, our first reaction might be, "God, you must be joking when you ask me to take up my cross and follow your Son." The vine and the branches can only be profitable when the pruning is accompanied by prayer. We can come back to Christ when we are sorely tempted to give up because of our weaknesses or when we feel ashamed of how we have reacted to God in the face of hardship and suffering.

Celine Goessl, SCSC

All of us are fragile, yet when prayer permeates our lives, it will become the sap from the branch by which the Holy Spirit supports us with a God-life that helps us remain faithful to Jesus, holding on to the faith that has been freely given to us. Let us take account of how our prayer life deepens from dawn to dusk every day. When we awake in the morning, we start our day by offering our entire selves in service to God, and when the activities of the day are over, we can sit down in a quiet space and thank God for all the gifts we have received that have strengthened us in our weakness. How good God is for sending us the grace to keep in touch with the life-giving presence of the Holy Spirit.

The important message of the resurrection continues day after day. Scripture reminds us, "As the Father has sent me, so I am sending you." We are called and sent as we walk in the footsteps of Jesus because he is with us and within us wherever we go.

God, prune us so we can bear good fruit
for you and for your kingdom.

Sixth Sunday of Easter

John 15:9–17

It is very important for us to remember that the most significant thing that Jesus asks of us is to love: love God, love ourselves, and love others. We have been given a model for doing this because Jesus showed us unconditional love as he hung upon the cross. The one condition for receiving the gift of love from God is that we are willing to share it by giving it away to others.

Love is a virtue that demands we give not just material things that we have received but, most of all, the gift of ourselves. Wherever we spread love, there God walks with us. This message is voiced very strongly in the Gospel of John: "As the Father has loved me, so I have loved you." What a wonderful concept, but what happens when we become stressed out by persons who are hostile to us or, even worse, show terrible hatred toward us? We might feel bitterness in our hearts and be tempted to fight back, using the Old Testament adage of an eye for an eye and a tooth for a tooth. It is important to remember that Jesus' love was not only given to people he liked. His love reached out as far as forgiving those who hung him on the cross and left him there to die a criminal's death.

I have heard a story over and over about a young child in a large family. She was the middle child, who thought that somehow her father and mother "sort of" loved her, and so did her sisters and brothers. Her family was not rich; in fact, they were barely surviving. Both parents had to work outside the home and were often not home when they were needed most. This child thought she was a burden to her family, and her life became very lonely. She finally met a wonderful boy who came to her and asked if he could be her friend. Later on, he said he could think of no one but her. Her loneliness faded away, and she became alive in a new way because of the love she felt from her friend.

That is what Jesus did for us when he showed his love and how willing he was to give his life for us. He went much further by saying

Celine Goessl, SCSC

what we heard in the last sentence of today's scripture reading: "This I command you: love one another." We cannot be truly human without love. I remember some of our older sisters telling the story of children in an orphanage who were so frail and almost lifeless. It happened that our sisters came to work in that orphanage. They began hugging all the girls and boys and showed by their attention how much they loved each child. Steadily, those children came alive and began returning that love to those around them. The children of that orphanage grew up to be kind and loving adults. The care and love of the sisters was passed on through those adults to many future generations.

Today, the word love is used in a number of ways and conveys a variety of meanings. The word might be spelled the same, but oh, how different is the meaning that we Christians have deep down in our hearts because through our faith, we learned that Jesus has given that gift to all of us. This kind of love does not always come easily. Go back to the story of the young child who learned love from another human being. Let us promise ourselves that we will make a difference in someone's life this week by the love that we show.

We cannot give to others what we ourselves do not have.

Ascension of the Lord

Mark 16:15–20

How many of you are left-handed? Well, you are in good company because God is left-handed too. This is a true story of a parishioner, who told me that he and his small daughter were sitting one night enjoying a spectacular sunset over Torch Lake in Michigan. "Isn't it beautiful what God has done for us?" he asked. "Yeah," his daughter said, "and to think that God made it all with just his left hand." The man was perplexed and asked his daughter what she meant. Her answer: "You know, Dad, that God could only use his left hand because when Jesus went to heaven, he sat on God's right hand."

At times, like this innocent child, we become confused about what the scriptures are really trying to tell us. We need to break open God's word so we do not miss the message that God wants us to have. Today's reading has two strong messages that address us:

1. We are called, by reason of our baptism, to bring the message of the Gospel to others.
2. The Lord will be with us as we carry out this important ministry.

Each of us is called in our own way. God has placed us on earth to accomplish a specific task, but we are not always clear as to what that task involves. The second reading from today's scripture points out the way in which different gifts are given to us. Some are apostles, some prophets, some evangelists, some teachers or nurses—the list goes on. In God's word, the body of Christ needs a variety of ministries to carry out the work that God calls us to do. Whatever the call today, we can, each in our unique way, be sure that we are called to bring Jesus' message to our world. St. Paul tells each of us that we are given grace according to the measure demanded by our life's future journey.

Our question might be, "How am I to carry out Jesus' ministry?" We are not all called to preach God's word, although some of us may

Celine Goessl, SCSC

be called to witness; as St. Francis says, "Preach the good news, and if necessary, use words." Christ has gone from the physical presence of people on earth, but he remains with us so we can walk in his footsteps even today. He is there with us when we may be tempted to infidelity or may feel the pressure to go out after work to drink with some of the crowd. Maybe there is a strong desire to engage in unethical business practices. So many things can arise in the workplace. Young people today will have temptations that we older people never dreamed of. Whoever we are and wherever we are, we need to make a daily decision to be witnesses of Christ because we are the presence of Jesus on earth.

We have another message from this Feast of the Ascension. Stop looking up! You will find Jesus but not by looking for him in the sky. He is not in some faraway place, as Bette Midler's song suggests ("From a distance … God is watching"). The music from her song is beautiful, but we all know better. God is not distant but in our midst.

At the end of the liturgy today we will be given a special blessing to go out and use our gifts to change the world. We ask Jesus to send the Holy Spirit so that we can help renew the face of the earth, which is in such need of renewal.

Will we know where to look for Jesus today?

Feast of Pentecost

Acts 2:1–11

We come to the conclusion of another segment of our liturgical year as we close out the Easter season. Unfortunately, this feast only lasts for one day. We do not celebrate the gift of the Holy Spirit often enough, so let us make today a true birthday solemnization of the church.

The beautiful gift of the Holy Spirit came into the world at the time of a Jewish feast, one of the three major feasts celebrated right after the Passover in the Old Testament. It seems to have been some kind of a harvest celebration, but it also was a day that the Jews commemorated the gift of the Ten Commandments given to Moses on Mount Sinai. This became a time that the followers of Jesus used in order to Christianize the already-a-feast-day in Jewish history.

This is an extraordinary time in the church year, when the apostles, along with Jesus' family, stayed in the upper room and from there had a transforming experience of wind and fire. Set in the midst of the Jewish feast, we find a great number of Jews gathered who experienced how bold the apostles were in coming forth to proclaim the reign of God in new and exciting ways. Peter's preaching was given a universal flavor as he proclaimed the Gospel to all nations, an invitation reaching out to the ends of the earth.

What does all of this mean to us as we celebrate the Eucharist today? It reminds us that on this very day, thousands of years ago, the Holy Spirit came into the hearts of believers of every denomination. There is now an inner unity through the Spirit, even in the midst of a struggling church that must celebrate its unity surrounded by culturally divergent expressions of many faiths that are visible in the world. We experience this variation even within our own families and in the surrounding cities where we live.

The same wind and fire is still blowing through our hearts today. The fire may have gone out, but if we reach deeply into our hearts, we know its heat still warms and strengthens our faith. Let us sit down

Celine Goessl, SCSC

in some quiet place, close our eyes, and become aware of the breath, fire, and noise around us. Let us inhale deeply and let the presence of the Spirit set our hearts on fire once again. Let us continue this breathing exercise for a couple of moments so that we all have an experience of what the apostles and Jesus' own family felt.

It is wonderful to be living in a time when we know the need that God has for us to continue the work Jesus began on earth. While Jesus was physically among his people, the breath of God remained in his body. When he ascended back to his Father, that Spirit was released to us. Consequently, you and I are now being sent on a very strong mission to go out into the world with the enthusiasm, passion, and energy given to us by the breath of God so we can bring the good news to all those we meet this week. We will not have the fanfare that accompanied the birth of the church, but we have faith, hope, and love and the unique gifts of wisdom, understanding, fortitude, knowledge, piety, counsel, and the presence of God that we initially received at baptism and had strengthened at confirmation. All this remains in our hearts so that we have something to pass on to those that God sends us on the birthday of our church.

Let us be among those who fly on the wind of the Spirit with fire in their hearts. Let us soar together into the dawn of the reign of God as our future destination.

Mentally, let us give the breath of God to all we meet today.

Solemnity of the Most Holy Trinity

Matthew 28:16–20

In today's Gospel, Jesus sent the disciples out to help people experience God as Father-parent. Our way of imaging God lies in our reason to see Father as Creator—one who maintains all that we cherish in life. When we speak of our brother Jesus, we glean from the readings of the church year that this person came to heal and to reach out to forgive but especially to give of himself. This is the One who fearlessly speaks out against injustice to the poor and the marginalized. Our gift of the Holy Spirit is shown through the energy we have to carry out our work as an act of love.

We know that God is a family of persons, a family of great significance. The brief passage shows us that a family can be in complete harmony and at peace with one another. This is an invitation for us to look at our own relationships as parents and children and extended family to see how our family life can be in harmony with the Trinity. Can we imitate the life of the Father, the Son, and the Holy Spirit and think about how the relationship to each person impacts our behavior with one another in our families?

God the Father planned us, created us, and put us into a specific earthly family to grow and to be loved. God the Son constantly offers us salvation, even if we have turned away from him and have chosen our own type of freedom at times. God the Spirit breathes into us an unconditional love that helps us see our parents and siblings in a new light.

Three is a special number that we find throughout scripture. At Christmas we met the holy family. Some of the first visitors at the birth of Jesus were three Magi. Then, when Jesus was getting ready for his public life, he went into the desert and was tempted by Satan three times. The story of three persons is also found in some of the parables; for example, the prodigal son, a story showing the relationship between a father and his two sons; and the Good Samaritan, who came only after the Levite and the priest had passed

Celine Goessl, SCSC

by. As we reflect on Jesus' coming closer to his death, we know that Peter denied him three times, and on the last journey to Golgotha, Jesus fell three times. As he reached the top of the hill, he was nailed to the cross, and as the sun faded and the earth became dark, three crosses were silhouetted on the hill. Finally, Jesus spent three days in the tomb. The number three is very familiar to us, and today we could read through some pages of our Bible and find other mentions of "three."

Take some time to ponder your relationship with these three persons of the Blessed Trinity. Do they have something to teach you about your own family life? This feast is not just about a mystery that we cannot comprehend, but it is also about a relationship having family dimensions. The Father is merciful and gracious, who sent the Son to save us, who in turn sent the Holy Spirit to take up residence in our hearts so we could live the kind of relationship that we see in God's family.

Let our desire and imitation of the Trinity show itself when we are kind and compassionate to our siblings. We cannot allow resentment to enter our hearts when, as parents, we make an effort to imitate the Trinity by bringing love into every relationship that we have. It is possible to carry out such a relationship, which is far beyond our understanding. We can become more intimate as a family because we share the inner beauty of family when we glimpse the heart of God.

A family that prays together stays together.

The Most Holy Body and Blood of Christ

Mark 14:12–16, 22–26

For more than a thousand years, the real presence of Jesus in consecrated bread and wine was a strong devotion in the lives of Catholics. Over time, other devotions developed, such as visits to the reserved sacrament, exposition, and benediction. At the time of the Second Vatican Council, the council fathers carefully made changes in the liturgy so that it became the center of Eucharistic devotion. It was at this time that many devotions related to the Blessed Sacrament had all but disappeared. The church community became poorer in its devotional life because such devotions had taught us how to engage in private prayer, which is a forerunner to common prayer. Many of our younger parishioners have been deprived of this ancient heritage of communal prayer by eliminating devotional practices, such as Forty Hours' Devotion.

One occurrence that has given us a greater reverence for the Blessed Sacrament is that for many years we have been able to receive Communion every time we attend Mass. Receiving the Eucharist is certainly not a prize for being good. Before we receive Communion at Mass this weekend, we will all recite the prayer together: "Lord, I am not worthy that you should enter under my roof ..." We come to receive Communion because we are sinners and need the bread of life. I received so often that it began to be a habit—until I talked to one of our RCIA participants. She told me she had gone back to her former church because she felt a deep yearning and need to receive the sacrament, but in the Catholic Church, she was asked to refrain from receiving Communion until she came into full union with the church community on Holy Saturday night. This woman taught me what it means to need such an intimate encounter with Jesus. We come to the table precisely because we are weak and hungry for spiritual food.

At the Last Supper, when Jesus told his followers to "do this in memory of me," he did not mean for the Eucharist to become a barrier

Celine Goessl, SCSC

between denominations. Yet we have a law that says only Catholics in good standing are welcome at the table. Why do we perpetuate such a barrier, particularly if those who wish to receive Communion are people of faith who truly believe that the consecrated bread and wine are the body and blood of Jesus? Today, our practices may be tidy, but what we celebrate is not. We do more than come to receive; we commit ourselves anew to become the Christ we believe in. Other religious groups believe as we do, and they have the same desire to make a commitment to carry Christ to others.

For Christians, the ritual performed by Jesus at the Last Supper and for all of us remembering what Jesus did then, the risen Christ becomes present to us as the Holy Spirit comes down upon our altars and allows Jesus to become present and to be eaten for our nourishment. Mark has preserved this sacred act and has handed it on to us. In his Gospel he made it clear that Jesus' action coincided with the Jewish Feast of Unleavened Bread and Passover, again connecting us with our heritage.

In this sacred action, heaven and earth become one.

The Season
of
Ordinary Time

Cycle B

Eleventh Sunday in Ordinary Time

Mark 4:26–34

In today's Gospel we are treated to two parables about seeds. They are very different but are complementary. It is good to read both of them to get a fuller concept of the reign of God. In fact, another parable of the sower and the seed at the beginning of this chapter will also provide insight to let us know that the proper soil must be prepared if we want to obtain a better yield.

In the first parable, the seed is planted and then the farmer simply waits for the harvest without doing much more to make it grow. He obviously has no doubt that the seed will die and new life will burst forth. The growth will be slow and will occur without the farmer's knowledge of how this will happen. We are reminded that our spiritual life will surely grow if we plant faith deep in our hearts. We should not become discouraged when we do not immediately discover how much we have grown in our faith. We need to be patient and to work toward developing the necessary qualities that will "grow" our faith. We know God will be with us to teach us how to help the reign of God become a reality during our lifetimes. Harvest, in the sense of this parable, is a symbol of God who provides the growth. That growth is God's domain, and we can only trust that God will gather all people who have been patient enough and who look forward with joyful anticipation to harvest time.

The other parable of the mustard seed sets up a contrast for us to think about. It is one of the smallest seeds but can grow to a mighty shrub or perhaps more like a weed that needs only the sun and rich soil to become large enough to provide shelter for small animals. Again, we need patience, trusting that God will provide for the needs of this tiny seed and will bring it to full growth, even though it had an insignificant beginning. In cycle A, I talked about wild mustard in our fields that was unwanted because if cows would eat it, their milk would be tainted. Such weeds would be good for nothing except to be cut down and burned. This parable very likely symbolizes a

Celine Goessl, SCSC

great kingdom that can offer life and protection to everyone living on earth. It can also tell us what happens when we tend the small seed of faith so that it will grow by leaps and bounds in our hearts.

For Jesus and for the people who read Mark's Gospel, the harvest time is very significant because it tells of the Second Coming of Jesus, either at the time of our deaths or in the end times. It is then that we will be gathered for the great harvest. The reign of God will be upon us, and we will rejoice to live forever in God's presence. We will have grown from small, insignificant persons into a huge body of Christ that enjoys eternal life when the time for a new heaven and a new earth happens.

Let us watch for signs as we break open God's word each Sunday. We will experience endless signs and growth patterns in our spiritual lives. Our future rests in God who gives us life and helps that life to grow, until God determines that it is harvest time. We will then enjoy an eternity where no person is small or of greater importance than others. We all will be equal in God's home.

*Live faith this week in insignificant ways, and
eternity will be your great reward.*

Twelfth Sunday in Ordinary Time

Mark 4:35–40

Entering into the season of ordinary time is similar to the disciples stepping into the boat with Jesus to have some quiet time after the work of the day made them weary. Perhaps they wanted to be alone with him and away from the crowds so they could enjoy his company. However, the stress of the hours with the multitude took its toll on their Master's psyche, and he immediately fell asleep from exhaustion. Still, just being with their good friend was enough reward for them.

They set out for the east side of the Lake of Galilee. Being seasoned fishermen, some of them surely knew of the possibility of sudden storms arising without warning, but the reality that they were finally alone with Jesus made them bold in carrying out his request to go to the other side of the lake.

Three elements in this story give us lessons from which we can learn: the boat, the water, and the storm.

1. The boat seems to be a favorite symbol of Mark. It is a place where Jesus can be more intimate with his friends and away from the crowds. The boat can represent the inner circle of friends and can, therefore, be used as a fitting name for the church. Boats also were the workplace for most of the apostles, and so they were familiar with this image.

2. Mark uses the concept of a lake that can be either a barrier or a means of transportation. He appears to use it as a barrier, which at this time in history shows the western side as Jewish territory and the other side as being the home of the "pagan" Gentiles. A boat could be used to breach the barrier between these two groups and bring them into close communication with each other through Jesus' efforts. Mark speaks of six crossings of the lake to teach the disciples that the followers of Jesus must be open to the acceptance of all, as the one body of Christ. The boat on the lake can symbolize

Celine Goessl, SCSC

the mission of Jesus and the church to overcome distances between denominations because we are all called to follow the way of Jesus.

3. Storms have been present in the church down through the centuries, even as they are present in the history of the twenty-first century. At the time of Mark, the church experienced a great tension between the Jews and the Gentiles. There is certainly no doubt in our minds today that the church is again in the midst of a number of storms: the sex scandal, pre-Vatican and post-Vatican theology, changes in the liturgy, moral issues that impact our society, and the like. What Jesus said to the sea he repeats to us today in the depths of our hearts. "Quiet! Be still!" and "Why are you terrified?" We are asked to listen to the gentle voice of Jesus. Storms in our lives are not necessarily bad unless we blame other persons or circumstances for our inability to face the turmoil that is part of our daily lives. Perhaps we are asked to become aware of our inadequacies, our unanswered hopes, the frustration of family life or work situations, and the poverty of our faith that makes our prayer life limp in the face of storms when Jesus is not a strong part of our faith. The Spirit of God is given to us today in the symbols of water and wind that tend to rock our small boats. This can remind us to call out to Jesus in our fear. Jesus is not asleep but is always with us and knows both our fears and our needs.

Calm our fears so we can experience the gift of peace.

Thirteenth Sunday in Ordinary Time

Mark 5:21–43

Last Sunday we experienced the power that Jesus had over the raging seas. Not only did he help the people in the small boat reach the far side of the lake, but he encountered the poor, possessed man and drove out an army of demons. Today we are back on the Jewish side of the lake and are greeted with another one of Mark's homey stories. It is full of tidbits of information, such as the gossip about expensive doctors and the lack of good done for a woman. Notice that he also adds the information about the age of the little girl. Take note of the number of times that "touch" is mentioned.

Mark's homey style pulls us into the story. We have a feeling of joy that Jesus has returned to our shore again, and we can readily place ourselves in the crowd as receiving his mercy. It is comforting to have Jesus so close once more. Our lives may have wasted energy, pain, and hurt, so we need to draw closer to him and even touch his garment. Feel the compassion for the woman who has been ill for so many years and was looked upon as unclean so that she no longer went out in public. No one could touch her, not even her husband or children. She was almost like a leper, living in her own home but separated from her family members.

Let us look more intently at this woman. She heard the great healer was in the neighborhood, so she left her home and went out into the streets of her town. I am sure she hid her identity as she made her way close enough to touch Jesus' garment. Her situation could not have been much worse; the nature of her disease made her unclean. It had been going on for twelve years at great medical expense, yet her present state was no better for it. She must have had a deep conversion of heart to be able to come out and think that if she could only touch the hem of Jesus' garment, she would be healed. The power of Jesus took into account her great faith, and she was immediately cured.

Celine Goessl, SCSC

The other account that we read about today is a report of a child whom Jesus brought back to life. These two stories play against each other simultaneously. Jairus asks Jesus to come quickly, but Jesus delays his journey to help another person. He delays long enough that his services are no long needed for the girl because she has died. He ignores the news and continues on his way because of the faith of her parents. Jesus' heart is touched by an outstretched hand, an appeal made in faith. Healing was at the center of his ministry, and the healing power that he showed is a mission that we are called to continue. When someone is terminally ill, medical skill cannot make him/her well again. What that person needs is the love of God made real for him/her through the care and concern of our touch. We receive the richness of God's blessing at every Eucharist, and then we are sent out to share that healing touch, that loving look, toward those who need us. Let us take time to look around this week and find someone who needs the compassion and healing of Jesus. Then let us remind ourselves that we have been called to be God's instruments of a faith-filled touch.

Someone is waiting for your loving touch this week.

Fourteenth Sunday in Ordinary Time

Mark 6:1–6

Mark puts Jesus' return to Nazareth right in the middle of successful stories about the miracles he performed and the astonishing power he exhibited in the surrounding towns. His neighbors could not deny reports of the marvels they kept hearing. They were most probably waiting to see what wonderful things Jesus would do in his hometown. Jesus came to their synagogue, and they accepted him there as well as in distant towns, but when they discovered that he was not going to work miracles for them, they criticized and condemned him. Jesus only wanted them to accept him into their everyday lives, but he soon discovered that their faith was very thin.

We can look at this incident and ask ourselves what it means for us in the twenty-first century in our own hometowns. If Jesus were to appear in our streets today, would we be overjoyed, or would we have the same condemnatory reactions to this ordinary man? The answer most likely lies within us as we look into our own hearts to determine the extent and depth of our faith. If we have a poor image of ourselves, how can we see goodness, wisdom, and wonder in another person? The task is to clear out the hometown streets within ourselves so we can become acquainted with the wisdom, goodness, and wonder that we hold inside ourselves. Only then can we see the prophetic gifts of those around us. Jesus wants to set up a hometown life within each of us, but when we do not accept ourselves with our own possibilities, potential, or redeemed humanity, how can we accept Jesus as a prophet in our midst?

The Gospel asks us to honor the prophets among us today. It calls us to appreciate persons we know well, especially those in our own families and among our own friends. It is a wake-up call to appreciate our spouses, our children, our neighbors, and our friends who are ordinary and who are the presence of God for us. Likewise, we can let ourselves become the prophetic presence of Christ for others so we will not miss opportunities to recognize God in our midst. Remember, the face of God is often the common face that is difficult to recognize but can become clearer because of the faith that is planted in our hearts. Take time right now to accept Jesus into your everyday life, and then enjoy the richness of a faith-filled relationship with all those you meet today. Such an experience will make you rich!

Let others be amazed at your faith in Jesus!

Fifteenth Sunday in Ordinary Time

Mark 6:7–13

We have now entered vacation time, but today's scripture reminds us that there is never a vacation from our baptismal duties of spreading the good news of Jesus. We are constantly sent out with the help and support of the Holy Spirit, who was given to us at baptism but with even greater force at confirmation. The message that Jesus gave to those chosen twelve ordinary persons is passed on to us. We really do not fully understand the word of God, but as we break open God's word each week, we realize that we are sent to live a simple lifestyle and are not to worry unduly about our physical needs. That is a difficult mandate in our consumerism society, where more is better and poverty is a negative word. To become a servant of God in a culture where selfishness is almost taken for granted is challenging and demands that we have an open and caring attitude. So much of what we accumulate in life is left unused or wasted. I know this from my own experience of moving often as I carried out my mission in life as a Franciscan sister. I have been amazed and chagrined at the accumulation of material goods that I have amassed as I moved from one place to the next.

One of the greatest ways to proclaim the Gospel is our silent witness to a simple lifestyle. Not too long ago, a bishop who had been called from the Midwest to take up residence in a diocese in Idaho said to me, "You know, it is easy to unpack a suitcase but not so the heart." We sometimes forget that the only luggage we can take with us into eternity is the love in our hearts with which we have reached out to others. Besides, have you ever seen a U-Haul behind the hearse in a funeral procession?

Today we are called to imagine we are one of the twelve, asked not to take a suitcase or money or even a sandwich, not even a change of clothes as we go about doing the work of God. We are asked to travel lightly and to stay wherever we are welcome. All of this is

Celine Goessl, SCSC

foreign to our modern life and will most likely stir up a feeling of responsible resistance to which God calls us.

It is interesting that the Gospel today says nothing about the content of the apostles' preaching, except that they were to call people to repentance. On the other hand, we are faced with great details regarding their lifestyle. This might remind us that the message we are called to share must be lived before it can be preached. We are all called and sent with the following threefold task:

1. Remind the world about repentance.
2. Rid our culture of anything that enslaves our humanity.
3. Bring people to Jesus, where they can experience healing and peace.

How can we simplify our lifestyles this week?

Sixteenth Sunday in Ordinary Time

Mark 6:30–34

There are two points that I wish to focus on this weekend:
1. The need to take times of quiet and rest
2. The response to interruptions in our workday

Jesus and the apostles had been out working without a break. They were tired and needed to rest. Jesus knew how they felt, so he took them off to a quiet place where they could relax and spend some time in prayer.

The importance of finding quiet times in our lives where we can be with Christ is so necessary that we cannot deepen our relationship with him unless we set time aside. God's voice is heard more clearly and concisely in moments of tranquility. Our entire lives are precious in God's sight, but we may never fully realize this unless we periodically find a quiet place to rest. There are three phases in Jesus' invitation: to come apart, to be alone, and to rest. Busy people will come to recognize that if they never take such periods of quiet, they will fall apart. Busy parents with small children know it is virtually impossible to withdraw and have such precious moments with Jesus until their children are asleep. One mom told me that she goes into the bathroom and closes the door, just to have some quiet time alone, but even then the children come knocking and asking her what she is doing. You may be in a similar situation, so look at what you do on Sunday, the day of rest that God requires. See how you can restore your energy by restful activities with—and even sometimes without—your children.

Our Gospel also shows what happens to the best-laid plans. Interruptions are bound to happen. Most of us could take a lesson from Jesus on how to handle interruptions gracefully when we are forced to make a change in our plans. No doubt Jesus was also weary, and after experiencing the excitement of the apostles returning from their ministry, he listened for a while and then proposed that they

Celine Goessl, SCSC

escape to a deserted place. So they got into their boat and headed downstream to a favorite spot for well-deserved peace and quiet. But the crowds were aware of this place of "R&R," so some got there even before Jesus arrived.

It is amazing how Jesus handles the situation. His compassion overrides his need for rest, and he immediately becomes a good shepherd to the sheep, who are without a true leader. Reflect on his response to the moment, and sense his compassion, unselfishness, and attentiveness to the needs of others. Take some time this week to follow Jesus' example—in his concern for others, first of all—and then allow some time to go to a quiet place alone for prayer. Try to be aware of people who are without someone to care about them, and become the presence of Jesus for them.

Think about how you spend Sunday as a day of rest.

Seventeenth Sunday in Ordinary Time

John 6:1–15

If we had continued reading Mark's Gospel, we would have found the same story of the five loaves and two fishes. This particular story is told six different times in the Gospels, so we know it was a common story of the early Christian communities and an important witness to the ministry of Jesus.

Today, crowds have come because Jesus has healed the sick. Phillip asked Jesus, "Where are we to buy bread for all these people?" Phillip commented on the economic impossibility of buying food for such a crowd. Obviously, he did not yet trust that God would provide. Then a boy—a person without status—came forward with five barley loaves and two fish, which was just enough for his own family. Jesus took the food from the boy, blessed it, and asked the disciples to distribute it to the crowd. We know the rest of the story because we have heard it often.

The miracle is initiated by a gift from an ordinary person. Miracles often depend on the gifts from within the crowd. We are aware of the needs of the poor on feast days, such as Thanksgiving when entire communities reach out to provide food. Yet there are always hungry people, and there is always a need to care for them, 365 days a year. It is summer, and around the country many people are harvesting vegetables or fruit from their gardens and fields. God provides enough to go around, but we do not always think so when we look at our diminishing farmlands, our food-bank lines, the starving children throughout the world, and the hearts of those in our own country who are without hope.

I believe that the real miracle in the Gospel story was that people began to realize there were poor people in their midst who had nothing to eat. Instead of keeping their provisions for their own families, they followed the example of this simple young boy and began to open their own baskets to share what they had brought with them. Not only were the baskets shared, but it appears that

Celine Goessl, SCSC

hearts also were opened to the needs of others. We all must open our eyes and our hearts to the needs around us so that Jesus can work miracles through us today.

Many people contribute to food pantries. Others might influence government policies so that the poor will have enough so they can live healthy lives. It is not enough to give a fish to a needy person; to teach that person how to fish is the goal for which we strive. Some persons have more than they need, but fear, or comfort, or the need for security and a sense of never having enough because they lived through the Great Depression of the '30s might keep them from sharing their abundance. Jesus speaks gently but unequivocally: "Give them the food you have."

We all have bread and fish to share as gifts, however small or great they may be. Please ask yourself today, "What bread do I have that I can share?" Offer your gifts to someone who hungers for bread for the body as well as for the soul. The fragments left over will be more than enough nourishment for your own deep hungers. (I am not speaking only of physical bread but of spiritual gifts.)

The signs we become this week are as important as the miracle we heard in the Gospel and perhaps even more so because they might be the only signs that the poor in our midst will see in their lifetimes.

Share something every day, even if it is only a smile.

Eighteenth Sunday in Ordinary Time

John 6:24–35

The bread-of-life discourse offers us a variety of directions to enrich our own desire for bread that can deepen our spiritual life. We will reflect upon three questions in this reading:

1. *Rabbi, when did you get here?*

    The crowd had followed Jesus to Capernaum. They had received bread that satisfied their natural hunger, but they still did not understand that Jesus was offering something with a greater depth than they realized. We too need to look at our motivation for following Jesus. Is it because many people are doing it or because we have felt a great hunger? We are here today to remind ourselves that we are not looking for material bread but for the nourishment that is satisfied by the teaching that God has for us.

2. *What can we do to accomplish the works of God?*

    Jesus performed many works through miracles that relieved physical suffering. He has already explained what such miracles were really about. If the crowd was asking for a miraculous repetition of what they already experienced, Jesus was saying a definitive no. He wants the crowd and us to know that he is bringing us something eternally better. The crowd following Jesus asked how he performed these wonderful deeds that they saw. Jesus tells us there is only one work of God that is important—the one to be done with the gift of faith that we all are given. Faith is given to us in order to pass it on to others.

3. The story continues with the third question: *What sign can you do that we might see and believe in you?* The crowd still did not understand but remained on a "natural" plane. Here we have an opportunity to measure our own degree of faith. Jesus gives many "signs," but they all lead to a deeper level than the crowd was ready to accept. Maybe we are also

Celine Goessl, SCSC

reluctant to go any further than just sit and wonder what this is all about. Once we look beyond the natural bread concept and truly comprehend the meaning of the bread that Jesus wants to give, and then we can see the sign today at Eucharist when Jesus becomes present in the bread and wine that we have offered during the presentation of the gifts at Mass. This becomes the true bread that we are given, but we must pay the price—through faith—of believing what Jesus is talking about.

The crowd continues to think on a natural plane as they ask Jesus to give them this bread. How do we understand this discourse about the "bread of life"? Jesus is not speaking of the Eucharist here, but he refers to himself through his teaching over all the years that he walked with people on earth.

As I mentioned at the beginning of this reflection, bread can bring great comfort, especially the bread of Jesus' teaching and the command he gives us to go out and be bread for the poor and the lonely and, in fact, all those who need someone to care about them.

This week bring "bread" to someone who needs love.

Nineteenth Sunday in Ordinary Time

1 Kings 19:4–8

Today we are using the first reading from the Hebrew scripture because it gives us a rich background for the discourse on the Eucharist that we read in the Gospels these past weeks. Sometimes we can feel like Elijah the prophet, who told God that he had enough. He appeared broken and at a low ebb in his life's journey and just wanted to lie down and die. But God sent an angel to nourish him so that in the end, he was able to complete the journey.

Many times in the bleak moments of our lives we feel like saying "I've had it!" Too many of us find ourselves crushed by the circumstances that block the paths of our journeys. In order to keep going, we all need food to sustain us. That is why it is so important to celebrate the Eucharist with the faith community each week—it is in this action where we meet God, who can fill us and give us strength to walk the proverbial forty days and forty nights until we reach our final destination. Food, of itself, is not an end, but it gets us to where we are going. Sometimes we might share a meal and go nowhere. Elijah's sentiments remind us that we have a long journey ahead. The Eucharist on a daily basis, if possible, is able to satisfy our deepest longing and help to carry us through down times in our lives.

One hears people today say, "Eat, drink, and be merry, for tomorrow you may die." More people believe this idiom than we would like to think. We Catholic Christians cannot be sustained by such a theory because it shows a lack of belief in life after death. The theology that we hear in today's Gospel (John 6:41–51) develops a strong faith in Jesus as our bread of life. But if we are nourished by this sacred bread, then we have a social obligation to go out and let ourselves be broken for the needs of the world, especially among those whose faith is weak and who might see us as the only nourishment for their journeys. It is a sobering thought that we, who eat the bread of life at each Eucharist, must then go out and be bread for others.

Celine Goessl, SCSC

As you receive Holy Communion this week, take the nourishment from this food to someone in need, and share it as you walk together to reach your final destinies. Think of the words of the angel to Elijah: "Get up and eat, else the journey will be too long for you."

What nourishment do we need for our journeys this week?

Twentieth Sunday in Ordinary Time

John 6:51–58

Last Sunday's first reading was the story of Elijah. He was worn out and just wanted to die. But an angel came to sustain him, and in the strength of the meal that was given to him, he was able to walk to the sacred mountain where he encountered God.

John speaks to us on various levels about the Eucharist throughout his sixth chapter. First, he begins on a material level, giving ordinary bread to more than five thousand people. As Jesus' lesson on Eucharist continues, he asks us to think on a higher level; he now speaks of himself as the living bread that came down from heaven. He gives us a symbol that is charged with life and meaning so that it will give us energy. Then what Jesus says calls us to rise to an even higher level. We are to pass from the physical evidence to the level of faith—to receive a sacrament. Here, Jesus' words are so strong that they shock the people. How can this mere man give us his flesh to eat?

Yet Jesus does not give any other explanation, even as his hearers are scandalized. Instead, he goes on to repeat his message three times, using a slightly different angle each time.

1. Jesus insists that eating his flesh and drinking his blood is the only way that we will receive fullness of life.
2. He tells us that this meal is a pledge of eternal life, promising to raise us up on the last day.
3. Jesus comes back to his opening concept of manna.

We know that we do not eat and drink like cannibals, but in the Eucharist we receive the body of Jesus in its eternally glorified condition. The word was made flesh; this glorified flesh has become bread for our journey.

There is a great difference between ordinary bread that we digest as it becomes part of us, and the Eucharist, which works the other way around. We are changed into the bread of life, who is Jesus.

Celine Goessl, SCSC

That is why it is so necessary to remember what we are to do when we leave church. We remember Jesus at Mass and then as we leave church, we are commissioned to "re-member" him in other persons who may need to be more closely aligned with him. We are to go out to continue Jesus' mission of mercy by bringing his presence to those we meet during the week.

It is important to spend personal prayer time with Jesus in order to ponder the importance of the Eucharist in our lives. It takes time to absorb such a mysterious gift and to determine how we are to share the Eucharist with others. In our prayers this week, let us decide how we are going to "re-member" Jesus for others and believe that he will give us the divine energy from this sacred bread to carry on his mission.

Don't forget to "re-member" Jesus for others this week.

Twenty-First Sunday in Ordinary Time

John 6:60–69

Everything was going so smoothly with Jesus and his followers until Jesus stood up and declared that he was the bread of life. Then came the complaining, the disbelief, the murmuring, and the turning away. People began walking in a different direction because the journey with Jesus had become too bizarre. Even good people, his most ardent followers, were offended and found his teaching hard to accept.

We know that we are the body of Christ, and we need to have the courage to acknowledge Jesus as he comes to us once more in our Gospel today. Will we serve Jesus and invite him into our lives? Jesus' greatest desire is to have us walk this road with him. He wants to be the bread of life for us so that we can know him as intimately as the apostles did. He wants us to follow him with our whole hearts, to be as much in love with Jesus as newly married people are in love with each other. We realize that our love, as great as it is today, must become even greater and deeper as time goes on. If we open our hearts each day with the prayer of the morning offering, we will begin to know the true bread of life and will find ourselves making decisions based on our desire to serve Jesus. We will discover the grace to forgive others, to be more active in our parishes, and to offer compassion to those in need. Before we know it, we ourselves will be the bread of Christ that is taken and broken for the world. That might be a scary thought, but I believe it is a wonderful practice as a way of showing our gratitude for the privilege of receiving Communion. When we say amen at Communion time, we are saying, "Jesus, I accept your word as God transforms me, changes me, and molds me so that my words, actions, and attitudes are a reflection of you." I am not sure we have this conviction each time we receive Communion. Sometimes I don't think about what I am really doing. All of us need to realize that God longs for us—longs to share words of guidance, comfort, love, peace, and forgiveness.

Celine Goessl, SCSC

Let us set our hearts on Jesus and exhibit a great longing for the living bread that has come to us in the Eucharist that we share, and Jesus will empower us with the capability of making our minds, hearts, and indeed our very lives into his own image. The wonderful gift that we carry with us as we leave church is that as Catholic Christians, we have a tremendous grace and power in the Eucharist, so we can and will make a difference by going out and sharing that gift with our families, our communities, and our entire world.

Open your heart, and let it happen!

Twenty-Second Sunday in Ordinary Time

Mark 7:14–15, 21–23

After listening to the Gospel of John, we once more return to the Gospel of Mark. The narrative for today is very simple:
1. A setting in which conflict is introduced
2. An explanation of Jewish purification customs, which is explained thoroughly
3. A criticism of Jesus because he does not observe the law
4. A response from Jesus

We will center on Jesus' response because he cuts to the core by explaining that his interest is in what comes forth from our hearts and not from some letter of the law outside ourselves.

People are usually judged by how they live and not by their ideals. Most of us have an ideal of living in a just and caring society. Some of us work toward this ideal in a peaceful and self-sacrificing way. When we look around at what is happening in our world, we know that too many persons seek to carry out their so-called ideals with violence as a way of moving forward.

The attitude of the Pharisees lurks within most of us at some time or another. Jesus asks us to be on our guard against outward rituals. Humans often look at appearances, but Jesus looks into the heart, and he will not be deceived. Some wicked things coming from our hearts seem quite neat and orderly to the eye and ear, but just because we are churchgoing Christians does not mean that malice is not present in our lives. The quality of our hearts, the innermost part of our beings, might be an area to which we need to give serious attention.

The heart can be the real source of the wicked things that crop up in our lives. Jesus lists sinful attitudes and actions that come from the inside out and create alienation from God. We heard in the Gospel about some who were obsessed with the danger of contamination from outside influences, from a foreign culture, or

Celine Goessl, SCSC

just from plain, ordinary dirt. It can be very comfortable to focus on external things so that we do not have to take personal responsibility for the evil that we sometimes propagate. It is surprisingly easy for us to come to Mass today and pray the familiar prayers and not be at all concerned about what is lurking in our hearts.

What are our motives for coming to Mass? Is it to fulfill an obligation of the law, to be seen by friends and neighbors, or to parade our latest styles? Perhaps it's out of an unhealthy fear that God will punish us for our absence. How great it would be to know that we are here with our faith community today and every weekend because we want to worship our Maker and show our love for God from the bottoms of our hearts! Hopefully, we come in order to express, from the depths of our beings, the teachings of Jesus in the face of the complexities of our lives in the modern world. Let what comes from within our bodies be pure love and the reflection of what we are called to be and to do as followers of our brother Jesus. Our hearts can then be mirrors of his image.

Let our hearts be as visible to others as they are to God.

Twenty-Third Sunday in Ordinary Time

Mark 7:31–37

So often we fail to appreciate our abilities to hear and speak, so we need a wakeup call from God to remind us that no gift can be considered a right or a possession that we take for granted. Today's Gospel shows us that each of our gifts has a purpose that is even greater than human communication. What we say and what we hear shapes who we are. As a Catholic community in a parish family, we are called to say thanks for God's gifts, but God also calls us to reach out in a special way to those who need us to share our gifts, especially to those who need the healing hand of someone who cares enough to be the presence of the Christ we meet in today's Gospel.

Jesus' ministry was to heal and to restore. At our baptism, we were given the healing presence of Jesus when the priest touched our ears and our mouths and said, "The Lord Jesus made the deaf to hear and the dumb to speak. May he soon touch your ears to receive his word and your mouth to proclaim his faith, to the praise and glory of God the Father." This part of the rite of baptism recalls the man in the Gospel who had a speech impediment. The use of fingers, saliva, and words are important sacramental symbols to indicate the divine power of God in our lives. Baptism brought us into the family of faith and showed us how deeply Jesus loves us. Because of that, consequences of baptism are attached to the commitment that we or our parents and godparents made. It is now our mission to go out and bring his faith to those around us. Not only must we compassionately reach out to those who are physically deaf or those who cannot speak or walk but also to the many people today who have ears but fail to hear and tongues but fail to speak of the wonders of God and of the good things in life. We all need the healing hand of Christ to help us hear and speak the language of love to ourselves and our neighbors.

This is also a wake-up call to express our concern and care for those on the margins of our society because they have physical handicaps. Inside each human person is a heart that yearns for

Celine Goessl, SCSC

relationship, for love and understanding, for companionship to replace loneliness, and for various forms of communication to take away the fear of silence. We might never know what happens inside each person when we reach out to him or her; it will become an untold story that will be revealed to us only in eternity. If someone in your family or among your acquaintances deals with such handicaps, you can be the one who figuratively proclaims, "Ephatha!" God asks us to be committed to the care of such people—those on the edge of society, those left behind in the name of "progress," and those who are vulnerable and forgotten by both church and society.

Find the face of God at homeless shelters, Vincent de Paul centers, AIDS homes, detoxification hospitals, or the Salvation Army. Let us thank God for our gifts of sight, hearing, and the ability to walk by sharing our gifts with others. When we reach out like this during the week, then we have something to bring with us when we come to celebrate the Eucharist on the weekend.

Do for others what you would like them to do for you.

Twenty-Fourth Sunday in Ordinary Time

Mark 8:27–35

Our scripture today brings us face-to-face with a basic question that each of us must answer individually. Having spent a great deal of time with Jesus, the disciples were challenged to identify him. Jesus asked them, "Who do you say that I am?" People today still think about this question because most of us long to know who Jesus really is. We can tell from this scripture passage that some compared him to prophets, or John the Baptist, or Elijah, but others saw him as a bit of a magician or a philosopher who came to town with strange ideas. There were even those who had a downright hatred for Jesus and saw him as a troublemaker, a blasphemer, and one who did not follow Jewish laws. Then Peter finally gave his best answer by announcing, "You are the Messiah."

The real question today is asked of each of us. Who is Jesus for us, and who are we willing to let him be in our lives? Like Peter, we often begin with a lofty ideal and then revert to more human ways of judging and thinking. Would Jesus need to put us with Peter, as he refers to him as Satan?

The final paragraph in the Gospel gives us a month (or even a year) of meditations to put things straight as we seek to know Jesus so that we can follow him wholeheartedly.

1. Jesus asks us to deny ourselves. This does not mean self-denial, like giving up chocolate, tobacco, or some type of entertainment. This type of denial tells us that we must get to know Jesus and take on his ways within the values of Gospel living.

2. Jesus asks us to take up our crosses. Around this time of the liturgical year we celebrate the Feast of the Exaltation of the Holy Cross, a great feast for us as Holy Cross Sisters. This feast goes beyond the picture in our minds of Jesus struggling beneath the weight of his cross. It really becomes

Celine Goessl, SCSC

a sign of repentance, a brand mark that sets us aside as those who are committed to a lifestyle as followers of Jesus.

3. Jesus asks us to follow him. Our Catholic way of life is not static but should cause us to be ready to move forward. Jesus gives us the energy and the courage to persevere in our way of life at all times, especially when the journey becomes difficult.

This reading creates a pattern that we will see again next Sunday and again later in cycle C of our readings, as Jesus speaks of his suffering, death, and resurrection. As we read these passages, we will sense that Jesus' followers misunderstood the meaning of discipleship and the need for Jesus to continue to instruct them and us, as we persevere on our journey of following him.

Who does Jesus say that I am?

Twenty-Fifth Sunday in Ordinary Time

Mark 9:30–37

I am constantly amazed at the response of the disciples, who had been with Jesus for three long years yet they did not even listen to him as he talked about his upcoming suffering and death. He had to stop them in order to ask them what they were talking about as they journeyed with him. At first their conversation appeared to be pious, as they talked about their relationship to Jesus. We are saddened because they were more concerned about who was the most important among them. Our concern here needs to be how much we are like that group of special followers.

Certainly Peter thought he was important because Jesus called him the "rock" and most probably proclaimed him the leader of this little band. John probably thought he was closest to Jesus because they seemed to have spoken heart-to-heart, and he had become Jesus' beloved. Andrew was one of the first to follow Jesus—would that not count for something? Judas was proud because Jesus entrusted him with the purse for the entire group. But Matthew kept the accounts. Each had his reasons to think he was the most vital person in the life of their group.

Then Jesus put an end to this nonsense. He needed to teach them a strong lesson. He went out to the street and found a child (probably a little girl), brought her back, and used her to tell them how much he valued each person. The sight of the uplifted face of this child must have made them feel foolish and their arguments empty! Hopefully, they realized that true greatness does not come from having power or by being better than others. What made them genuinely great was that they were given the opportunity to be of service to others. Contrasting their status to the presence of the small child in their midst had shown they lacked trust. This fact must have made them feel very insignificant and ashamed.

What lesson can we glean from this story? The true test of discipleship for us is to listen, to observe, and to be open to life,

Celine Goessl, SCSC

as this child was. Can we take this lesson to heart and reach out to others, even to those in our own families, in a way that shows how much we treasure the virtue of humility so we can become simpler in our thinking and acting? An attitude of importance does not make much sense when we look at Jesus' example of his treatment of others. So often we have seen that God has no favorites but that each of us is equal in God's sight, and that is all that matters.

> *Be as simple as children and as wise as*
> *the great people of the Bible.*

Twenty-Sixth Sunday in Ordinary Time

Mark 9:38–43, 45, 47–48

Mark is trying to tell us something that even some church leaders today are not willing to take seriously. He says that any person of goodwill who graces the world with the love of Jesus is worthy to be part of the church. The misguided notion that only our church has the real truth and only its members can be part of the body of Christ seems out of character, as far as Jesus is concerned. Why, then, do we have such a weak ecumenical spirit, which was one of the priorities of the Second Vatican Council more than fifty years ago? Jesus shows us in the Gospel today that his tender heart rejoices in the beauty of goodness, no matter where it is found or who proclaims it. The questions we might ask are "Does Jesus say that there are no outsiders? Does everyone belong to the body of Christ, even the Protestants, the Muslims, and the Jews? Why, then, are we not one in spirit and in truth?"

This thought makes us turn the spotlight on ourselves. The idea of a little child is brought back again this week. Reflecting on becoming as children during these coming weeks makes us ask ourselves where we belong. The thought of cutting off our hands or feet or tearing out our eyes is not something that Jesus advocates. That is self-mutilation in a literal sense, but as we contemplate more closely what this text is telling us, we can gather some very important insights:

1. Hands are meant for greeting and welcoming, for serving and giving, for healing and uniting. Our hands belong to Christ by reason of our baptism. If we use our hands to withdraw from good deeds, if we have close d fists that do not reach out to others, then we have already cut our hands off from Christ.

2. Feet_are meant to help us go to carry on Jesus' mission of standing firm and bringing the good news to the poor. If we use our feet for running away from our duties or for marching

Celine Goessl, SCSC

to the sound of terror and war, surely our feet do not belong to Christ.

3. Eyes are the windows of our souls that shine forth with the love of God to all we meet. They are the windows through which our hearts have contact with the outer world. They bring light into the darkness of today's sinful world. Dark, shifty eyes filled with hate or prejudice is not part of God's plan for us.

Heaven or Gehenna? Where will our journey lead us? Gehenna was a place outside of Jerusalem that was the city's garbage dump. Even more than that, it was a place under a curse because in pagan times, child sacrifices took place on that spot. However, in the scripture today we can look upon it as a garbage pit of wasted time, treasure, and talent. If we accept the love and fellowship that Jesus offers to his followers, then God demands that we eliminate from our lives selfishness and prejudice against other denominations and persons. This is a radical call of Jesus to all people. Jesus values an inclusive mentality. All people of goodwill journey side by side. For us, this means that anyone who is not against us is for us. Think of what we can do this week to strengthen the bonds of ecumenism in our families, our neighborhoods, and our parishes as we follow the values of the Second Vatican Council.

Who, really, is our neighbor?

Twenty-Seventh Sunday in Ordinary Time

Mark 10:2–6

Today's Gospel offers us two distinct lessons. I don't know how these two are connected, so I won't even try to connect them in this reflection.

1. Mark gives a strong message to us about the indissolubility of marriage and says there are no exceptions. He tells us something not found in the other Gospels—that women can also divorce for good reasons. There is still great controversy regarding divorce and remarriage among us. As people live longer today, there are those who are faithful to their vows for sixty or more years. Spouses who remain together longer than ever are to be praised and thanked.

    However, there are also those who might not have been mature enough to marry when they did or who hid their addictions and behavioral problems. Such problems have caused unbearable suffering so that the ideals they promised on their wedding day cannot be lived. We have a process of working with such cases that we call annulments. Some people may choose to go through this process. Even Pope Francis has a compassionately gentle way of dealing with these people. He is helping to make the process of annulment less traumatic.

    As a pastoral administrator in parish work, I have helped persons walk the journey of undoing something that might not have been a true marriage because of circumstances. This step needs the care and compassion of persons who are educated in canon law and can help diocesan marriage tribunals to facilitate the process. It can happen so that the church, suffering with individuals who have found it impossible to live out their commitment to marriage, can dissolve the covenant. This is done when it can be proven that a true sacramental marriage never took place because of the

Celine Goessl, SCSC

inability of a spouse to make a permanent commitment. The church is called upon to alleviate the trauma connected with broken marriages. Today, much more care is taken to prepare couples thoroughly before they come to the altar to seal their sacramental covenant. That is the reason why people are required to take their premarriage instructions seriously.

2. The last section of today's scripture might be overlooked when people are concerned with divorce and remarriage. This may have been a way of diverting the Pharisees in their trickery against Jesus, but it may also have been a way to share the gentleness and compassion of our Savior. It can indicate to us how we are to receive people who suffer greatly at the hands of other people. The disciples of Jesus wanted to have parents take their children away and not to bother Jesus because they thought he had more important things to do. Jesus stops them and takes the opportunity to tell us that children are the people who have a greater inclusion in God's kingdom when they die. He is telling us that we are not to stop anyone from coming to our church. We have no right to place obstacles in the path of someone's faith journey. There is no right or wrong way to approach Jesus because he wants to welcome everyone.

Both of these lessons show us how to accept people as they are and to welcome them as equals in our parishes.

The reign of God is a free gift for all those who want it.

Twenty-Eighth Sunday in Ordinary Time

Mark 10:17–30

Mark gives us three stories related to how we are to deal with worldly possessions. We begin with *the story of the rich young man* who has the desire to follow Jesus. He appears to be very enthusiastic, but underneath his fervor, one can sense his need to accept the reign of God by using his own preconceived opinions. Jesus seems to respond a bit harshly by asking the man why he calls Jesus good. Then Jesus continues to ask about living the commandments, especially those that refer to social relationships. Perhaps he wants to set up a covenant relationship with the man. Finally, Jesus asks him to renounce his wealth as a condition for becoming a follower of Jesus. Looking into the man's heart, he might have seen no room for accepting the reign of God.

From this follows *the conflict between wealth and the reign of God.* Surely Jesus loved this man and wanted him to clean out his heart so Jesus could fill it with gifts to help him. In another place in scripture, Jesus tells us that where our treasure is, there our hearts will be. The man turned away, and we do not hear from him again, so we will never know what he finally decided. The disciples must have felt sorry for him. They realized that salvation is completely dependent on God, and that it is easy to let worldly possessions consume one's time and energy. Jesus went on to explain about the difficulty of a camel passing through the eye of a needle. Of course, this was not to be taken literally, as the eye of the needle was a place in a mountain pass where a camel and his master passed through only with great difficulty. Jesus meant to emphasize the problem.

We now come to *the benefits of renunciation.* Once more we encounter Peter, who has become the spokesperson for the small band of apostles. He was assured of the benefits of a future life with Jesus in heaven, but all of them were told about the hundredfold in this life. Jesus' explanation brings out the riches that are present. We might be surprised to see the inclusion of persecutions as a benefit.

Celine Goessl, SCSC

There is a lot of wisdom in this Gospel! What Jesus is saying might have frightened the rich young man—and us too. Most of us today have far too many riches to comfortably divest ourselves of all the creature comforts that we take for granted. We live in a consumerism society and might be considered upper-middle-class people. When we stop to count up our riches, they are many: a roof over our heads and food on our tables; a loving family and many friends; different clothing for all seasons of the year; a fine education; and transportation to help us live a mobile life. However, all these commodities need not keep us from attaining the reign of God. If God is our most precious gift, we will be able to live more simply while we enjoy God's gifts. We will come to realize that what we are given in this world, we are asked to share with those who have less.

The lesson we learn from these three stories is that wealth brings with it an obligation to reach out to others. If our own hearts are filled with possessions, we don't have room for God.

God calls us to share from our abundance
so God can reward us with more.

Twenty-Ninth Sunday in Ordinary Time

Mark 10:35–45

All the scripture readings at this time of the year are anything but ordinary. Each week we are confronted with extraordinarily serious obligations if we wish to be disciples of Jesus. Today, Mark shows us three facets in our call to discipleship:

1. *We will need to suffer.* We know the journey that Jesus walked was filled with sufferings. What he did, he asks us to do. We are asked to "drink the cup" and "be baptized so we can more readily repent and accept hardship." When James and John asked for the privilege of sitting with Jesus, one on his right hand and the other on his left, the response was only that they must suffer.

2. *The role of placement in the reign of God* comes as a second condition for discipleship. The disciples of Jesus were very slow to learn this role. We read about many people in church history who wanted to be first. In dealing with our fallen nature, we all want to be "somebody." Let us thank God for giving us Pope Francis, who has a strong desire to humbly follow Jesus. We would do well to take him as our model so we can carry out today's Gospel message.

3. *The role of leadership in the church*—Jesus gives us two words to carry out this duty: servant and slave. Servants in the time of Jesus were commissioned to wait on table and to carry out other domestic services. The duty of a slave was in a lower realm than a servant. Jesus told his followers and us that longing to do everything humanly possible to obtain a top position of authority will bring us nothing but emptiness. Here again we go to Pope Francis as our mentor. The entire world sees him as a servant. On the other hand, those in leadership positions within the church hierarchy have been exposed for their lifestyles of privilege. One of the first things Pope Francis did after taking office was to

require the leaders at the Vatican to change their habits and live a simpler lifestyle. This carries out the ideal that we find in scripture that the first will be last and the last will be first.

The history of our church has been badly scarred by power, prestige, and possessions within the hierarchy but also within the lives of the laity. Calling for the Second Vatican Council, Pope St. John XXIII began a new direction in Catholicism to help us return to the values and practices of the earlier centuries. There still needs to be a cycle of renewal that did not quite catch on after the council ended. Today, thankfully, we are called to a deeper prayer life and a more solid program of education, especially for adults. Many parishes and dioceses are concerned about efforts to lead local communities to be more faithful to the spirit that permeated the Second Vatican Council. We can do much to help our community by providing good education programs for adults as well as for children. However, knowledge is not enough; we need to take what we know and put it into action.

As we look back at the three duties that Mark gives us in his Gospel today, let us take time this week to flesh out those duties and honestly decide what we can do as we put the gifts God has given us at the disposal of our parishes' needs.

Would there be enough evidence by our actions
for a court to convict us of Christianity?

Thirtieth Sunday in Ordinary Time

Mark 10:46–52

I recall when cataracts were growing over both of my eyes. What a frightening experience to feel the loss of sight! That gave me a glimpse of how Bartimaeus must have felt because of the total blindness that he experienced.

We know that even if we have eyes and can see, that doesn't always mean that we see what is most important in life. There are so many ways in which physical blindness is not the worst catastrophe, when we think of what spiritual blindness does to us. We are sometimes victims of all sorts of blindness; for example, hatred, pride, jealousy, anger, or greed.

When Jesus opened the eyes of people in his day, it was not only to an awareness of blindness in those who needed the restoration of physical sight but also to those whose lives had grown dim because of sin. At times we are such people, and we need to cry out, "Jesus, have pity on us." This is referred to as the Jesus Prayer. It is a wonderful model for us to use because sometimes we are blind before God, and we need to become beggars because we are unaware of our blindness. The Jesus Prayer helps us to stand in God's presence with Bartimaeus as we yearn to say, "Lord, I want to see!" This man was blind but he prayed, and because he persevered and believed that Jesus could cure him, his faith gave him the gift of sight.

We will notice that he did not follow the injunction of Jesus, who told him to go his way because his faith had healed him. No, he became aware of a new light, so he cast off his old way of sitting at the gate to beg. He began walking a new path in union with Jesus. Today we are given that same opportunity to cry out to Jesus in our need and to believe that he will heal us too. The best way to proceed is to leave our old sinful ways behind and find strength and zest for

Celine Goessl, SCSC

life that will help us walk in the new light of faith. If we are ready and courageous enough to take this step, God will open our eyes to new possibilities. Let the cry of the blind man—"Lord, that I may see"—be on our lips and in our hearts often this week.

Continue your journey of faith, and go wherever God leads you.

Thirty-First Sunday in Ordinary Time

Mark 12:28–34

During the past seven Sundays we recognized that Jesus was on a journey to Jerusalem, where he would be put to death. Today we learn that he has reached his destiny. As the group was traveling, Jesus continued to teach his disciples so they would carry on his ministry after he was no longer physically among them. Today, and for the next three Sundays, we will be given insights into the obligations of a disciple because we are called to become ardent followers of Jesus so these obligations will bring about the reign of God here on earth.

Jesus, in one succinct statement, asked all of us to put our priorities in order. He told us that love comes first. The other two ministries of worship and practical daily living will only have significance if they are a response to God's love.

An unnamed scribe comes to follow Jesus in Jerusalem. He has an open mind and heart. Jesus, who looks into the depths of all hearts, saw this openness and rewarded him by saying, "You are not far from the kingdom of God." Nothing is as powerful as love! We know it becomes a powerhouse of peace, tranquility, and grace for us to become all that God calls us to be.

We are called to love God with all the strength that we have, and if that is not enough to ask, we are also summoned to love others as we love ourselves. The phrase in the Lord's Prayer that points out this guideline is "forgive us as we forgive others." The love to which we are called makes us leave our own wants behind as we reach out to the poor and needy around us. When this kind of love is evident in the Christian community, people "will know that we are Christians by our love," as an old hymn states.

Celine Goessl, SCSC

What is most important in life? What do we need to do in order to live the Gospel truth of this Sunday's reading? What will you and I do this week to bring about the closeness of the reign of God in our families, our workplaces, our neighborhoods, and our churches?

We will find no greater commandment than to love.

Thirty-Second Sunday in Ordinary Time

1 Kings 17: 10–16
Mark 12: 41–55

What a gift to be given such meaningful scripture passages right after we were reminded to reach out to the poor in love! We know about the great sums of money that are wasted on sinful exploitation of the poor and marginalized in our country. Jesus' obvious measure is not from appearances such as those that were made by guilty exploiters. His obvious measure is not from such sinfulness, but he penetrates the depths of our souls to seek the motivation and hidden intentions of our actions. If only all citizens would be convinced that God wants our hearts more than our possessions and that the poor and marginalized cry out for love even more than for material goods.

Our liturgy today celebrates the lives of two widows. First, we encounter the widow of Sidon, who shared her last meal with the prophet because he begged her for a little sustenance. Then we meet the woman in the temple who comes up to the money container to give two tokens of love. She could have kept one and placed the other in the box, which would have indicated that she was giving half of her possessions, but she obviously knew that heaven was not in the business of calculating, so she was willing to let go of her last penny to show her thanks to God for his gifts.

God is looking for our lives, not for our possessions. We are called today to look at others and at situations in our lives with the eyes of Jesus. Let us take time this week to put on the "eyes" of our Lord so we can see life and the masks that we wear as Jesus sees us. The two widows teach us that love must be our guiding force and that, just as Jesus, we need to give ourselves to God totally and unconditionally. This is not possible without the gift of God's grace, which we are given so freely merely by asking. As we surrender to love, we will be rewarded for recklessly giving all to the one who gave all to us.

Celine Goessl, SCSC

Look at the second widow in the Gospel again. She came in unobtrusively and walked up to the thirteen big metal money chests that were apparently shaped like upside-down trumpets. When coins were thrown in (paper money was not used yet, so there could not be a silent collection), there was a resounding echo of how much each person gave. The widow's tiny two coins must have just tinkled a bit, and then she turned away and was gone as quietly as she had come. Jesus then turned to his followers and used a phrase that was surely to become an important pronouncement, which silently said to the listeners, "Please pay attention." Jesus said, "Amen, I say to you ..." He calls us to look into our own hearts with his eyes and to see behind the outward show so that we can read our inner hearts and give to God what belongs to God. This is a big order for the week! It reminds me of the farmer who was praised by his pastor for his generous support to the church. The farmer merely said, "The way it is, whenever I give God a shovel full of anything, God shovels more back in my direction. You see, God has the bigger shovel."

Give back to God, not from your abundance
but from your poverty.

Thirty-Third Sunday in Ordinary Time

Mark 13:24–32

We can be absolutely sure about only one thing and that is, one day you and I will die. By the time many of us return home after work each evening, it is dusk or even dark. Winter speaks to us of darkness and death. We know that the only way we can see the blossoming of flowers and leaves on the trees next spring is to go through the dark months of winter so that we can share in the patterns of new life when spring arrives.

People seem to have lots of questions about death. Just the other day I read about the reemergence of the idea of limbo. That makes me wonder what I think about such a strange concept or even about the concept of purgatory that I learned as a child. Do these concepts fit into my experience of a God who loves unconditionally? Many of us try to say yes to God each day. Yet we need to acknowledge the selfishness that holds us back from totally enjoying God's love. Let us ask ourselves if we really love God with our whole hearts, our whole minds, and all our strength. I have to admit that this is not always true of me. I know that sometimes my love needs to be purged of selfish traces so I can end up totally open to God's unconditional love.

Let us not forget about purgatory as a state of punishment! Our God is not interested in punishing us when we have struggled to overcome negativity and striven to accentuate the positive during our lives. Besides, purgatory is not a place but a state of mind. Often, I believe God gives us that final opportunity to be cleansed of our sinful ways just before we die, even as we enjoy the happiness of knowing that we are in the embrace of God for all eternity.

But what is the point of praying for the dead? We believe that we are united to all people as part of the body of Christ. Just as my hand can relieve the irritation of a muscle cramp, or my finger can relieve an itch in my eye, in the same way my prayers can benefit the pain of other members of the mystical body of Christ.

Celine Goessl, SCSC

Let us take a new look at eternity and put aside the worry about when death and/or the end of the world will come. We are asked to live each day with the knowledge that we are loved by a God who already embraces us. When the day of our transition from earthly life to eternal bliss comes, it will be like the time that a fig tree comes into full blossom in the summer. Enjoy winter as it sets in around us and know that down the road of our faith journey, summer will surely come.

Reflect on which season of the year you like the best.

Feast of Christ the King

John 18:33–37

Today we come to the end of another church year; it closes on a sad note with an incident taken from Good Friday. We encounter two leaders, Jesus and Pilate, who can both legally claim kingship but in such different arenas. Jesus is the one who touches the hearts and minds of people to draw them into a loving embrace, while Pilate appears to be out of touch with such intimacy as he questions Jesus about his regal ministry.

We leave the Gospel of Mark and turn to John for our reflection today. John sometimes uses irony to get his point across. Pilate demands to know if Jesus is a king, but he does not get a direct answer to his question. Rather, Jesus calmly but solemnly sends a question right back, which puts Pilate on trial. After two thousand years, Jesus' challenge to Pilate still rings true today. We are still asking Jesus who he is. Why do we continue to ask, and what motivates us to do so? Do we really want to know who he is? If we do, then some challenges confront us.

The predicament confronting Pilate has definite parallels to ours. Pilate is disturbed, under pressure, indecisive, and anxious not to rock the boat. Jesus appears to be reaching out to Pilate, calling him to look at his way of life and to reconsider his set of values. At the end of the church year, we too are called to consider our lifestyles and our values that could have become skewed by the values of the world in which we live. As in the time of Pilate, we also have to deal with unjust use of power, corruption, and exploitation by both church and civic authorities. What is our response?

All we need to do is to look at Jesus as he stands before Pilate, simply dressed, haggard from a sleepless night in prison, being questioned by a ruthless leader who cares nothing about human kindness or a heart reaching out in love. Jesus' reign has nothing to do with ambitions of power, prestige, and possessions. The only thing he wants is to walk humbly with us, to touch our hearts, and to show us how to be truly free so we can live in peace. After the long journey, we want to enter the reign of God through the path of the cross and suffering, by seeking to imitate our King as we make room for him in our hearts each day.

Jesus is the model—the perfect witness—who gives us courage and strength to undergo everything in God's name. I would like to end on a personal note. One of the founders of the Holy Cross Sisters, Mother Theresa Scherer, has asked us to be courageous and strong. This is a clear call to us to live a life that will prepare us to be happy as we step into a new church year with hope. Come and join us, as together we all commit ourselves to the one who is our truth and our salvation.

Leave behind old habits, and step into a new
church year with a clean heart.

The Season
of
Advent

Cycle C

First Sunday of Advent

Luke 21:25–28, 34–36

Luke approaches the beginning of a new liturgical year in a very different fashion, as compared to the other evangelists. He tells the story of Jesus, which we have heard many times. But strangely enough, he starts by talking about the *end* at the *beginning* of Jesus' life. As we reflect on this New Year, we might wonder why he is writing about the end times.

This lets us see the last days as the beginning of a new era. Some of us tend to be futuristic, letting go of the past and being happy to walk into the future before we experience it. That is what Luke is doing as he talks about the new life that will come with the birth of Jesus. He begins by showing us how the entire universe is in turmoil, and a new life has to come so we can go on living. We need time to improve the quality of our lives, to turn ourselves around, and to take a path where we will be taught how to live life in a better way. Luke used the terrors in our universe as a backdrop to contrast what will happen when this baby, Jesus, comes to show us how to live. During these next four weeks, we are given time to begin that task.

Jesus tells us to read the signs of the times. It is a new beginning for us, a time to start over. Perhaps this year we can do much better so that we won't be caught by surprise as we prepare for his Second Coming. How gracious God is to give us time to begin anew so we can come to a deeper understanding of our relationship with Jesus as he comes to us in new and exciting ways.

What are signs of God in our lives that help us get ready for this new coming? This is a somewhat harsh Gospel, where we are given a vision of terrible things in nature, of frightful things we are about to experience if we look deeper into our hearts with the eyes of faith, rather than only with our physical eyes. It is a time of darkness, of quiet, of taking into account how we have left the path we were shown at our baptism, when we became priests, prophets, and royal people. Now is the time when God calls us to "stand erect and raise our heads." Our redemption will come in the form of a tiny baby, born in poverty and without fanfare. What Jesus will become will slowly be shown to us after we pass through the "valley of darkness" and come to recognize the light of the world through the eyes of our faith.

We know that this Gospel was written for people who were suffering persecution. Today, the persecution that we suffer might not be visible because we have become accustomed to the frightening signs of evil all around us. It is our task to walk through the powers of this world so we may be cleansed. It is then that we will be able to see the newness of life that God sends to us in the form of a baby. Otherwise, we could not truly recognize such a gift.

We return to these weeks of Advent every year in order to appreciate the first coming of Jesus at our baptism, and we hold the light we were given then so we can see clearly the Second Coming of Jesus as we enter eternity.

What are the signs of God in our everyday lives?

Second Sunday of Advent

Luke 3:1–6

We continue to recognize God's signs as we reflect on today's Gospel, which is set on a worldwide stage. John cries out in the wilderness on the one hand, and the commercial Santa Claus cries in his own wilderness on the other hand. Both of these voices ring in our ears, and their effects reach the wilderness of our minds and hearts. Which Advent path will we take as we wander in the wilderness during the time between now and Christmas? We all have paths to straighten wherever our hearts have veered off from the loving voice of God. We can celebrate Advent properly only if we know of our need for a Savior.

It is significant that the story of the coming of Jesus begins in the wilderness, a place where it is difficult for life to survive, where wildlife searches us out as worthy prey. It reminds us to look ahead to the beginning of Lent, when Jesus goes out into the desert. Although Advent is more a time of joy than of penance, it still calls us to live out our commitment, knowing that Christmas is about more than food and drink, presents and hilarity, comfort and excess. It is about preparing a path to let God have a greater say in how we live our lives. Will we hear the right voice in the hustle and bustle of all that faces us in our commercial world?

Preparing a way for God demands more than cosmetic changes; it requires a major change of heart. Let us dig down into the roots of our beings. Perhaps we can center on our relationships with our families, the Christian community, and our friends. Is the voice of God calling us to spend more quality time with them as we cut down on other less significant commitments? In the physical realm, we might be called to eat healthier foods, especially as we come closer to the rush of Christmas parties. In terms of our spiritual growth, God calls us not only at this season but all year long to develop a deeper prayer life. We are asked to reach out to the poor and the marginalized instead of centering our attention on buying expensive gifts for friends. This might demand a complete change of heart in helping us set up priorities.

We all have paths to straighten wherever we discover we have deviated from the ways of God. The wilderness of our twenty-first-century lifestyles can bring frustrations and failures, sandstorms of fear in a violent world, and shadows that conceal the wild animals or compulsions that have gripped us and leap out to claim our allegiance. Unless we face these things honestly, we will not come to realize our need for a Savior. Remember, into the wilderness, "Come, Lord Jesus!"

Give yourself quiet time this week so
you can hear the voice of God.

Third Sunday of Advent

Luke 3:10–18

This is a season of questions, and the big question today is, "What is it that we should do?" People crowded around John as he called them to repentance. It is here that they asked what they had to do. This also gives us another reason for our call to discipleship and what it means, especially at this time, when we are in such a frenzy about shopping and decorating, forgetting about the Advent spirit of looking deeply into our hearts and listening to John the Baptist, who insists on some stringent principles.

"What, then, shall we do?" There is no word about getting gifts, or jumping on the bandwagon of a specific cause, or getting hooked on television ads that tell us what we need. John simply asks us to eliminate any grandiose expectations of what we need to be happy. We are to take time to notice and appreciate the ordinary things in life, to slow down enough to look at people and at nature that surrounds us. We are called to strengthen our prayer life through reflection on the gracious presence of the God within us and in the hearts of those whose lives we encounter each day. We are told to make positive efforts to be honest and forthright and to be content with what we have at the present moment. This is what will bring joy to our hearts on this Sunday of rejoicing as we gently journey toward Christmas.

"What, then, are we to do?" Preaching alone never converts anyone. We are to make God's presence visible on earth by what St. Francis says: "Go out and preach, and if necessary, use words." Both Francis and John give us simple answers to this question. They could be saying to us, "Do not eat too much junk; be kind to your enemies; go for a walk in the woods; do not worry; share as you stand in solidarity with the deprived poor among us; or pray and work diligently for an end to war and the killing of innocent life."

"What should we do?" John's answer to us would be the same as he gave to the soldiers, police, tax collectors, church leaders, and ordinary townsfolk. Look into our hearts and let go of all negativity, all violence, all intimidation, and all sin that keeps us from knowing the real Jesus when he comes into our daily lives. John made it plain that he was not the Christ. He could not change human hearts. He could only baptize with water that could wash the dirt away from the outside of the body but could not change the minds or the ways of people. In the end, the authorities came and arrested him, threw him in prison, cut off his head, and put it on a silver tray. He lost his head because he had not been able to eradicate the sin that sits deep down in human hearts. It is only Jesus, who has come, who is here with us now, and who will come daily to bring the joy that will open our hearts when we make room for him.

Today, John insists that the best is yet to come. Look for the best in yourself and in others so that joy may abound in our world. This happens when we carry out the difficult question, "What do you want us to do?" It is solidified when we accept the God of love who desires to reach into our hearts ... the God of life who will come to beautify the wintry branches of our lives that bear no fruit ... the God of light who will brighten the dark depths where we live in fear. It is only the light of God who will replace darkness with the gifts of joy and peace that happens when Jesus is among us.

Make room for Jesus by being happy with
the simple, ordinary things of life.

Fourth Sunday of Advent

Luke 1:39–45

Today our scripture focuses on God's gift to us in Jesus Christ. The spotlight turns to the woman who brought Christmas into the world. We have a second woman who was also important because she was responsible for preparing the world for such a wonderful gift. In our reflection today, we need to center more deeply on these two women and their roles in carrying out the will of God. Mary started out on a long and arduous journey, without counting the cost of traveling south along the Jordan River and then up into the mountainous area of Jerusalem. This had to be a dangerous and very exhausting trip for a pregnant woman to undertake. She knew she was on a mission, sent by God, to help Elizabeth. She most probably didn't even think of counting the cost because she was sent by the Holy Spirit. This is a clear story of how the Spirit moves throughout the world and how the Spirit's voice stirs up hope and faith.

That is what happened when Mary came to Elizabeth with her "shalom" greeting. What a beautiful visitation—two women in distress, giving themselves to each other as they carried out the will of God with bold stirrings of joy and strong signs of the presence of the Spirit in their lives. This holy encounter poses some questions for us to think about. How does this meeting of two faith-filled women make a difference in our daily lives? What meeting with others will God ask us to carry out in the all-too-brief time between now and Christmas? It calls us to listen to the Holy Spirit with greater intensity since the time is so short. Take time to answer a few questions that impact your own life.

Whose voice greets you with "shalom"? Does your voice stir up joy in those you meet? Is the Spirit's power visible through you? What is ready to be born in you as you wait for the birth of the Savior? We need to make room inside ourselves for God, for the word that will become flesh through the coming of Jesus. Like Mary and

---

Celine Goessl, SCSC

Elizabeth, we need to give ourselves to God so that God's word can enter us and, through us, become present to the world.

This week will be full of visits, greetings, travels, and perhaps reaching out to the poor who need sanctuary. We cannot wait for greater strength before setting out on our journey, nor can we wait to see more clearly where God is calling us to go. Let us follow the example of Mary and have the courage to go to those who need our loving touch. It is the perfect time to begin our own story of Christmas by responding to that which grips our hearts as we read the scriptures today. Let us use our voices to stir the hearts of those around us to greater joy and delight as we share the God within us. Both Mary and Elizabeth have been models for us. Pass on the gift of "shalom" to others—the greatest gift God has given to us.

Jesus desires to grow within us.

The Season
of
Christmas

Cycle C

Feast of the Holy Family

Luke 2:41–52

This is the only story about Jesus' youth. It indicates that Jesus showed extraordinary wisdom in his childhood, although he was relatively unknown for the next three decades. The scripture centers on family-life values.

The holy family is again on a journey in observance of the Jewish Feast of Passover. We might see this feast inserted in the church year at this time because of the hectic life we experienced in trying to keep Christmas in perspective as family values erode due to the commercialism of our time.

This year, let us make family life a priority. We can glean the virtues of family life from today's Gospel. It is a transition of Jesus from childhood to adulthood. He is still a child, obedient to his parents, but already he carries out God's will with an adult concern as he sits and converses with the leaders in the temple. That is why, when Mary and Joseph find him after searching for three days, Jesus tells them that from now on, his priority is to do the work of his Father. Yet he obediently returns to his home, where he learns more about family life so he can hand on to us the values by which we should live.

When we think of what this means for Jesus, we realize that he grew up in a closely knit family in a small Palestinian village. Regardless of where we live today, family life needs to take on the values that we learn from this small, insignificant household. Today, we pray that government organizations will support family values, but our faith plays a much more important role in helping to build a solid family life in the face of social mores that are not that much help in carrying out family values. We are all aware of today's situation as we look around and see so many homes broken through violence and addictive behaviors. Single-parent families abound, and that often leads to lack of time to love and care for children. Children absorb values from their parents, who teach by the way they live and work

Celine Goessl, SCSC

and pray. Positive life patterns are present as well as negative ones, and children's minds are quick to absorb both.

We look at the family of Jesus and the things that were not easy for them. There was a solid life of worship and respect, but they also suffered loss and anxiety and the hardships of poverty. Mary must have often thought of Simeon's prophecy, as he told her that a sword would pierce her heart. Joseph surely had a lot of anxiety when he did not completely understand what God was asking of him.

This is also true of our own family life. We struggle with adversity as we live with uncertainty and the many troubles that we face every day. However, God is our support in all that we must endure and will bring joy and peace to our family life. We only need to ask for God's guidance.

What do we need to be happy and peace-loving families?

Feast of the Epiphany

Matthew 2:1–12

These days can be dreary when we look up into the night sky and cannot see any stars because of the banks of clouds. It makes the reflection on the star of Epiphany shine even more brilliantly in the darkness of our imaginations and our world. In fact, there is so much faith, hope, and love in that star that we can imagine it bursting into our imagination with startling effects. Like the Magi, the inner star of our faith calls us to search and discover the presence of Jesus in our hearts and in the life around us.

Three groups of people are in today's story from the Gospel of Matthew:

1. Herod and the political men in Jerusalem

   These were the power-hungry people whose primary religious ideal was their own advancement. They were a desperately insecure and selfish group, which made them blind to the brilliance of that star.

2. The scribes, priests, and religious leaders, who kept their noses in their books of the law

   These were the consultants who pored over their books to find the name of the town where "the King" would be born. They didn't even think of taking the journey to see Jesus, because they lived in a world of theory and could not step out onto the road of reality.

3. The courageous Magi, who came from the east to bring gifts to the newborn baby

   These were the wise people who were searching for Jesus, who saw the star of Bethlehem and accepted it as a sign from God. They quickly got back on the road and trusted that their faith would take them to the Savior they sought.

There is another threefold symbol upon which we can reflect: gold, frankincense, and myrrh. Here, we enter the picture so that we

Celine Goessl, SCSC

can also bring gifts to the Christ child. Our gold is the commitment to continue God's work here on earth, for God has only our human hands to carry out the Christian ideals of justice, peace, and joy that the world desperately needs. The frankincense is our recognition of Jesus as our true priest, who gives us the Eucharist as our food for the journey. The myrrh is our belief that Jesus has conquered death and anoints us so we too will enjoy eternal life with him someday. By receiving these gifts, we have the light of Christ to pass on to others, especially during this season. We might not have the gold, frankincense, and myrrh of rich and wise persons, but we have what they symbolize—the precious treasure of Jesus in our hearts, which can inspire and touch others so their journeys during the year will be rich with the presence of Jesus.

Every gift we have to offer Jesus has already been given to us.

The Baptism of the Lord

Luke 3:15–16, 21–22

Luke differs from the other Gospel writers because he does not specifically talk about the actual baptism of Jesus. Luke wants the people to be clear about the fact that John was not the Messiah. He portrays John as the one who would bring the Old Testament to conclusion so that Jesus could inaugurate the new life in the Spirit.

We now look at the importance that Luke places on the prayer of Jesus throughout the rest of his life on earth. Luke makes it clear that Jesus was found in prayer before any major event in his life's journey. He prayed as he stepped into the public arena in today's Gospel. He also prayed before he chose his apostles. When they began journeying with him on a daily basis, he stopped with them to teach them how to pray. Later, he prayed at the time of his transfiguration on the mountain, at the Last Supper, and on the cross.

This makes us realize how important it is for us to develop a solid practice of prayer. Scripture tells us to "pray always." It will take the rest of our lifetimes to carry out that task, because we cannot continue to live holy lives without the support of a prayerful life. It is by prayer and in prayer that we are empowered to carry on the mission of Jesus, as God sends us out to share the good news everywhere we go. Prayer is the food we are given to carry on our discipleship responsibilities. Prayer needs to permeate our family lives, our work and play, our relationships with others, and our faith lives in the Christian community. Prayer is the most powerful and important part of daily life.

Prayer life today has done a paradigm shift from when we were children. In the past, it was important to say prayers, and many of us were good at wearing out our prayer books by leafing through the pages every day and reciting the words that we found there. I was very good at saying prayers, and for years I considered myself a prayerful person. It was only as I was working on a doctoral degree in the 1980s that I learned how to pray. It was humbling to realize that I had used the words of other people all my life to be in contact with God. When I took the course on prayer, a whole new world of spirituality opened up for me, and God's gift warmed my heart and my entire being with an astonishing awareness. I had been envious of my non-Catholic friends who could pray so simply from their hearts when I struggled to find my prayer book to be able to pray.

Many parishes are offering adult faith-formation classes on prayer. We need to look for their offerings or find something in neighboring parishes to help us learn how to talk to Jesus in our own words. Children today are taught to pray spontaneously in their faith-formation classes. Learn from them how to become childlike again so you can develop a relationship with the Trinity that will deepen your God-life and show you a greater response to discipleship. Jesus says in scripture, "See, I make everything new." That is what we strive to experience! It will take a lifetime, but it is worth the effort and the time because it will prepare all of us for a happier life in this world and in the next. Added to that it is the extension of our own baptismal commitments.

Prayer is the most powerful moment of life.

The Season
of
Ordinary Time

Cycle C

Second Sunday in Ordinary Time

John 2:1–11

Jesus' purpose of coming to earth was to change people and their lives, just as he changed water into wine. This Gospel is a personal invitation for us to change our ways as Jesus calls us to a new way of life. A few weeks ago, we experienced the beginning of a calendar New Year and perhaps made a few resolutions that we might already have forgotten. One big mistake in our lives is when we run short of life-giving ingredients and forget to turn to Jesus for a fresh supply of what we need. Today he asks us to come to him with open hearts and empty hands so he can give us the wine of love and joy that will renew us.

The Hebrew system of strict law is represented by the six stone jars. Water from these jars was used for the ablutions for Jewish feasts. Stone jars were considered very clean. Yet such an exaggerated insistence on ritual cleanliness left the people with hearts like jars—made of stone. Jesus wants to pour new wine into our hearts so that our hearts of stone will turn into hearts of flesh. Remember, there was a set of six jars, one short of seven, which Christians consider the number of perfection.

Now that we are invited to turn our hearts from stone into real flesh, we have what we need to be successful and happy because we are gifted by God. God calls us to use our gifts to produce new wine. With softness in our hearts, God surely looks on us with love. We are appealing to God because we are unique, talented, and beautiful. We need to see ourselves as God sees us, not just as jars of ablution water but as vessels of precious wine, mirroring the image of Jesus within.

Let Jesus talk to you about your personal life this week. Is it true that after some years of marriage, we lose our dreams of a happy life? For all of us, our love might have dried up by the fact that we have lost our original fervor and no longer have the sparkle for life. Have we let our lives become humdrum daily boredom? John is telling us that we need to be refreshed so we can become new wine. Let Jesus

Celine Goessl, SCSC

touch the water of your life as you become good wine through the inspiration of today's Gospel.

We read that this is "the beginning of his signs at Cana ..." John used the word "sign" because for him, a sign is a stronger concept than a miracle. A sign reveals to us the power and glory that Jesus brings to the world. It is the forerunner of what we experience in the Eucharist. A purpose of these reflections before we come to Sunday Eucharist is so that we have something to offer at the presentation time of the Mass. Today, we can offer our hearts of flesh!

We are not stagnant water but precious wine.

Third Sunday in Ordinary Time

Luke 4:14–21
Isaiah 61:1–2, 10–11

There is nowhere we can walk without leaving the imprint of who we are—good or bad—upon the earth that we tread. When Jesus walked into the synagogue and was handed the scroll that had the famous words of Isaiah, the people who heard him would never be the same again. When Jesus enters our hearts and our homes, life for us will never be the same. And when we enter the lives of others, please God, let it be said of us that they will never be the same again. We have the imprint of God's good news that we have become and that we are asked to pass on to the world.

Jesus chose the prophecy of Isaiah very deliberately to tell the people who he was. Read the first reading of today's liturgy, and let this passage sink down into your heart. The second verse tells us that the Spirit comes to proclaim "a year of favor from the Lord." That year was a jubilee year, proclaimed every fifty years. For the people of Jesus' time, a jubilee year was the time to let one's own ground lie fallow and to return any land that might have been extorted from another person. God comes to us every day to bring a year of favor in which all debts are erased so that we can begin anew. I will use this passage for my funeral liturgy, which I have prepared ahead of time, indicating to people that for which I want to be remembered. I also prepared the liturgy for my funeral long in advance so that I would try to practice it every day of my life. Hopefully, when it is read at my funeral, my friends and relatives will be able to say, "Yes, the Spirit of the Lord helped her to do good in her lifetime."

However, the physical journey with the Spirit of the Lord upon us is only half of the story. There is also the inner journey that must take place every day. Each of us needs to look deeply into our hearts, where we can hollow out space that will provide room for Jesus to place the Spirit within us so we can walk as jubilee persons. We need to take time to let our baptismal commitment grow deep roots

Celine Goessl, SCSC

so we can bring glad tidings to the poor, liberty to captives, sight to the blind, and freedom to those who are oppressed. That is a task of a lifetime!

Who in the world needs our love and care? Nothing paralyzes persons as much as guilt complexes that they may have learned when they were young. So often the rules we were asked to follow set up guilt within us that we have never completely redeemed. A strong source of captivity is the anxiety we might experience, especially in our day, when terrorism is so prevalent. Jesus calls on us to be present to those who are prisoners to guilty feelings.

This week, let us relax and put smiles on our faces. The outer composure helps us to let go of our chains of guilt so we can help others unlock their chains and be set free. Jesus will favor us once we know of his love, care, compassion, and forgiveness in our daily lives. Let us leave an imprint on the earth as a legacy for future generations.

Can others follow in Jesus' footsteps by following in ours?

Fourth Sunday in Ordinary Time

Luke 4:21–30

The first thing that strikes me in this passage is that people can be so fickle in changing their minds in a very short time. After Jesus read from the prophet Isaiah in last week's Gospel, he sat down and apparently charmed the local people who accepted him so favorably. They loved what they heard and were proud that he was one of their own. They must have thought what a blessing it was to have him come from their own neighborhood or family. That is what they said with their lips, but deep down in their hearts, there must have been another message. Otherwise, they could not have changed the course of their actions so swiftly.

Jesus went on to tell them how they failed to appreciate their heritage. He spoke not to condemn them but to show them a better path to travel. This took courage, even at the risk of being rejected. Most probably there was already gossip in the streets, the local bars, the workshops of the town, and even in the homes of the people. They could not understand why Jesus would perform such spectacular signs for strangers and foreigners and not take care of his own people. By the end of this short passage, they were already silently saying of him, "Shame on you!"

Did people come to the synagogue with hidden agendas? Is that why they could make such a turnabout so quickly? However, this does not stop Jesus, who is on a mission beyond the confines of Israel, even to the extent that he is perceived as uncaring about the people in his own town. What happened that day in Nazareth was a statement of rejection that Jesus would experience many times, from the hill of his own town, where they attempted to kill him, up to the hill of Calvary, where he is taken to his death without even trying to walk away or to escape.

We can take many directions with this message today. Jesus simply walked away from those who misunderstood him. Do we walk away from fruitless arguments and disagreements, especially when our tempers are out of control? Perhaps it is easier to complain about what we do not have than to show gratitude for what we have. Jesus challenges us not to allow bigotry, narrow-mindedness or discrimination to hamper us in our commitment to discipleship. We will need to look into our own hearts and eradicate any hidden agendas as we come to Jesus today, asking for help to be prophets in our own humble ways so that we can stand up and be counted as persons who put others' needs before our own. What can we expect when we carry out God's will? Some people will praise us, but some will gossip about us. God calls us to a mission that we must follow, knowing that we might become targets of hostility or rejection. If so, it just might be a sign that we are true Christians.

No prophet is accepted in her/his own town.

Fifth Sunday in Ordinary Time

Luke 5:1–11

The words of Mary that we read last month continue to echo in my ears: "Do whatever he tells you." It also reminds me of the model that I have tried to follow for several years. All of us, by reason of our baptism, are called to do whatever Jesus asks of us as we adapt our hearts to the fact that we are all called and sent forth.

This Gospel is about Peter and his reaction to the work of Jesus. He drank the water, which was turned into wine, and it didn't make him think about what Jesus had done at the wedding in Cana. He certainly was not really impressed. He saw Jesus cast out demons, and it astonished him, but it didn't appear to affect him. But now, he experienced the catch of fish! That was different, because he was a fisherman. He knew that one only went fishing at night and stayed in shallow water, where the fish would take the bait. Yet Jesus appeared to them and asked them to do the impossible—to put out into the deep in the middle of the day! Peter could have said, "But who are you, a carpenter? What do you know about fishing?"

Suddenly, Peter was touched and knew he was standing in the presence of God. He was ready to do whatever Jesus asked, to be a fool for Christ's sake. This might tell us that it is not very good to be too near to God because God might ask us to do impossible things. It is too dangerous to touch God, for fear of what might happen. But Jesus says, "Do not be afraid. Follow me and you will make a tremendous catch like you have never known."

We notice that they brought the nets to shore, most likely sold their catch of fish, and then left everything and lost their lives as ordinary fishermen to win a new life of going on a mission with Jesus. That is the risk to which Jesus calls us today. This is a dangerous journey of faith because Jesus catches us and sends us into a very different form of ministry—of catching people whose lives will never be the same, once we share our faith with them. Just as Peter's response was that he realized he was a sinner and not worthy to take on this new ministry, so we are also sinners, called to leave our past behind, because God reminds us that we have been baptized and gifted. We need to go out and use our talents to make God's presence known to others by the way we live our relationships with God. This week, do whatever he tells you, even if it sounds preposterous.

Where will we minister today in God's name?

Sixth Sunday in Ordinary Time

Luke 6:17, 20–26

We may have reflected on Matthew's Sermon on the Mount, but today we are asked to look at Luke's version, which is shorter and simpler. Luke indicates that Jesus is preaching on a flat stretch of land where many people were gathered. Jesus' disciples were among the crowd, and Jesus took advantage of their presence to speak directly to them. This sermon was obviously meant for those who already had a relationship with Jesus.

Luke speaks of only four beatitudes, using the word "blessed." He follows these four with a corresponding woe:
1. The poor are contrasted with the rich.
2. The hungry are the opposite of those who live with plenty of food.
3. Those who are sad are compared to those who are happy with superficial lives.
4. Those who are looked upon with hate are paralleled with those who are praised.

In this way, Jesus deals directly with what is happening in the lives of his contemporaries, as well as with us. Another reason for Luke's blessings and woes might be that he wants to show us that suffering in this life can be a means of redemption.
1. Physical poverty can give us a reason to see how we must totally rely on God for everything.
2. Hunger can lead us to look at spiritual hungers so we see how the Spirit will satisfy our hunger.
3. Weeping can tell us about who is in charge of our lives and who will bring comfort.
4. Hatred can mellow our own hearts and prepare us for the joys of heaven.

Celine Goessl, SCSC

We are not blessed because we experience difficulties, but our experience can lead us to deeper values as we follow Jesus. He will give us the grace to anticipate the wonderful gifts of our future lives with him in eternity. Contrasting blessings with woes will also teach us to view the pain of the present with the reality of the future.

1. The poor will look forward to the joy of eternity, but the rich will have already received their rewards.
2. Those who are hungry will be able to view their emptiness in such a way that spiritual nourishment can become their satisfaction.
3. Those who mourn can come to Jesus for their comfort, while those who rejoice now might find their sadness waiting for them after death.
4. Those who are hated and reviled by others will have boundless joy someday, while those who were well thought of will be blinded by their own pleasures.

Jesus was very radical in his preaching as he showed that his greatest mission was to the poor and the downtrodden. There may be moments in our lives when we feel at a loss because of all the misery that has entered our lives. We might be tempted to doubt God's unconditional love. Besides our faith, we have the gift of trusting in the works of the Lord.

In faith, we accept the word of God.

Seventh Sunday in Ordinary Time

Luke 6:27–38

On this Sunday, we are given time to celebrate love through the feast of St. Valentine. How fitting to have the Gospel in which we talk about authentic love as Jesus sees it. Jesus calls us to radically turn our lives around so we can see beyond the hurts and injustices we must face. As we continue the Sermon on the Plain, Jesus makes it clear that we need to love as God loves. We often hear "What goes around comes around." But God says, "Turn the other cheek." God does not encourage abuse, but if we know anything about the ancient practice of striking someone on the cheek, we realize it is awkwardly impossible for such a person to continue his/her abuse. Romans struck with a backhand slap and used only their right hand. If one turned the other cheek, it would be physically impossible to strike again with a backhand slap, thus making one equal to the abuser.

Jesus asks us today to consider the level of our love. Loving people live by different standards than what the world teaches them. Jesus does not expect the impossible, but he simply gives us examples of what loving people do naturally. He tells us to stop judging other people and to live by the Christian principles planted in our hearts. We know that this Gospel calls us to begin again by taking small steps to break our stony hearts, so God can replace the stone with a heart of flesh. Think of the Golden Rule—never do to others what you would not want done to you. Jesus tells us that this rule does not go far enough because, first of all, it is a negative statement and limits our Christian response.

Jesus seems to use a formula that was later used by his followers. He took, he blessed, he broke, and he gave. At some point, I began to realize that God repeats these four actions when God relates to us. We cannot skip to stage four without going through blessing and breaking before we have something to give. That might entail many disappointments, failures, and breakings before we can even begin to let go enough to then bless and give. But Jesus, through each of

---

Celine Goessl, SCSC

us, definitely has something to give to the world. Our mission from Jesus this week is to love one another, have compassion for others, and keep ourselves in the background. That will certainly be a gift of love to others.

Listen to what Jesus asks of us this week.

The Season
of
Lent

Cycle C

First Sunday of Lent

Luke 4:1–13

Do you have a place you can call your own personal desert, a place where you can be alone and take time to empty yourself so God can fill you this Lent? It has to be difficult for parents with children to find such a nook in their lives. Perhaps the only place they can go is to the bathroom, and even that is not off limits for small children, who constantly want to know where you are and what you are doing. Perhaps this Lent we will find time, a place, or even a segment of our hearts where we can create a wilderness or a desert. It will help us to continue our journeys together.

Once we find such a space, let us reflect on the three encounters that Jesus had with Satan. They reveal three things to help us deal with evil tendencies within ourselves:

1. The study and practice of the scriptures (*One does not live on bread alone.*)
2. The proper use of authority and power (*Power and glory belong to God.*)
3. True worship of God (*We cannot presume that we know God's will for us.*)

Satan tempted Jesus to rely on his relationship with God in order to get what he wanted. This is an extremely selfish approach. Sometimes we focus on our culture's standard of living so we can use our religion to insist that God is taking care of us. We ask God to break the usual order of creation to make sure we are selfishly served. We can also ask the Holy Spirit to use her power to give us mundane things or powers that we do not need.

Many nations, governments, and even some religious authorities are focused on expanding their power. We can be taken in by such a temptation to use the powers of the world to bring about God's reign, instead of relying on God. Power easily corrupts when it is not used in a positive way.

Celine Goessl, SCSC

The third temptation appears to be the most difficult. We might want to use our relationship with God as a wedge that lets us think that God will not allow us to be harmed or will save us from pain and suffering. Jesus makes it clear to us that while our relationship with God will not save us from destruction, it will protect us from forcing violence of any kind on others.

Some of our Native American tribes have a custom called *potlatch*, the practice of giving back to the Great Spirit a complete sense of gratitude for all that was given to them. They invite guests to their homes and give gifts, sharing their possessions with those who need them or who would like them. This is symbolic of their gratitude for God's blessings. (A more extensive explanation of potlatch can be found in the *Encyclopedia Britannica*, which gives a thorough picture of this custom.) Are we willing to follow the Native American example by giving away something each week during Lent to show our gratitude for God's great goodness to us? Giving frees the spirit so that we can be more resistant to evil.

Welcome to Lent and to the journey ahead!

Second Sunday of Lent

Luke 9:28–36

Mountains are spectacular places. They offer a new perspective because the higher we climb, the wider our view of the world around us. I think Jesus often walked up a mountain so that he too could have a place that would expand his human mind and give him a new perspective on life and the direction in which God was leading him.

We ask a difficult question today. Why did Jesus take specific disciples with him as he climbed the mountain? It could have been because they were so entangled in the darkness of this world that he wanted them to have some new insights or new light to flood their hearts so they would be ready for the leadership and the journey to which they were being called. It was they who needed to be strong leaders in the church during the first century. Peter needed experiences he could keep in his memory in order to be the rocklike support for others in those first days after Jesus ascended into heaven. James was the first one to taste martyrdom, and he too needed the memory of this event from which he could draw hope, to endure the transfiguration of his own body. John was the one who would survive long after the others. He would need inspiration to write his Gospel, which would bring the light of revelation to the people. When God gives any one of us a moment of insight, it is because of a future strengthening for the work that we will be given from God.

This was very likely a turning point in Jesus' ministry, when events became frightful. He needed time away to make decisions regarding the future direction of his own human journey. The mountain was a place of peace and quiet, where he could gain positive energy to go back to face the harsh reality of life. The message of the transfiguration was to be a definite connection between what happened on this mountain and of trudging up the mountain to Calvary. There is no shortcut to glory, and the road we all travel

Celine Goessl, SCSC

is one that takes us through the mystery of the cross so we can experience God's glory with greater intensity.

We usually see this as Jesus revealing his glory to the disciples, but there is another significant side to this experience—the disciples are now truly able to see! Living life to its fullest depends, to a great degree, on how we refine our ability to see. There is so much awesome beauty around us in nature and in people that often escapes our sight. God is with us, to help us envision with greater clarity the experience of ordinary events of our day, particularly in nature and in the smiles of other persons.

Today, the Gospel helps us see more deeply our need for prayer. As a follow-up to last week's reflection, we might find a mountain or a lake or a desert—someplace where we can go to pray regularly. I heard about a man who was very ill in the hospital, and his wife prayed constantly for his return to health. She was supported because everywhere up and down the halls of that hospital, she could hear the prayers of people for their loved ones. Let us thank God this week for the small and great miracles that we experience around us. Let us ask Jesus for the gift of sight to see deeply into our own hearts, where miracles happen every day.

Let us not be blind to the miracles in our lives.

Third Sunday of Lent

Luke 13:1–9

A few strange things are said in this parable. First of all, what is a fig tree doing in a vineyard? Even at that, a fig tree takes about seven years to bear fruit. Yet it sounds like after only a few years, there is no fruit, no life, and no future for this tree. I would continue to think along these lines, but underneath such strangeness, I find some hard facts that relate to my own spiritual life.

My father used to stand out in the fields after a day's work on the farm. He looked over the crops that were growing. I'm sure he was thinking about what he had done and what was left to do before he could be assured of a good crop in the autumn. Thinking of him reminds me to take his example as I come to the end of the day and look back over my spiritual gains. I ask myself how well I fertilized my heart and my mind with the patch of "earth" that God gave me by grace so I can bear good spiritual fruit.

How can we cultivate the little patches in our lives so that our hearts do not go the way the barren fig tree might have gone if the gardener had not been so diligent and positive about a favorable outcome? We are given many opportunities every day to bear fruit. The short parable of the fig tree is intriguing because it tells us that God always gives us a second chance—and a third and a fourth, if we need them. Each Lent is that extra chance to care for our hearts, to soften them as we receive the seed of the good news. It is time to let Jesus, the gardener of our lives, loosen our roots, water us with his life-giving word, and then wait for us to respond. How patient he is to wait for long periods until we are ready to bear good fruit. God expects us to grow through prayer, through the grace of the sacraments, and through an appreciation of the gifts we are given.

This parable is very positive. It reminds me of the time when I was speeding down the road, and as I came around a curve, I saw a police car in the bushes up ahead. Of course, I immediately slowed down but kept watching as I passed the car and stayed the course as I continued my journey. A rush of adrenaline convinced me that I needed to be "uprooted." I was given a second chance because the trooper apparently did not have radar pointed toward me. I learned from that experience, and I have thought of it often when I am on a straight stretch of road and am tempted to speed. I am not going to do that anymore; no, I will carefully tend to what I should be doing. I believe that the patience that I am to practice will bear fruit in the long run.

Perhaps we can learn from the growing crops in the earth or the virtue in our hearts. Things that sprout rapidly might last only for a short lifespan. The seed of the hardwood tree can take up to two years to sprout above the soil; the virtue that I try diligently to grow in my heart may take a lifetime. Slow growth can develop mightily and will last for an eternity.

The lesson we can take with us today is to let the gardener of our soul dig around the roots of our spiritual lives, water the tiny sprouts of virtue, and ask Jesus to let life grow in and around us. Easter time will then bring a wonder-filled harvest.

What needs to grow before Easter arrives?

Fourth Sunday of Lent

Luke 15:1–3, 11–32

This is the story of the prodigal son but should more aptly be called the parable of the two brothers. The story begins with the one who left home to have the time of his life. The last part describes the one who stayed home to take care of his father and their property. The action is very simple: a young maverick demands his share of the family fortune, which he promptly goes out and squanders on loose living. He returns home, ashamed of what he has done, and he is greeted by his father, who had to endure taunts from neighbors about his unworthy son. The father probably went out to the top of the village hill every day to look for his son as he waited for him to come home. Finally, when the young man comes back, the father shows tremendous love and compassion. The older son resents all this attention focused on his wayward brother and refuses to have anything to do with the celebration. At this point, we are expected to call for an end to this deep and complex literary masterpiece so we can continue with living a profitable life.

The parable talks about forgiveness from a number of different angles. It shows us a God whose manner of forgiving is absolute and complete. God does not hold grudges, regardless of the sin we have committed. God just comes with open arms and embraces us with indescribable caring. For any of us burdened with remorse or guilt, here is an example of a great ending to the story of our sinfulness. It is also an example of the wisdom of self-forgiveness. We can get on with our lives after huge mistakes by not making excuses but merely by forgiving ourselves and making an effort to make amends. We too can return "home" and live with humility and a greater understanding of the God who loves us unconditionally.

Let us be warned that if we do not forgive ourselves or others, we will have damages to face. We cannot make God "small." Like the older brother in today's Gospel, we can harbor resentment and cling to our hurts, but all the while, we will hurt no one more than

Celine Goessl, SCSC

ourselves. Think about the relationships that are destroyed, families that are torn apart, and entire nations that are damaged by wars of vengeance, just because we hold grudges and nourish them by our refusal to forgive.

Today is the time for us to open our hearts to forgiveness—forgiveness by God, forgiveness by us, and forgiveness by others, regardless of who is at fault for damaging relationships. Think of the misery we cause ourselves when we do not forgive and the anguish we endure because we nurture resentments. Blaming others for the ills of our world is really quite pointless. Being open to choosing the better options in all hurtful situations shows us a wide door to freedom, a door that we need to open every time an opportunity presents itself.

Lent is a time for growing in appreciation of the wonderful truth that every person has a place in the heart of God. This story can very well be our own story, drawn from real life. We only need to look at the various shades of the two sons in our own personalities. Have we been disobedient and selfish persons, or are we people who humbly own our weaknesses and ask forgiveness? Have we held grudges and been unwilling to forgive one another, or do we know that at times we are less than who God calls us to be?

What is coming home to God all about?

Fifth Sunday in Ordinary Time

John 8:1–11

I would like to center my reflection on two symbols today. The first one is hands, and the other one is stone. One of our recent popes said, "Hands are the heart's landscape." We can look at our own hands and at the hands of others and become aware of some of our inner attitudes. In this Gospel, we look at the hands of those who brought the woman into the circle at the temple gates. They were cruel hands that roughly dragged her and exposed her to the public eye. Their *beckoning hands* called bystanders to come and support them in their accusation. Her *trembling hands* indicated that she was ashamed and wanted to cover up her guilt. *Accusing fingers* continued to wag so much that they could hardly cover up the hypocrisy in the minds that were attached to the fingers that pointed in her direction. They addressed her as "this woman," as though she had no name, no rights as a human person. Their *fingers became balls of angry hands* as they clenched upright hands into *angry fists.* I wonder where the *guilty hands* of the man who committed adultery with her were hiding.

Now let us turn our gaze to the *gentle, relaxed hands* of Jesus. He does not point fingers or clench an angry fist. No, he uses his hand to write something in the dust. Was he writing their sins or just trying to distract them and draw attention away from her embarrassment? Or, in his playful mood, was he doodling, as we sometimes do when we are bored or uninterested? He might have been telling the accusers that he had no time for the hypocritical strain that he sensed in their actions. Hands can be used for good or for evil. Take time to look at your hands and ask yourself what good you can use them for this week.

The other element is the part that *stones* play in this reflection. In scripture, there is a prophet who begs God to take out of peoples' hearts *the stony* elements and replace them with living flesh. People in Jesus' time were still living by the laws that were written for

Celine Goessl, SCSC

Moses on *stone*. They worshipped in a *great temple of stone,* perhaps a clear symbol of their hearts. Then, into the temple built of *sacred stones,* the people with *stony hearts* dragged a woman who was about to suffer a cruel fate of being stoned to death. But the curse of the stone would change when the Spirit of God rolled back the *stone of death,* and the tomb carved out of stone became a womb of life.

The prophet Ezekiel says, "I will give you a new heart, and put a new spirit in you: I will remove the heart of stone from your bodies and give you a heart of flesh instead." Hands and stones! Take a stone this week, and reflect on what the stone in your hand can do to bring you closer to God and give you a new lease on life.

A friend gave me a small gift—a prayer rock. An attached explanation reads, "Just put me on your pillow. At night when you climb into bed, your rock will hit you on the head. It reminds you to kneel down and pray. Dump the rock on the floor and when you get up in the morning, you will stub your toe as a reminder to say your morning prayers. Make your bed and put the rock back on your pillow." What a unique reminder of how God might want to talk to you!

Make a rock gift for each member of your family.

Holy Week
and
the Season of Easter

Cycle C

Passion (Palm) Sunday

Luke 23:1–49 (This is the longer version, encompassing the entire Passion.)

We are confronted with the greatest of all Christian symbols, the cross, without which we cannot be true followers of Christ. I would like to share with you an ancient Russian folktale for our reflection. I read this many years ago, and the concepts of the story have remained in my heart.

It happened that there were two thieves who were caught in their crime and had to make restitution. For their punishment, they each were asked to take a cross and carry it across the desert. Eventually, they would come to a city, where they would be forgiven. They began the faithful journey, trudging along with the heavy crosses. By the third day, they were in agony—it was hot, and they had little water left for their nourishment. The journey was long, so they sat down to rest. At this point, one thief decided to cut off the bottom of his cross so it would be lighter. The other liked the idea so he simply made his cross thinner in order to carry it more easily. After some days, they encountered a very wide river, which they had to cross. It was dangerous and contained flesh-eating fish. Again, their creative minds helped them on their journey. The first thief tried to stretch his cross over the water but it was too short, so he died in the desert. The other thief's cross stretched over the water but when he stepped on it, it was so thin that it broke under his weight. He fell into the water and drowned.

Let us put ourselves into this ancient tale. What cross has Jesus asked us to carry, and what will happen if we try to alter it? Perhaps we will need our cross to walk across the space between earth and heaven! What are we to do? Will we either continue to carry the cross that Jesus gave us, or will we try to take an easier route to our destination? Jesus walked the road to Calvary for us, and now it is our turn to walk with him as he helps us by lifting some of the burden from our backs.

Celine Goessl, SCSC

What have you done during the Lenten season to show that you are ready to take up your daily cross? If you have participated in the events in your parish to help you carry your burdens more faithfully, you will understand the story of the Passion with greater clarity. If you have not taken advantage of the steps that your parish has laid before you, you still have time during Holy Week. We are all given a few more days to turn our lives around so we can face God and listen to the call, telling us what we can do.

The Holy Week Triduum is a sacred time for us to make our final preparation for the joy of Easter. On Holy Thursday, we can come into our parish churches with the entire community to celebrate and appreciate the gift of the Eucharist. What happens on our altars on Thursday night also took place with the apostles in the upper room. There will be the washing of one another's feet before we come together at the table to celebrate the gift of Jesus' body and blood. It will be food to strengthen us for the days ahead. On Friday, we will hear the reading of the Passion one more time. Let us put ourselves into the midst of the scene of Jesus' death and burial. Holy Saturday is a day of quiet waiting. Then, after sundown, we will gather once again for the beautiful liturgy of resurrection. If any parish has an RCIA process, this is the time when we invite our elect to come into full communion with us. Please be with the parish community to welcome our new Catholics and celebrate sacramental life with them. Easter Sunday will have much deeper significance if we have walked that journey together.

We ask everyone to greet our neophytes tonight.

Easter Sunday

John 20:1–9

The Synoptic Gospels speak of the women who went to Jesus' tomb early on Easter morning. Only John tells us that Mary Magdalene went alone. There were no angels, no gardener present in John's story. Why is it, we ask, that the lone woman was the one chosen to run and tell the apostles that Jesus was alive? Unlike *The DaVinci Code*, written by Dan Brown, this is not fiction; it is John telling us what actually happened on that morning. Only later will Mary Magdalene return to the tomb and find the gardener, whom she begs to help her. The man calls her name, and immediately she opens her eyes of faith to the gift that God has given to her.

It is not the usual topic on Easter to reflect on a cemetery, but we slowly become aware that our faith did not begin at the stable in Bethlehem or at the baptism of Jesus in the Jordan. It didn't even begin at Calvary but at the empty tomb in the middle of a cemetery. Have you ever thought of a cemetery as a place to celebrate Easter Sunday? Whenever I go home to visit my family, I make a trip to the local cemetery to treasure the silence and remember all those from my past who have left their bodies behind and are now in heaven, enjoying their reward with Jesus. I walk down the road to the plot where there is a big stone with the name "Goessl" carved into it. I take precious time to reflect on who helped me develop my faith life. It was the holy bodies of my family, friends, and neighbors who have been laid to rest in the cemetery until the final resurrection. My faith teaches me that these persons are alive and are celebrating Easter right now with the risen Savior. It also shows me where my body will lie some day, but the grave will be empty because death is only for an instant of passage from this world to the next.

Take time this week to make a visit to the cemetery where your family is buried. Feel the excitement in your heart at the faith that has been given to you because you believe in the miracle of resurrection. After the visit, either physically or in your mind, write your own

Celine Goessl, SCSC

Easter story. Let it contain all the ups and downs of daily life and how you dealt with them. Search your heart because your faith lies there. Perhaps there are those among us who will be encouraged to begin writing a journal of their personal, daily thoughts, where they write down what they find in their hearts each day. Go back and read the story in your journal next year at this time, and thank God that you have become an "alleluia" person who lives the life of resurrection each day in a richer way.

Write things in a journal that you want
to say to your future family.

Second Sunday of Easter

Acts 5:12–16

Let us reflect on Luke's second book, showing how the early church community survived after the resurrection. This passage opens with "many signs and wonders were done ..." The apostles lost no time in carrying out the mission given to them by Jesus. The Acts of the Apostles summarizes the events that occurred in order to assure Christians of a place to gather to enrich their lives as followers of Jesus. We are told that converts increased steadily, and the spiritual and corporal works of mercy were daily experienced by the people. Since we have just experienced the same movement in the parishes that had RCIA people baptized and receiving the fullness of sacramental life through confirmation and the Eucharist, we rejoice in the fact that the same ministry is carried on even in our day.

Luke wrote this book sometime in the AD 80s. There were only a handful of eyewitnesses to Jesus' life left on earth by this time, so Luke took on the task of teaching about the life that would help the small community flourish. It became obvious that the presence of the Holy Spirit was very important to the early church. She was the driving force that compelled the church to continue its mission of salvation.

Growth in the early church was evident, because people shared their possessions and talents as they gathered to pray together and to be nourished by the teaching of the church leaders. We can appreciate how the formation of new Christians came to be the driving force to help our neophytes know how important storytelling is, so all could know Jesus more intimately.

Without the stories in the Acts of the Apostles, much would have been lost to posterity regarding the everyday lifestyle among the Christian community. We have a solid foundation of our history, and it is now our task to carry on the mission of preparing future generations. We have the same tools of faith that the apostles had.

Celine Goessl, SCSC

Let us take time this week to read the Acts of the Apostles slowly and meditatively. Then we can think about what is happening in our own parish communities. Make a list of actions that you can glean from the scripture reading and place that list on the left side of a paper. Then go back and use the right side to list similar activities that are present in your parish. Compare the two lists and perhaps make some recommendations to your pastoral and finance councils and the various committees that are active in your parish as to how the parish can come closer to the Christian ideals enumerated in scripture.

We know the church is still growing today, but we encounter obstacles we must overcome. If we go back and imbibe the spirit of the early Christians, we will be able to help enrich life in our parishes, our dioceses, and the universal church. We are called to use the signs and power of the Holy Spirit to bring the good news to everyone through our words and actions.

Signs and wonders continue to be visible through our hands.

Third Sunday of Easter

John 21:1–19

We now realize that the scene where the apostles have been switches from the upper room, where the doors were locked, to the open air by the Lake of Galilee. Seven of them had come with Peter to the shore because they had decided to return to their former jobs as fishermen. By now it was light, an indication that not only had a new day dawned but that it was a new time in their lives. They were eager to put the events and trauma of the past behind and slip back into life as it was before Jesus had called them to follow him. Their eyes were still laboring under the dark of night, and they failed to recognize their next encounter. They saw a man on the shore who told them to cast their nets on the other side of the boat.

Now they were to experience an entirely new miracle that would have meaning connected to the shared experience with the risen Christ. Recognizing the miracle of their catch of fish and knowing immediately that the man was Jesus, they quickly came to shore, where the focus was on the meal they were to share with Jesus. All of them filled their stomachs with the fish Jesus had prepared and their hands with the bread he gave them. Jesus may have asked them, "Do you like this food?" And they would have assured him with the answer, "Yes, oh yes!" Jesus then asked some important questions.

He asked Peter, and he also asks us, "Do you love me?" Peter gave a quick answer, assuring Jesus that he, indeed, loved him. What did Peter really mean? Did he mean that he loved him because he loved to be with him, or did he love Jesus because Jesus kept the small group well fed with bread and fish? Again Jesus asked the same question, and Peter repeated the same affirmation, perhaps meaning, "I really love your lifestyle." But then he would go on with life and not live as though there was a tremendous love that burned in his heart. Jesus asked a third time, to give Peter the triple opportunity to express his love after he had three times denied even knowing Jesus.

Celine Goessl, SCSC

There remains Jesus' same question to us: "Do you love me?" That is a powerful call, put very clearly to us in today's Gospel. We say we love Jesus, and we regularly come together to witness this love by sharing the bread and the cup at the Eucharist. We pray and sing together, but do we return home after Sunday liturgy and then fall back into our old ways? When we labor through the darkness of night and our nets come up empty, are we still convinced of the fact that we are loved? There is one who stands on the shore of life and waits for us, day after day, in order to tell us of his unconditional love. It is the Lord!

Is our love genuine?

Fourth Sunday of Easter

John 10:27–30

Our Gospel today is filled with the fact that we each have a vocation. God has entrusted to Jesus the vocation of a shepherd. Even the word *pastor* is derived from the Latin for herdsman. Today the discussion of vocations is not limited only to religious vocations. We all have a vocation by reason of our baptism. However, I want to talk about the religious vocation of sister, brother, and priest because I am most familiar with the baptismal commitment that I have lived for many years.

God has created us for a specific purpose in life. Although we cannot be positive of that purpose, we know that there is nowhere we can walk in this life without leaving footprints of who we are on the path we choose to take. Look at the lives of so many persons who are generous in giving of their time and talents to the poor and the marginalized. In our society, which lives with lots of noise drowning out the silence, we need to live wholesome lives. Little room is left to hear the voice of God. Today, God still calls many to religious life. We are asked to open our hearts to the possibility of a call to vowed life or to join vowed persons as associates in mission. We need to think about what that call might include as we look at the future of religious life. Perhaps God calls men and women, single and married, to become associates who will have the opportunity to give time and talent in spreading the Gospel of Christ as they walk side by side with someone in religious life.

We might be unaware of the gifts we have, or perhaps we are afraid to take the risk in faith to open our hearts as God calls us to a special service later in life. We can be true shepherds by preaching the same way that St. Francis preached—by example, and only if necessary, by word. What have we done lately to foster a broader concept of a vocation in the church? This needs to be the concern of the entire Catholic community. Parents are called to create a climate within their homes in which Christian values are lived and

Celine Goessl, SCSC

encouragement is given to family members to follow the call in a way that we have not thought of before. God does not knock on every heart, asking people to join a religious order, but if we are so inclined, then we must be generous enough to give a positive answer and to inquire of persons in religious life about various forms of commitment today. Otherwise, how will the need of a strong flock in future generations be met?

One of the most precious symbols of our tradition is Jesus the Good Shepherd. He calls us to discipleship, not as dumb sheep but as courageous shepherds at times, and as faithful sheep who know how to follow the Good Shepherd at other times. We are called to do our part to help build the reign of God in our own pastures. This is not just "sheep talk" but a call to become part of the faith force that works untiringly and lives for the good of the sheep. Many go astray. The church needs people like us to give our lives to God in some form of religious commitment or covenant. If you would like to know how you can do this, ask a sister or a priest more about living a closer-knit community life with them in prayer and in ministry.

Every religious community has various forms
of commitment to a lifestyle for us.

Fifth Sunday of Easter

John 13:31–35

Sometimes I feel that John goes in circles and repeats himself so much, but this week one thing is certain: John is very clear about who and what we must become if we want to be called Christians. The scene today places us at the Last Supper. Judas has just left and obviously, a new era has begun. We are called to love!

This is an invitation to look deeply into our hearts and determine if we can truly call ourselves Christians. We do not define ourselves by enumerating a list of beliefs that we follow, or a body of doctrines to which we subscribe, or even to membership in a particular denomination. If we want to be known as Christians, our fundamental goal is to love as Jesus loved. We must learn how to love others; that means not just friends, family, or neighbors but all of humanity. As a child, I was told I didn't have to like everyone but I must love all people; there is a difference.

There is no way we can hide our lack of love with good intentions. These intentions break into pieces if we gossip maliciously about others. If we want to be real Christians, it takes a commitment of a lifetime. Our family or our parish can be known as a wonderful place where social activities, super liturgies, and fantastic ministries are thriving. But if it is also a place of competition, bad will, prejudice, and gossip, the externals of religion mean nothing without the basic foundation of authentic love.

The best way to understand love is to go through the pages of scripture and find examples of what Jesus did to show his love. For him, love calls us to help others, care for them, and offer our service whenever we can. It means encouraging others when they are close to despair, affirming them, and offering them forgiveness for their failures. That is the basis for salvation far more than private holy practices or denominational rules.

For Jesus to say "Love one another," we know that this new commandment is not as explicit as the Ten Commandments, with

Celine Goessl, SCSC

"Thou shall" and "Thou shall not." We have no set guidelines or protocol about the kind of love that Jesus asks of us. It is more the practice of having healthy relationships with others so that we become responsible for one another. The commandment to love places a radical demand on us, not the flimsy kind of love that the world tries to convince us to believe as authentic love.

This week, let us try to make it a daily practice to reflect on our degree of love. We can put love into practice with members of our own families, our next-door neighbors, people in our workplaces or communities, and even with strangers living on our street or in our neighborhoods. A friendly smile costs nothing, yet it can light up the world for someone who needs attention, care, a word of encouragement, or an affirmation.

Let others say of us this week, "See how they love one another."

Sixth Sunday of Easter

John 14:23–29

For years I was entrusted with the responsibility of pastor in parish life. I often sat with families who were going through the wrenching pain of saying good-bye to a loved one who was dying. In today's Gospel, we have Jesus gently breaking the news to his close followers about his impending departure from this earth. It is no wonder that they were so numbed by this revelation that they could barely understand what was going on. Yet in either case, it was not abandonment but an offer of a deep peace and of walking more faithfully with God. This might be something too difficult to comprehend for those without a long history of spirituality. It is not a promise to rescue people from future pain and hardship but rather a promise to bring us through seemingly impossible trouble as we journey toward eternity.

The peace that Jesus promises includes the knowledge of being sure that we are loved unconditionally, which flows in abundance when we open our hearts and allow God's healing presence to come to us. Peace that the world might strive to attain would mean the absence of war, an avoidance of conflict, and easing the tension and restlessness that afflicts our bodies. This is not the peace of the Lord. The question we ask is whether or not we are at peace with ourselves. If we place barriers in our lives that prevent God's love and peace from flooding our hearts, now is the time to decide how we can break down those barriers between Jesus and us or between other persons and us.

Fear touches our lives just as it touched the lives of the disciples when they were told that they would soon be separated from Jesus' physical presence on a permanent basis. We now have an incentive from today's Gospel to begin each day by reflecting on the presence of Jesus within us and by taking time for prayer and quiet listening. Do not let personal fears that keep you from seeing your own goodness or the fear of other persons keep you from seeing how

Celine Goessl, SCSC

you are the image of God. It is profitable to stop three or four times a day to converse with Jesus. We must remember to give Jesus the opportunity to respond to our conversations by taking an equal amount of time to listen to his voice.

Let us continue to see Jesus with the eyes of faith.

The Ascension of the Lord

Luke 24:46–53

Luke has given us a Gospel about the life of Jesus on earth and a news report on the foundation of the early church. The Ascension today acts as a bridge between the two, as well as a finale to the Gospel and an opening to the Acts of the Apostles. Both of these books give us insight into the importance of the mission that Jesus left for the apostles and for us. As Jesus returned to the right hand of God, he left behind the ministry of preaching forgiveness in his name. This appears to be an impossible task, but to inspire and assure us, Jesus promised the presence of the Spirit of love to be implanted in our hearts, that we would always have the courage and the energy to be his presence from now until eternity.

This was certainly a difficult paradigm shift for the apostles, a sad and wrenching departure in which Jesus tells them to be glad, because "if I do not go, the Spirit will not come." G. K. Chesterton once wrote, "The test of greatness is—what did the person leave behind to grow?" Jesus is the prime example of what and how to leave something precious behind. I think of my own parents and what they left behind for their ten children. Primarily, it was an ideal that we could do whatever we set our minds to accomplish. What a supportive example! Actions speak louder than words, and our parents showed us by their example how they carried out this maxim many times during their lives.

Jesus blesses his apostles as he takes leave and reminds them of their powerful mission to be witnesses. With this, Jesus also gives us a promise that the Holy Spirit will journey with us if we continue to live good spiritual lives.

In essence, the message of today's Gospel is:

1. Jesus returns to God in heaven.
2. A power from heaven comes down to help us be witnesses to Jesus' mission.

Celine Goessl, SCSC

3. We can look forward to the return of Jesus as he brings us home.

His admonition was that we "stay in the city until you are clothed with power from on high." We all need to take time to wait for the grace of God to become manifest in us. This is a direction for the week. Let us make a daily visit to Jesus, either in the silence of our hearts or in front of the Blessed Sacrament, and stay until the Spirit manifests herself to us. Such a visit gives us the opportunity to reflect on the power that will be given to us to live healthy spiritual lives in the coming years.

Are we ready to welcome the power of
the Holy Spirit into our hearts?

Feast of Pentecost

John 20:19–23
Acts 2:1–11

Today we need to read both the New Testament reading and the Gospel of John. It is exciting to realize that Pentecost happens every year and involves each of us as we develop an ever deeper intimacy with God. The readings today have three messages for us to ponder:

1. As with the disciples, we too must let the Holy Spirit direct our lives. During this past week, I set aside time each day to pray for one gift of the Holy Spirit. It was a constant reminder that the Spirit is with me for a renewal of her presence, which I received in baptism and again in confirmation. This feast asks me to appreciate that holy presence. (You may have noticed that I refer to the Holy Spirit in feminine terms because, going back to Hebrew and Greek, the third person is spoken of in feminine terms.) I am reminded that Jesus asks us not to count the cost of giving ourselves to God without reserve.

2. We are asked to cultivate the spirit of forgiveness. Just as the apostles were given the opportunity to let forgiveness be an important part of their personal lives, we are challenged to be compassionate, tolerant, and patient with ourselves and our neighbors. Although this process takes a lifetime, others should be able to know us by our attitudes of love and forgiveness.

3. We are asked to observe Pentecost every day. The Holy Spirit who was breathed on the first disciples is also breathed into our hearts, if we ask this to happen. During your prayer time each day, sit quietly and inhale the presence of the Holy Spirit, that she may be with you as God sends you out to bring the good news to the world. We desperately need to have such a Spirit to give new life and enthusiasm to God's people. The fire of God's love is so necessary to our transformation!

Celine Goessl, SCSC

I would suggest that we use Cardinal Newman's favorite little prayer as our own Spirit prayer each morning.

Come Holy Spirit
Make our ears to hear
Make our eyes to see
Make our mouths to speak
Make our hearts to seek
Make our hands to reach out
And to touch the world with your love. Amen.

Feast of the Holy Trinity

John 16:12–15

Today we look at God as being alone, because God is only one but can never be completely alone because our God is also three. That is a confusing statement and much too difficult to explain. For a better understanding, let us consider what it feels like to be alone. If persons eat alone, sleep alone, walk alone, work alone, or live alone, such a life can become unbearable.

Some time ago I read about a person who was so alone and lonely because no one ever shook her hand, patted her on the shoulder, hugged her, or even touched her. She became very depressed and spent the last dollar she owned, not on food but on a beautician so that she would have someone to touch her and make her feel worthwhile, even if just a for short while. Loneliness must be one of the most frightening feelings in life. In working with prison inmates, I am told that one of the most dreaded times in their lives was to be put into solitary confinement and left for hours without anyone coming by, as though the whole world had forgotten them.

If you have ever had the feeling of being completely alone, this can change your entire personality. We tend to dry up and to hear voices inside and outside of ourselves but have nobody with whom to attach those voices. It is not good for us to be alone; in fact, it is terrifying. Some of us know what it feels like, even when we are with others, to feel trapped, as though we are alone and no one cares. Some people experience the feeling of being trapped between two walls during their lifetime—the wall of their mother's womb and the wall of the earth where their bodies are laid when they die.

Of one thing we can be sure: we do not have to stay with such a feeling because our relationship with God is one of our primary joys. God's love is never so neutral that it cannot beckon us to be united with the Trinity. Perhaps we need to challenge our ideas about God. Some may think of God as being aloof and distant up in heaven, with little connection to us. Others may think God does not care how we feel or how we live. Let us set aside some time today to think about God. Let joy fill our hearts as we think about how much God cares for us with unconditional love. Pray to the Holy Spirit dwelling within for a fire that can last for many years, even as that same Spirit came to us last Sunday. Let us sit quietly and tell God how we long for God's presence that will bring joy and draw us closer to the one who created us. God walks with us as we follow in his footsteps, as he enlivens our spirits and calls us to a higher purpose in life.

As Christians, we take time this week to be committed to experiencing the Triune God within ourselves. Our response to such a reflection will inspire us to pour out our love on others so that those with whom we live, work, and play will never feel alone.

This is a wonderful way to give glory to the Father, the Son, and the Holy Spirit.

Reach out to someone who is lonely and needs a loving smile.

Feast of the Body and Blood of Jesus

Luke 9:11–17

I remember the time when I worked at a local food pantry. As I walked around the room, helping the poor put food in their bags to take home to their families, I felt like Jesus out on the hillside, asking people to sit down and then telling the disciples to pass out food to them. What an experience to know that Jesus was asking me to do the same thing he called the disciples to do. The Gospel, especially the book of Luke, constantly reminds us to take care of the hungry. Providing food from a local food pantry or Meals on Wheels each day is good, but it is not a substitute for going to Eucharist on Sunday. We are called to do both.

The stories told in the Gospel follow the same format as the shape of the Eucharist on Sunday.
1. We come together.
2. We are taught by the word of God.
3. We eat.
4. We are dismissed.

Jesus shows us how important it is to bring abundant life to others. Such a story tells us that nothing we ever do is neutral. Going around helping families fill their baskets at the food pantry is not just another job to be done; it is definitely a ministry to be accomplished with joy. That was exactly my experience, and it called me to help God be a life-giver for the day.

Bread is a very common element in our diets and a very relevant symbol of hope for our broken and hungry world. When we think that half of our population suffers from the shortage of "daily bread," we realize it is little wonder that Jesus chose bread as a sign of his presence and care for us. Luke, the grand physician, seems to have been fascinated by food. Every chapter in his Gospel has the mention of food or eating. Jesus also appeared at table with friends, being with people as a guest or leaving the table and going out to bring

Celine Goessl, SCSC

more abundant food to the people to whom he was sent to be their bread.

When we eat ordinary bread, it is changed into us, but when we eat the bread that Jesus gives, we are changed into him. We become what we eat. I remember one of our celebrants at a parish where I was the pastoral administrator, who told the congregation that he and I and another sister went out to eat at a Chinese restaurant. My fellow sister, he said, had chicken stir-fry. Everyone chuckled because they knew she was a quiet person who was too "chicken" to boldly step out into the limelight. He then said he had pork stir-fry, and again the people laughed, because he was very overweight. Then he said, "And what do you suppose Sister Celine had?" I had shrimp stir-fry, of course, because I am vertically challenged. From all practical deductions, we had become what we ate. When we receive Communion this week, can it also be said of us that we will become what we eat? I challenge both you and me to go out this week to become Christ to all those we meet. Have a wonderful week.

Do people see by our lives that we go to daily Eucharist?

The Season
of
Ordinary Time

Cycle C

Eighth Sunday in Ordinary Time

Luke 6:39–45

Luke has just finished his Sermon on the Plain. Immediately, he launches into three parables that continue to tell us about the proper behavior of a true Christian. Luke's stories indicate that he might have been a physician in his professional life. Therefore, the examples he chooses often have something to do with leading healthy lives. The people to whom Luke was preaching would not hear anything new, but they would be asked to give an account of their treatment of other people. This entire chapter talks about our attitudes and actions toward other persons.

Three parables give us a model of how we are to treat others:
1. The first parable shows how ridiculous it would be to try to teach others about that of which we know nothing.
2. The second parable asks us to reflect on our own failures and sins before looking at the faults of others.
3. The third parable tells us that we can bear fruit only when we have healthy attitudes in our hearts.

Earlier we talked about blindness and how difficult it is to spend our days and nights in total darkness. The blindness that Luke speaks of is the spiritual inability to see things as they really are. He uses light and darkness to indicate how much one can see or cannot see. Sensitivity to the needs of blind persons calls for us to reach out to them in their blindness, but not before we first take care of our own inability to see. We must find a way to cure our own spiritual blindness so that we can help others with greater ease.

The second parable tells us to take the log out of our own eyes so that we can see clearly enough to remove the splinter from someone else's eye. If we concentrate on our own faults and weaknesses, we will not have time to see the faults and weaknesses of others. The point of these parables is to practice one of the maxims that the great scholar Socrates lived. He told us that we have two eyes and two ears

Celine Goessl, SCSC

and only one tongue. We don't have to explain anything further to know what he meant. This week we might try to open our ears and eyes wider and keep our mouths closed.

The third parable speaks in agricultural terms that people of Luke's time understood from everyday life. Persons are compared to a tree that bears either good or bad fruit, depending on how the ground was cultivated and nourished during the growing season. Every season is a growing season for our spiritual lives, so we need to cultivate and nourish our hearts in order to produce the good, not only for ourselves but for those with whom we live, pray, work, and play.

The last verse of today's Gospel sums up what Jesus was teaching us through these three examples. Read it again, and center your prayer on what is most important in your situation at this time in your life.

Trees, logs, and blind people have important messages for us.

Ninth Sunday in Ordinary Time

Luke 7:1–10

For the next two weeks we will reflect on some extraordinary healings of Jesus. He raises two persons from the dead, but it is the circumstances surrounding these miracles that make them special. Today, we center our thoughts on a slave who is near death. We are not told very much about the slave but only about his connection to a foreigner, a Roman centurion. The lesson we learn is indirectly concerned with the sick man, but our primary attention is drawn to the centurion, who asks for the miracle.

As a Roman, he does not feel worthy to approach Jesus directly, so he sends some people under him who have a high regard for him as their respected commander. Next we hear that he sends a second group of people, his friends—again, he does not go directly to Jesus himself. The centurion is a man of power who supports and rewards his clients for their faithful service. He has a grasp of Jewish law, so he realizes that asking a Jew to come to his Gentile home would render the visitor unclean. When Jesus discovers the implication of this situation, he immediately recognizes the deep faith of this foreigner, as well as those who have come to beg for a miracle in the name of their leader.

Some Romans recognize the extraordinary power that Jesus has over death. The centurion, realizing the favor he is asking of Jesus, goes out onto the road to meet him before he gets to the house where the dying servant lies. The centurion tells Jesus that he is not worthy that this holy man should even come into his home, but if he would only pronounce some healing words, the centurion was sure that his slave would be healed. Jesus again indicates the importance of his mission to all people, including the Gentiles. It makes us realize that Jesus has come for the salvation of all, not only a small segment of the population.

The faith of the centurion shows itself by the fact that he has a great love for his slave and is willing to step out of his comfort zone to

Celine Goessl, SCSC

ask for help from Jesus. Jesus' reaction is to say that he has not found such strong faith, even among the people of Israel. Could he say the same about us today? Let us invite Jesus to look into our hearts and measure the amount of faith that we carry within ourselves. We recite an important prayer every time we celebrate Eucharist. It is taken from the remark of the centurion. We say it just before we approach the altar to receive Jesus in the Eucharist. We say, "Lord, I am not worthy that you should enter under my roof, but only say the word and my soul shall be healed."

Let us ask Jesus to help us increase the amount of faith that we carry within our hearts. Can we measure up to the foreign centurion who has not been given the grace-filled moments that we have been offered these many years? It is not enough to merely recognize the power of Jesus to cure us; we are called to follow the example of the centurion as we place our trust in the power of Jesus.

Lord, we believe. Help our unbelief!

Tenth Sunday in Ordinary Time

Luke 7:11–17

The account of this miracle is only found in the Gospel of Luke. Here we find three amazing remarks that lead us to see Luke as a possible physician. We read of surprising details full of information regarding the specific nature of the young man's illness.

Three sets of details actually precede the miracle itself:

1. It is clear that the impact of the story is not centered on the miracle of raising a man to life but on the mother, who is a widow, and on the crowd who accompanies her.
2. Jesus obviously feels deeply about the plight of the woman who has no one to support her. She will become destitute because of her situation. Jesus compassionately raises the son to life and gives him back to his weeping mother.
3. There is more to the story than merely an understanding on the part of Jesus and a sympathetic word that he shared with the woman. He recalled the Old Testament story from 1 Kings 17, which is used as our first reading in today's liturgy.

The fact that this story centers on a widowed woman shows Jesus' deep concern for the marginalized in society. Jesus stopped the funeral procession because he had compassion for the woman and was concerned about her future. The story takes place at this point in Luke's Gospel so that, when John's followers asked if Jesus was the one that John said was to come after him, whose sandal he was not even worthy to unfasten, they would have an answer to take back to John regarding the Christ. Jesus simply told them to relate to John what they had heard and seen. Jesus let John know in very clear terms that he was the one, how his mission was being carried out, and how he used the power God had given him.

If you had been among the crowd in the funeral procession, what would your response to this miracle have been? A Methodist minister once had a conversation with me about miracles. He said

Celine Goessl, SCSC

that Catholics were so concerned about keeping rules and following patterns of conduct that they did not take time to recognize miracles in their lives. I did not believe in miracles as so many people of other denominations did. It was just not part of my religious upbringing. However, today I have a better understanding of what this man tried to tell me; I see miracles in life ever so often. My mind and heart are much more open to see what God is doing in me and in the world today.

One of the important miracles I learned from Luke is his great compassion and care for women in society. He was concerned about women who are still being oppressed in so many ways today. I also realized how he was a proponent of life in all its forms. The scriptures speak of the beauty of life from conception to natural death. Today, there is a lack of respect for human life, so we need to preach by our lives that authority over death belongs to God alone. Pro-life is very necessary, but it must be broad enough to include all of life. Abortion is only one facet; there are also concerns about war, violence, possession of lethal guns, and hospital and clinical ethics in the terminally ill and the elderly. Let us place life into the hands of God, and let God decide when, where, and how each of us is to live and die.

God, you care deeply for us; look with favor upon our lives.

Eleventh Sunday in Ordinary Time

Luke 7:36–8:3

After some thought and prayer, I want to share a topic that is dear to my heart; it tells of my experience as a woman in the Roman Catholic Church. It is unfortunate that none of the Gospel writers was a woman, because we don't have a clear, feminine perception of the story of Jesus. Luke comes close to it, especially when he tells the story of a man with a corresponding story about a woman—Simon and Mary.

In the story today, we meet Simon, master of the table. He is a Pharisee who had the initiative and organizational ability to invite guests to a banquet. It is significant that the Pharisee is named but the woman in the story is without a name. She is an anonymous person, and having no name, she is considered an "evil" person. How did she get such a bad name? Bad names do not just happen! Such information most probably was spread by good people of the town.

This bad woman seems to have had a need to get her life together and come to some type of reconciliation within her. She came in to the banquet, uninvited, and she went to "confession." She did not kneel behind a screen but came to the feet of Jesus with tears, touches, and kisses. Jesus does not ask her how many times she had sinned, but he read the depths of her heart.

Jesus' response is to tell a story, a tactic that he often uses. He used the story of two debtors to bring out his point of reconciliation. Jesus asked which of the two showed more love. Was it Simon, who appeared to give a "head" answer, or the woman under the table, who showed that her heart was in the right place? What a challenge! We can look at the scene and wonder how we might feel at that table. We may be with Jesus at Sunday worship, but if we bring in cold judgments and unfeeling principles as we approach the banquet table, we might find ourselves too uncomfortably close to Simon. Can we accept that Jesus may be far closer to the heart of someone who is barred from receiving him in Communion because of an unfortunate divorce? Perhaps we need to reflect on Simon, even though it would be easier to identify with the woman. Jesus seeks out the "Simon" in each of us. We don't like the fact that we are all sinners and must acknowledge the traits of Simon in us.

What can we learn from this encounter with Simon and the unnamed woman? As we reflect on this story, it might be better to love extravagantly than to live according to the law without love. Of course, the best thing is to live justly and love tenderly at the same time.

We, though many, are one body in the Lord.

Twelfth Sunday in Ordinary Time

Luke 9:18–24

The scripture begins today with Jesus going away to a quiet place to pray. Often when we are told about Jesus at prayer, that means something important is about to happen to him and his mission. An important question will arise from Jesus' lips when the disciples join him. It will be a further description of discipleship to which the apostles—and all of us—are called, because what is true of Jesus will also be true of us. Today, the important question is, "Who do people say that I am?"

Jesus waits for answers from his followers. They are quick with a variety of remarks they heard from those outside their intimate group, anxious to tell Jesus what others are saying about him. Jesus lets them carry on the conversation for a while, but then he turns the question around to ask who they say he is. At this point, their response is not as candid as it was to the first question. They were so free to say what others voiced, but when it came to their answers, they very likely had no idea what to say. Finally, Peter spoke up as the leader of the group, telling Jesus that he was the Messiah. Did Peter really know what he was saying, or was this some answer that did not have a connection to what was stirring in his heart? Even more so, did this answer have any connection to the faith of the early Christian community? Was such faith in Jesus and an understanding of him as the God of salvation a personal response from the heart of this simple fisherman?

Jesus went on to talk about discipleship and what it meant to anyone who would be called to carry on Jesus' mission after his death. He says clearly that anyone who wants to follow him will have to be ready to follow completely, meaning it would include the cross in their everyday lives. Jesus not only talked about the moment when he would be nailed to the cross and left to die an ignominious death, but he also included the injunction of taking up one's cross daily,

Celine Goessl, SCSC

including all the small or big struggles, with the same determination that he accepted whatever God gave him.

Would we have had an answer to Jesus' second question? This is something we can reflect upon as we prepare to offer a gift to Jesus when we come to church this weekend. If we look more thoroughly into the life of Jesus and still want to be his disciples, then we are ready to give a simple answer to his question. It will need to have greater depth than Peter's answer, and it will have to be said with greater conviction, now that we have a better concept of what Jesus is truly asking us.

One more question needs to be asked regarding a response by Jesus' disciples. That question is the one that we must ask Jesus: "Who do you say that I am?" Sometimes we can live on a superficial plane and not really accept responsibility for our desire to follow Jesus. This question needs to send us off to prayer, just as Jesus took time and space to reflect on his life when something important was about to happen. Our prayer will need silence so we can listen attentively to the answer that Jesus will give us. Openness to the answer will also help us answer Jesus when he asks who we think he is.

This week, something of great significance will happen to us as we struggle with our personal answer from the heart of Jesus in connection with our hearts. If we want peace, we need to spend time working out our relationships with Jesus so that we can be true disciples, ready to do what God wants, without counting the cost.

Who does Jesus say that I am?

Thirteenth Sunday in Ordinary Time

Luke 9:51–62

Today we rejoin Jesus on his journey to Jerusalem and come to a new milestone. Scripture says, "He resolutely determined to go to Jerusalem," knowing for certain that he was walking to his death. According to Luke's tradition, he places some of Jesus' pertinent educational lessons into the framework of a journey motif. This passage shows us what is demanded of anyone who wishes to follow Jesus. The shortest route to Jerusalem is through Samaria, so that is the route he takes with his followers. The messages he leaves with us are obviously paradoxical and symbolic.

To follow Jesus, we must leave what is comfortable and familiar and launch into the unknown with a great amount of risk. We might be enthusiastic in following him wherever he goes, but we need to know, right from the start, that Jesus does not offer even an ounce of security. Might we think that his call is harsh? Following him is not a journey for sissies! There is no wiggle room for making excuses, because such a reaction might indicate a halfhearted response and rob us of the satisfaction of responding to the call of God. Life as a Christian requires full-hearted commitment with responsibility for our actions. If we have a habit of making excuses, now is the time to look at our actions, take into account what we must do to change, and then set our sights resolutely on the path we are about to take.

In Samaria, Jesus and his men were met with hostility. Does this sound familiar to your experience at times? Remember—Jesus has promised us opposition and even persecution if we really want to be his faithful followers. John and James were ready to call down fire from heaven. Yet the only fire that Jesus will call down is the fire of the Holy Spirit. What else does he ask of us as a condition for discipleship? "Leave the dead to bury the dead." The fourth commandment asks us to honor parents, but is it possible that spreading the good news is more urgent than doing what siblings might be called to do? Sometimes family tasks are our duty because

Celine Goessl, SCSC

we have not received a mission of something more demanding. "Foxes have holes and birds have nests, but Jesus has nowhere to lay His head." Our present address is transitory, and we must move on at times because our hearts long to follow Jesus wherever we are called. Another admonition is, "No one who sets a hand to the plow and looks to what was left behind is fit for the reign of God." If we know anything about farming, we realize that one hand was used to steer the oxen, while the other hand had to hold onto the plough. Any farmer will tell us that this takes concentration and coordination to achieve a straight furrow.

Each of our calls is unique, but the variety of ways in which we follow Jesus demands that we let go of everything that holds us back from being faithful followers. Is there a barrier between God and you? Your call in the Gospel today is to remove any barriers—no excuses!

Have a faith-filled journey with Jesus this week.

Fourteenth Sunday in Ordinary Time

Luke 10:1–12, 17–20

If I, as a pastor, were preparing to send people out on a mission, what would I give them to take along? Jesus had the answer when he sent the seventy-two out—just take two things with you: a fellow-companion and peace. When we go to work each day, is peace in the presence of our coworkers enough for us? Jesus had other "strange" instructions that we might find difficult to carry out. He told the seventy-two to go barefoot and speak to no one on the way. They were to trust Jesus completely by leaving home without any provisions. It would be quite foolish to tell people today to go to work on a bicycle; to take no wallet or credit card, not even insurance; and to isolate themselves from other people.

What do we make of these strange directions? They seem to indicate a sense of urgency. The seventy-two were to trust that God and good people would look after their needs. As Christians, we go to our work every day with this sense of urgency to promote the values of human life. We must be keenly aware of the state of the poor and marginalized so we can reply to crises with compassion and tenderness of heart. That is of greater importance than to hold to policies that are contrary to our Christian values. We need to live, showing that God is sufficient for us and that God is to be trusted, because we have experienced how real God's love is for us. We sense from this scripture that the way Jesus sends us out to carry on his work has more to do with our lifestyles than with what we say. I have often said that St. Francis lived with the value of preaching and if necessary, he used words. People today are looking more seriously for those who are witnesses than for teachers and preachers. Have you heard the saying, "What you are thunders so loudly that no one can hear what you are saying"?

It is time for us to do a reality check. How do we exhibit a mature Christian attitude? Are we more concerned with church governance, ritual, buildings, or numerous controversies of the day than with

Celine Goessl, SCSC

being the loving persons that Jesus calls us to be? Today, we are the seventy-two disciples, invited to go out and witness against the evils of our time, to work together to make sure that the cause of Satan will collapse. This task is risky, but bringing peace to our war-torn world is the call of God to each of us. Both the beginning and the end of Jesus' remarks indicate that hostility and failure are to be expected. It reminds us of what St. Teresa was supposed to have said to Jesus, "No wonder you have so few friends if that is the way you treat them."

We are aware of what the reign of God means. Jesus calls us this week to bring in the harvest of what others have planted. By reason of our baptism, we are sent to be gatherers and peacemakers. Together, let us do our share in building a world where trust and peace can take root and produce a great harvest.

This week, let us give away some of our
possessions that we really do not need.

Fifteenth Sunday in Ordinary Time

Luke 10:25–37

The story in today's Gospel is so easy to understand but so painful to put into practice. It forces us to look at ourselves and to think about the quality and quantity of our love. To make the best use of the story told by Jesus, we need to put ourselves into the picture and decide which of the characters we would like to emulate. I believe a beginning point of our creative interpretation of the Good Samaritan is that the very road from Jericho to Jerusalem runs right through our own neighborhoods or cities and is strewn with all kinds of wounded persons.

Let us look at the masterful choice of characters in the story. The priest and the Levite are the religious characters who hold positions of great esteem in their society. There is also the Samaritan, who is a despised foreigner and is considered lower than a pagan in the eyes of religious authorities. Let us not forget that there is another character of whom we know little. We only know that he portrays those who "lie on the road half dead." In our experience, this character could be a single mother, an irresponsible parent, an alcoholic, an AIDS victim, a thief, an illegal immigrant, a human-trafficking pimp or john, or a homeless person. Anyone who is in need demands our attention and compassion.

Jesus' stories are never just stories. They are invitations to enter into the scene in order to find our place and discover anew what faith in God requires us to do. The first step is to pay attention to other people. We open the shutters of our hearts so that fresh, new ideas can enter and take root in the depths of our beings. Right now, with whom can you best identify in the story—the priest, the Levite, the Samaritan, or the person who lies in the ditch? How does being that person make you feel? Feeling is empty if it does not call us into action. The titles and roles of each of these characters mean nothing in the end. What is important is the truth of who they are, deep down in their hearts.

Celine Goessl, SCSC

The real question is not "Who is my neighbor?" but "How can I help others this week?" Religious profession or priestly presence as leader in worship does not make us worthy of heaven, and showing piety does not necessarily indicate that we are intimate friends of God. Neither does being seen as an enemy, or a person who does not go to church, or a drunk lying in a gutter on some lonely city street mean that those persons are not lovers of God and as such, lovers of others. God looks into our hearts and takes into consideration what is there in light of eternity.

Our present pope, Francis, has come out with some concepts that we have not heard since the Second Vatican Council, which ended more than fifty years ago. How do we regard other denominations or anyone who does not strictly espouse the Roman Catholic faith? Think about such a call to us in view of today's Gospel story. Can we draw conclusions for what Jesus asks us to do in the field of ecumenism? Perhaps we Catholics are the ones who lie wounded and dying in the ditch. The real gift of today's Gospel is to allow the power of this word to challenge and change us, remembering that self-righteousness is much more treacherous than selfishness.

Check out your spirit of ecumenism.

Sixteenth Sunday in Ordinary Time

Luke 10:38–42

Let us ask ourselves today how this Martha/Mary story fits into our everyday lives and what Jesus is telling us about priorities—how we need to decide what is of the greatest importance. Many of us at some time must have experienced the fuss and fret of these two women as they clash with their Ideas of what takes priority. Martha is so hard-working that it has to be frustrating to see Mary sit around, idly listening to and conversing with their guest. But if we look at the situation from the heart of Mary, why does Martha have to be scurrying around with unnecessary tasks when this important guest has only come to get away from the noisy crowd for a little while, so he can be renewed and refreshed for the journey ahead?

Let us put ourselves into the story of being a guest at Martha's home. We came to visit with someone we love and have longed to see, and although we are treated with great hospitality, we are annoyed at her rushing around. We just wish she would sit down and have a quiet conversation with us in order to ease our tired bodies.

We have also been at Mary's home. The moment we stepped inside her house, she guided us to a resting place, where we sat and laughed and talked for hours. We are beginning to get hungry. The room gets cold because windows need to be closed or the fire needs to be stirred up. We feel uncomfortable, even though we are having a good time. Do we have to choose between these two treatments? I wish I didn't have to, because Martha's hospitality is so heartwarming. However, I would prefer the opportunity to learn from this guest who has just entered and warmed my heart with his love.

Martha appears to act like a digital watch, always in action, chasing one moment to the next and not taking time to slow down and be present to the moment. It is like a picture of our times where we are constantly and frantically in search of some instant experience but not patient enough so our bodies can rest. On the other hand, the Mary virtue of being quiet and listening is not encouraged in our

Celine Goessl, SCSC

culture today. The more noise and the faster the pace, the more we enjoy life—or do we? We need some training in the art of quietness. It would be a wonderful practice for all of us to sit down today and become attentive to quiet sounds for even five minutes. Listen to things you cannot see or to the wind that sighs on a warm summer day. Become aware of the gentle pitter-patter of soft rain on the ground or of the birds singing gently in the distance. The experience of these gentle sounds is but an echo to the rhythm of life within us. Let us become conscious of our breathing or our heartbeat, which is far more soothing than the anxieties that often plague our psyches.

Have you ever gone on a retreat? It is a time and a space that one sets aside, goes off to a quiet place, and learns all over again how to listen and receive the gifts of God to which one has not paid attention for a year. We need to take time to let God visit our lives and find out how necessary it is to sit in the presence of Jesus and just be. Let us give ourselves time to think about what we cherish most in life and whether it will give us a better chance to get ready for eternity.

Come aside and rest a while.

Seventeenth Sunday in Ordinary Time

Luke 11:1–13

We are in transition this Sunday from breaking open the word of God to looking at our own personal prayer life. Since this is our focus, we pause now and look at the place that prayer held in Jesus' life. Prayer is truly part and parcel of Jesus' ministry. He is often spoken of as going aside into solitude in order to sharpen his awareness of a deep connection to his Father. It is after a night of prayer that Jesus chooses from his followers, a small group of twelve apostles. When he is faced with conflict and opposition, he takes time for prayer so he can look at the consequences of his own life as the anointed one of God and calculate the cost of discipleship.

Jesus' followers were obviously impressed by his prayerfulness. That is probably why they wanted to pray as Jesus did. It was a golden moment for them to peer into his mind and get a glimpse of his relationship to the Father. The Lord's Prayer is not so much a prayer formula as an expression of a solid Christian relationship with God. Let us take some time today to peel back some of the meaning that might underlie the various phrases of this all-too-familiar prayer.

Our Father ... We do not come to God as individuals, but as family because we belong to the family of God through the gift of the Holy Spirit given to us in baptism. As adopted children we can call God our "Father," a very personal way of saying that God is the source of our lives.

May your name be held holy ... conveys a tenderness and warmth of speaking of the one we know loves us unconditionally. For this reason, we offer a sign of adoration and praise because of the holiness that we encounter when we come to know God through a sacred name, just as God holds us up through the sacredness of our own personal names.

Your kingdom come ... shows that we long for a world of deep peace and justice. We want God's kingdom to come into our world,

Celine Goessl, SCSC

knowing that it is our duty to help this happen by the way we share the food and resources of our planet, provide a place where the talents and gifts of all are nurtured, and where people care for the poorest and most handicapped. We pray to be surrounded by God's reign, where we can live in such a special society.

Give us this day ... We pray as we come with empty hands, dependent on the hand of God to sustain us and give us only what we need for the day.

Forgive us our sins as we forgive others ... This concept that faces us every day because we are in need of forgiveness. However, it is interesting that we ask God to forgive to the degree that we forgive others. It is a reminder of the woman who loved much because much had been forgiven her.

Do not subject us to the test ... This says, please take us by the hand and lead us through every danger so we will be free from the evils of this world.

By giving us this formula for prayer, Jesus put a human face on God and showed us an intimate way of conversing without having to use a multitude of words. This week, pay special attention to the words you say whenever you pray the Our Father.

Pray this familiar prayer, using our own words.

Eighteenth Sunday in Ordinary Time

Luke 12:13–21

The important virtue for those who grew up during the Great Depression of the '30s and the rationing of food and other materials during World War II was "waste not, want not!" Depression continues today with the great number of unemployed and the poor becoming poorer and the rich becoming richer. This hastens the chasm between the two groups, so there seems there is no longer a middle class in our country. We might think that this Gospel is a condemning message for the rich, but we can be poor and also greedy. All of us at some time might be tempted to associate our personal value with our possessions or attempt to gain prestige through what we own. Are we stretching our credit cards beyond their limits or letting our homes become warehouses?

What Jesus is telling the brother who demands a share of his inheritance is that he needs to be aware of what worries him most. The man who ran up to Jesus was obviously frustrated, wronged, and tortured by family greed. He must have been so full of anger that he could think of nothing else. His heart had a reality blockage, so much so that he could only think about the "things" that were his due.

This story reminds me of a story that I once heard about sickness and death and how they came into our world. The story points out that in the beginning, no one ever died. God gave people life for a while in this world and then sent a beautiful messenger from heaven with the invitation to come back to God so they could enjoy life to its fullest. The messenger was so pleasing that people could not resist and were happy to switch from life on earth to a higher life. Then one day, a messenger was sent to a very rich person who had just filled his granaries with a bumper crop. In fact, he had built new granaries to house his treasure. That very night the messenger came, but the rich person said he was not ready because he still had a lot to do on earth. The messenger went back to God, who asked where the man

Celine Goessl, SCSC

was. The messenger explained that the man had too much to do to be able to answer the invitation. Then God became sad and decided to send sickness and old age to people before he would issue an invitation to them to come home. God knew that some of us would amass too many strings, attaching ourselves to earthly possessions, so God cut the strings one by one to prepare the hearts of the people for a journey into eternity.

When the man came to Jesus to demand that his brother give him the share of his inheritance, maybe Jesus refused because he did not want the man to have so much that neither life nor death would make any sense to him in the end. That brings to mind two comments for us to reflect upon this week.

1. There are no pockets in a shroud.
2. No one has ever seen a U-Haul attached to a hearse.

What counts when we die is not possessions, prestige, or power but the persons we have become during our lifetimes by practicing the virtue of love.

What can we take with us when we die?

Nineteenth Sunday in Ordinary Time

Luke 12:32–48

Two sentences in this scripture passage have significant meaning in our lives:

1. "Where your treasure is, there will your heart also be."
2. "Those to whom much is given, of them much will be required."

These two sentences seem to fit together as the hand of God weaves patterns in and out of our lives in order to shape our future. When we view life through such a lens, we know that we and others both can read our hearts by what we consider a priority.

The second sentence indicates that greatness is measured by knowing how to receive from God that which we can freely pass on to others. Let us look into our hearts and count up the tremendous gifts that God has given us, and we will know that our actions speak louder than the words coming from our mouths. Jesus is concerned about our hearts—that place within us that is the fundamental source of the way we live, as well as the gifts we give to others. Let us remember the unique and generous manner in which they were given to us.

Peter questions Jesus. From the response he gets, we know that those who have been entrusted with greater responsibilities will be more accountable and that they will be more richly rewarded if their hearts are in the right place. If we have been given such a large reservoir of gifts and do not pass them on to others, our punishment for not using these gifts might well be in proportion to how we refuse to share. Our having received gifts calls us to be faithful stewards. This is not an option but something we owe God through others for the goodness that God shows to us. Being a good steward is required of those who are given the keys to a better life. How many keys do you have in your pocket?

Celine Goessl, SCSC

As Catholic Christians we are given many gifts and corresponding responsibilities. As Americans, we are also well endowed with material gifts. That tells us what is expected of us. The Gospel challenges us to place our hope in God and be ready to answer our call to holiness, placing our trust where it belongs and keeping our hearts ready to answer the Gospel mandate.

Yesterday's gifts do not give us a right to demand gifts tomorrow. Today is what we have, and we cannot cling to them as though there were no tomorrow. Tomorrow will begin the process all over again, and so we are constantly living in a cycle of receiving gifts in our hearts and emptying out all the goodness that has been freely given to us.

Flow with the cycle of receiving and giving.

Twentieth Sunday in Ordinary Time

Luke 12:49–53

What a strange lesson we hear today! I don't think any of us goes out and seeks to become unpopular. We do not stand up to be counted when there is an unpopular topic on the table. We feel better just remaining part of the silent majority because we might lack the courage to speak out. Today's Gospel gives us a strong jolt and makes us sit up and take notice that conflict and stress are part of daily living. A song from the past reminds us that we were never promised "a rose garden" throughout life. On the contrary, today Jesus promises that our journey through life will be strewn with crosses on a regular basis. In walking such a journey, if we want to follow Jesus, we cannot be looking for an escape route.

Such a message makes us sit up and take notice, knowing that we are on the edge of a life story that shows how Jesus was able to rock the boat, even when it was unpopular, knowing that people would hate him for what he would say or do. These words in the Gospel are hard and frightening—Jesus saying that he came not to bring peace but to create division. This appears to contradict many other portions of the Gospel. Yet we often feel that our faith is the greatest comfort in life. When comforting aspects of Catholicism become shaded as we become involved in environmental concerns, in standing up for just social issues, or in walking with the poor and marginalized, particularly with illegal immigrants, let us take to heart today's message and realize that Jesus calls us out of our religious comfort zone into the line of fire. We sometimes need comfort, but we also need a balance of the uncomfortable because we have a broader agenda than merely working with the niceties of life. If scripture does not shake us up once in a while, then we might need to examine if we are truly listening to the real message of Jesus Christ.

We can draw positive energy from the tension we experience between comfort and discomfort. Fire sorts out and purifies our intentions. The images we find in this Gospel are ones of testing

Celine Goessl, SCSC

and purification. We need to be drawn from a superficial life down into the depths of purifying values. If we take God seriously we will be led through fire and water that will not always feel soothing. It might be time to look at our personal faults and determine if we have outbursts of anger that need to be challenged into energy for creative actions. Any forms of addiction we might be fighting need to be moderated. If my present creed is "I believe in me," then I will do anything for comfort, and I will worship at the shrine of my inner self.

Truth is difficult to face. When a family acknowledges alcoholism in a member, when a community realizes the racial inequalities in its midst, when a nation admits its economy is based on the oppression of the poor, there are bound to be blowups. This is precisely what Jesus is saying when he tells us that he has come to bring fire to the earth so that all sinful tendencies can be burned up, and then we can live in the peace that he speaks of so often throughout scripture.

Sit up and take notice of conflict.

Twenty-First Sunday in Ordinary Time

Luke 13:22–30

Recently I was with a group of people who were discussing the difficulties that immigrants have in the USA. The Gospel this week tells us something about people who want to come to the United States to work in order to provide for their families. I have listened to innumerable stories of immigrants, and they have given me so much on which to reflect.

Jesus gives an answer that we should consider when thinking about those from Mexico who have come to live with us, to become our friends, and to work side by side with us. Jesus says the gate is narrow but it is open. In today's story, an anonymous person from an unnamed place came to ask how many people would be saved. He might well have asked, "How many of your immigrants will stop to get a visa, a green card, alien registration, or a Social Security number?" Jesus' answer was very telling. He says the gate is open with free entry. There are no formalities, no bribes or taxes, no watchmen or guards at the border. There is nothing except the gate that is open but narrow. He knew what this meant because he himself was going that same way through the narrow door of death and walking the narrow path that led him to Jerusalem.

I also remember stories from our families and our religious sisters in Europe during the war, when they were warned to get out, leave their homes, and not to take too much luggage with them but go through the door while it was still open. The path leading them away from their homes in the middle of the night was narrow. If they were not ready to leave immediately, they would be lost or somehow, they would disappear. Would those who were saved be few, or would there be many? They could only give an answer for themselves and do what they knew they had to do in order to be saved.

Notice that Jesus does not answer this person's question for a good reason. Such calculations are not that much help. Jesus only calls our attention to the goal in the life of all Christians, "Enter

Celine Goessl, SCSC

through the narrow door" in imitation of him. God does not have favorites, so we cannot pin our faith and hope on the fact that we pay our dues and show up for Sunday Eucharist. The test of Sunday worship and our faith is how we live once we go through the narrow door of our church building. At the end of each Eucharist, the priest tells us to go and serve God by serving one another. The real question that we need to ask ourselves is, "How do we live at home, behave at work, or treat our family members and neighbors during the week?"

As affluence increases and as technology provides more and more conveniences for us, we tend to become spoiled, and along with all the material goods we have for enjoyment, we might tend to want our spiritual life to run along the same lines. What road are we walking? What door is open to us, even though the gate is narrow and the road leading to the door is difficult to find?

Think about the journey you are on and the road you are traveling. Then ask Jesus to help you to let go of all kinds of worries and burdens. If we live simpler lives, are generous, and care only for that which will help us pass through the narrow door, we will not have any reason for asking Jesus about questions of calculation. Let us look once more at our brother and sister immigrants and see from their example and by the way we live our lives how we might better fit through the narrow door.

Last week and today, can you hear what
you might not want to hear?

Twenty-Second Sunday in Ordinary Time

Luke 14:1, 7–14

Guess Who's Coming to Dinner? This old movie can tell us a lot about cultural stereotypes and attitudes toward anyone who is not a white, middle-class person. The movie showed that whoever gets invited to dinner is a long-standing, sensitive issue, and today we realize such an attitude goes all the way back to the time of Jesus. It seems obvious that Jesus was invited to dine with a leading Pharisee, not because the Pharisee wanted to reach out to Jesus in love but because he wanted to get a closer look at Jesus' actions and words.

An example from contemporary society can show how painstakingly a bride and her mother work to seat the wedding guests at a reception. Proper etiquette plays an important role in seating guests. We worry about people's status in life and whether those placed in close proximity will cause conflict and arguments. Such banquet scenes are as familiar to us as they were in Jesus' time.

Jesus might also be teaching us about who should be invited to our home for dinner. Do we really want to hear that we should invite marginalized folks, or would we rather invite those from whom we might derive some benefit? Jesus seems to be somewhat impolite. Does that surprise you? We have seen that he is not always polite because he tends to live outside the box. Just two weeks ago we listened to the message of Jesus bringing fire upon the earth. There was the suggestion of setting households in conflict against each other. In every Gospel for the last few weeks, we heard a less-than-polite message. Today, we are told to bring the poor and the lame, the blind and the crippled to our tables. That is a radical choice—a choice that we must make every day, whether it is at table or in our interpersonal dealings with one another.

With this setting in the context of a meal, Jesus entered the Pharisee's house. He knew that he was being watched closely. He was also watching the guests closely. Then, once again he proceeded to turn their world upside down. Earlier in this Gospel, Luke showed

Celine Goessl, SCSC

Jesus criticizing the religious leaders for choosing the best seats. We can follow the suggestions about taking the last place and then being called up higher, but then we must be ready to have the host or hostess leave us at the bottom seat if he or she wishes. This example can undermine our unreal sense of importance, but in the long run it shows that real status in life comes from the eye of God.

Mealtimes are when we can gain social acceptance, tie up frazzled relationships, and gain entrance into the lives of others by our conversations. Mealtimes at home with my family were very important. We never sat at the top or bottom of the table because those seats were reserved for our parents. None of the rest of us had permanent places, and we took any chair that was available. Inviting neighbors who dropped by or friends we brought home with us to stay for dinner was a weekly occurrence. They always felt welcome. To this very day, I am always tempted to invite anyone to share food and table talk at my home. I believe that the banquet table of heaven will be akin to this example—a table filled with the joy of life and a God who dons an apron to serve us. Such a banquet will surely be full of daily surprises.

Take a look at the pattern of table manner that is part of your daily life. Is it similar to the Pharisee's table or to the kind of table that Jesus encourages us to have?

Enjoy meals and table conversations this week.

Twenty-Third Sunday in Ordinary Time

Luke 14:25–33

After having dinner at the home of the Pharisee, Jesus resumed his journey to Jerusalem, where he would die. Here again, he gives us a glimpse of Christian discipleship but this time from a different perspective. The demands of discipleship intensify as he calls us to carry out our baptismal commitment. Jesus does this with two illustrations:

1. He tells us if we are going to do some type of construction, we need to survey our resources and decide if we can finish the job.
2. If we are going to battle, we need to calculate the chance of success, and if it seems likely that failure is upon us, we need to prepare for peace instead.

What an appropriate reading that fits right into the conundrum that we face in our world today with its endless wars. It is good for us to contact our congresspersons and demand that this scripture be taken to our hearts and to the hearts of the entire US government.

Looking more seriously at the demands of discipleship, Jesus tells us that anyone who seeks to follow him must pay the price of carrying the heavy burden of daily crosses. This message might make us feel uncomfortable if we are truly making an effort to stand up for what we believe. But if all we have to show is Sunday Mass and Communion and a few prayers during the week, we are not really walking the journey with Jesus. Following him makes radical demands on us and has the power to transform us when we put Jesus first in our lives.

Jesus certainly knew where the road was leading, but the great crowd following him had no clue. That is why he turned around, stopped them, and asked, "Do you really know what you are doing? Are you ready to walk with me? Do you know the price that you must pay?" We need to hear Jesus asking us these same questions.

Celine Goessl, SCSC

When we look into our own hearts, we might see very different answers calling us to admit why we follow Jesus. Do we want to profit by getting more things, having better lives, getting rich or getting healthy again, or finding security that the world cannot or will not offer?

We are called to think in terms of the reign of God, which can call us to give up everything, even our own families, and live the kind of life that will set us at odds with our societal value system or the cultural expectations of the world in which we live. Carrying our cross does not only refer to daily aches and pains in life, a marriage breakdown, illness in our families, and problems with adolescent children or financial losses. Carrying our cross refers to what happens to us when we consistently live according to the Gospel of Jesus and are transformed by the courage and determination that calls us to have complete confidence in God.

If we say that we would like to follow Jesus but ask what that will demand, how much it will cost, and what we can expect as a reward, then we are asking the wrong questions. The world is full of wishful dreamers—for example, someday I will lose weight, give up smoking, or pray more fervently. We cannot arrive without taking the necessary steps. This tough and demanding side of discipleship is difficult but we have the role model of Jesus to follow. This week, let us make the effort to walk in the footsteps of Jesus, and we will end up as happier, more peace-filled people!

Reflect on the joys of discipleship.

Twenty-Fourth Sunday in Ordinary Time

Luke 15:1–32

A Lamb! A coin! A son! How are these items connected, and what do they have in common? In these three parables there are significant losses, but the result of each story is the same. Rejoice! What has been lost is now found, so we have reason to celebrate. When we gather on a weekend, we come for the celebration of the Eucharist because we realize that there were losses in each of our lives during the week. As we gather, we are reminded that each of us has been found through the death and resurrection of Jesus.

Many people are lost every year. We only need to watch the news on television to come face-to-face with a lost child who has been stolen by an unconscionable pimp to be ushered into human trafficking, a spouse who has lost someone in the military service, a family who has been told that their beloved is in the hands of terrorists, or a single person who has lost a job. Sometimes we have reason to rejoice, but all too often, most of the lost persons are never found. Families try desperately to find children or victims who are terrorized by asking for help from the government or the police force, by putting their photos on the computer or their images on cereal boxes or milk cartons.

Fortunately, in the parables today, each of the lost has been found. Perhaps we can listen in a new way by turning our attention to those who remained as others were lost. Have we ever thought of the ninety-nine sheep that had to be left alone, or to the coins in a woman's apron pocket that have not disappeared? What about the son who stayed home and was faithful to his father? It is the lost in the story that gets all the attention and privileged treatment. Pay attention to your reaction when you listen to these stories today at church. In your own heart, do you think all of this is a bit lopsided? We need to pay attention to what shocks us. The shepherd, the woman and the gracious father appear to react in exaggerated or even foolish ways.

Celine Goessl, SCSC

Look back at the opening verses of the Gospel. Tax collectors and sinners gathered around Jesus, and that made the Pharisees and scribes complain. He gathered irresponsible and shameful people. Many Christian groups today would share such consternation if their leaders were to associate with the scum of the earth. They are likened to the ninety-nine good sheep and the nine safe coins. What we need to learn is how the mercy of God plays itself out in our daily struggles with evil. Obviously, we all work to keep within our reach what is most valuable to us. Jesus did too—the stories are told as a way of answering the criticisms against him. In the criticisms about Jesus eating with sinners, he wants us to know that he is in each of the lost persons.

In the world today, a lot of lost persons are adrift, morally or spiritually, or in need of some type of healing. Jesus sends us out from the liturgy to find those lost persons and give them hope by our encouragement and support. God is good to the wicked. God calls us this week to go and do likewise. When we hear that our government plans for millions and then tramples on the one, or that multinational corporations manipulate the thousands with no sympathy for the individual, or that in a cruel world of competition, one finds no compassion, then remember today's Gospel that tells us which direction we must take.

Be compassionate with someone who is lost.

Twenty-Fifth Sunday in Ordinary Time

Luke 16:1–13

Our Gospel today is a very strange parable in which there are many problems to be solved.

1. What is happening in the life of the manager? The owner caught his manager embezzling money, so he is about to fire him. The distraught manager decides on a plan that will put him in good stead when he is without employment. Is he truly cheating his master or does he just contact each client and reduce his own commission without lessening the money owed to his manager? In this way, people will be his support group if he does not find another job.

2. Is this parable really about the manager, or is it a lesson about the master? If the focus is on the manager, he would not be praised for his shrewdness. If it is on the master, he might be showing the same example that the father showed in the parable of the prodigal son.

3. Regardless of whether the manager was embezzling or was just a poor manager, he is still dismissed and now has to give an account to his master. He is thinking of his own future and by lowering the debts of clients, he knows that the clients will owe him favors.

The parable appears to have one main focus—when there is a crisis in life, one must act decisively in order to create a future for oneself. Basic choices have to be made, and the manager uses creativity in order to become a beneficiary to those with whom he dealt.

The parable goes on to say that we cannot serve two masters who have such opposite lifestyles. If we are centered on Jesus, we must place our confidence in him alone. But if our main focus is on earthly possessions, then we will not be able to act as Jesus would act. The situation is similar to the one that faces the Christian community.

Celine Goessl, SCSC

The Second Vatican Council, in a document titled *Gaudium et Spes*, set an agenda for social concerns. Later on, Pope Paul VI stated that if we wish to live in peace, we need to work for social justice. Since that time there have been numerous statements from Rome that have concentrated on the same agenda. The manager is praised for the manner in which he decides to use material goods. He knows that money is necessary for life, but he also knows that material goods are meant to be shared. When we reach out to those who do not have enough to live decent human lives, then we resemble the manager, and Christ has every reason to praise us for our efforts.

As we look further into what is happening in the field of social justice today, we must help to create a paradigm shift in our value system so we can use funds to provide jobs for the unemployed. This gives us opportunities to work for just wages and decent living conditions for the poor and the immigrants so they can see themselves as good people. As we look around and see how we have raped our environment, we are asked to care for the earth and all of creation. These are not only political concerns but also moral values that we must uphold.

Jesus calls us to make good use of possessions that have been entrusted to us. When we are faithful in smaller things, it will help us to know how to take on greater responsibilities. If we truly want to follow Jesus with all our hearts, we will use our energy to serve God and trust in God's unconditional care for us.

Let us become first-class disciples of Jesus.

Twenty-Sixth Sunday in Ordinary Time

Luke 16:19–31

During the last few weeks we have concentrated on some of the pitfalls of giving too much attention to material possessions. Luke is the only Gospel writer who gives us the parable in today's reading. He tells us about a rich man who lived extravagantly in this life, as compared to a poor man who did not even have enough means to live a decent human life. Both died, and now we encounter a reversal of roles. This message should cause some discomfort because it speaks directly to our hearts as we reflect on two very opposite situations.

The rich man lived an overly comfortable life, dressing as a man of royalty and having an overabundance of food at his disposal. Lazarus sat at the rich man's gate, begging for necessary sustenance. The parable tells us that when both men died, the rich man found himself in Hades, and Lazarus was taken into the "bosom of Abraham." We listen in on the conversation the rich man had with Abraham as he asks for help. Lazarus should come and relieve him of the great thirst he was experiencing. Abraham's answer is a warning to us to take time right now to care for the poor in our midst. We will be judged on our failure or our concern regarding the poor among us. Do we even recognize those who are poor so we can compassionately care for them? There are many Lazaruses today who offer us the opportunity to share our possessions and time with them. Our greatest sin is the failure to notice these people who are close to the heart of Jesus. If we do not recognize them, it might be because we are guilty of the common saying, "Out of sight, out of mind." It doesn't have to be a matter of treating the poor cruelly; our failure would be that we have not recognized the poor as our brothers or sisters, and as a result, we do nothing for them.

The poor we will always have with us. They will continue to suffer if we neglect them. We have numerous opportunities to care for their needs, but first we must be able to see—to recognize them in our own cities and neighborhoods. God calls us to do something

Celine Goessl, SCSC

for them during our lifetime. These people are giving us the chance to reach out in love, to overcome our selfishness, and, in so doing, to secure our own eternal salvation.

A second part to this parable teaches us a deeper lesson. We must strive to be converted before we die. The rich man was heard begging Abraham to send Lazarus to his five brothers, who were also living in opulence and were guilty of the same sins as their brother, who was now suffering in Hades. Great wealth can cause blindness. Having someone come back from the dead to show them their wrong doings will not be enough to convert them. They already have enough to help them reverse their behavior if they can open their eyes and hearts to the gifts that God wants to give them. A voice from the dead would not be convincing enough to reverse their sinful lifestyle.

Let us take time this week to reach out to those who need our help. Food pantries and homeless shelters need our help, but more than that, there are people who need our presence to show them that we care enough to pay them a visit, to take time to talk to them and to help alleviate their loneliness, or just to simply be present to them with a smile or a friendly greeting.

Now is the acceptable time.

Twenty-Seventh Sunday in Ordinary Time

Luke 17:5–10

We have two symbols to explore this week. The first is a *mustard seed as it relates to faith*. The description of faith as a seed shows us that it needs to grow. Growth in faith can be better understood if we relate it to growth in the stages of human development. We began life as children, when we were nourished, clothed, and served by other family members. As children we absorbed culture and values from those around us. We didn't question our faith. The scene of our adolescence was a growing period, when we began to reflect abstractly and wanted to have our own way of putting all the pieces of the puzzle of life into place by ourselves. In our faith lives, we became aware of alternative views and perhaps rejected family values or traditional forms of rote prayer. The limitation at this stage of life was the tendency to reject whatever we could not understand and to dismiss what we had never experienced. Finally, the mustard seed grew into adulthood, and as we became sufficiently certain of our destinies, we were ready to plunge into unknown relationships with total commitment. The seed that comes to final maturity can then seek the reign of God above anything we seek for selfish reasons. It is a lifelong struggle to let that mustard seed grow in our hearts until it reaches maturity and makes us ready to accept God for all eternity.

The second symbol is that of *a table*. There are many tables in Luke's Gospel, but none seems as lonely as the table in today's reading. We are told of a small farmer who has one servant for manual labor and for waiting at table. The farmer's life is unexciting, humdrum, and very, very ordinary. There is no womanly presence and warmth in this setting but only drab, bachelor-like business. The food is very probably unexciting but functional. The master does not even offer a word of thanks, and the servant doesn't seem to expect it. Duty is done, another day is lived, and life goes on.

Luke has other tables that show excitement—succulent beef (the fatted calf) being carried in, and the table includes wonderful family

Celine Goessl, SCSC

reconciliation. At another table sit those who have foolish pride in their hearts, and they vie for positions of prestige. Do you remember the picture of the sinner on her knees, weeping tears of gratitude, while the cold hearts of those gathered at table are passing judgment on her? Then there is the air of solemn quietness to provide time for listening, such as happened in the house of Mary of Bethany.

The life of prayer brings us to sit at every one of Luke's tables. Prayer can go on for long periods at a humdrum, unadorned table, where the faithful go through the motions but there is no exciting celebration. Sometimes our faithfulness seems to be stuck in a pattern of nothing glamorous, only a quiet faithfulness because we know that God sits at table with us.

Luke gives us a rich catechesis on faith today. We have an opportunity to think and pray about many aspects of our life and growth in faith as disciples of the Lord. Once more we experience ourselves in an upside-down world of Jesus as he calls us to be faithful disciples. We let the life of faith grow and mature in us.

Jesus, plant our faith ever deeper in our hearts.

Twenty-Eighth Sunday in Ordinary Time

Luke 17:11–19

Three distinct themes seem to emerge in today's Gospel. The first is that of a lone person who returns to Jesus after he is cured. He becomes a model of the faith that we talked about last week. All the lepers were remarkable people because they all had the courage to approach Jesus to beg for a cure, and they all had faith and hope. They all obeyed Jesus, even before their cure was visible.

The second theme includes the Samaritan. Because he was a foreigner, he would not be permitted to come to the priests in the Jewish temple. He would have been unwelcome and surely would have been thrown out. That is most probably why he left the others and turned back to Jesus in order to thank him for the gift of the clear and clean skin he experienced. The other nine went to the temple priests and then back to their families and most likely to their former businesses and way of life. It doesn't say so specifically, but I suspect the tenth never went back to his old way of life. Because he had a heart full of gratitude, he got the full benefit of healing in both body and soul. Jesus told him that his faith had saved him—not his skin but his entire being; not merely on the surface but in his heart and his mind.

The third theme is the disappointment of Jesus that he could not give the fullness of his gifts to the other nine. Only the Samaritan was given something better than a cure; he was given the assurance of eternal salvation. The original listeners were probably surprised by the fact that their stereotyped "foreigner" was held up as an example to them. Even today, we, who are removed from the dynamics of ancient prejudice, are taken aback. Is it because we still have prejudices that we need to overcome? Whom do we consider a foreigner today? On the news we are often confronted with those who risk everything in order to cross our borders and come into the United States, only to be shunned as they experience discrimination.

Celine Goessl, SCSC

It is a challenge for us to dig deeply into our hearts and to decide which of the lepers we would be. Would we be too busy with the new possibilities of a restored health and so we would forget to come back to our healer? The real test of our love for God flows from the ability to recognize the countless blessings God gives us every day. The more we thank God for these blessings, the more open we will be to receive greater blessings and, in the end, to be given the same eternal salvation that was afforded the lone Samaritan. Each night before we go to bed, let us think about the blessings of the day and give thanks to the One who deserves our praise.

Today, our faith has saved us.

Twenty-Ninth Sunday in Ordinary Time

Luke 18:1–8

Last week we began an instruction on the qualities of prayer. Today and next week, we will continue serious teachings on our prayer lives. We need to be grateful for this opportunity to look more deeply into our hearts and take account of how we pray and how it relates to the parables of Jesus. Especially in our culture, we have become so accustomed to instant results that this habit appears to spill over into our spiritual life as well.

When we look at the qualities of the poor widow, let us reflect on three **P's:** *perseverance*, *persistence*, and *patience*. Instead of becoming impatient with a delay to the response of the judge, this woman comes back day after day, week after week, until the unjust judge can barely sleep at night because she has pricked his conscience with her persistent request. She does not relent or turn away and go home when her voice is not heard. What a great model of patience she is for us!

We, on the other hand, are so accustomed to our fast pace of living that we have little tolerance for any delays to our requests. We have come to expect quick fixes for our problems and instant gratification for our needs. The three virtues mentioned above do not come easy for us. That is one reason why we must look to people in third-world countries with admiration. They have not been accustomed to instant gratification and so respond with more patience as they refrain from complaining. We need to change some of our habits and take time to let our sense of dependence on God grow to maturity. Each day we pray the Our Father several times. The petitions of that familiar prayer need to sink into our hearts so that instead of saying "Thy will be done" and then acting as though "My will be done as quickly as you can," we must listen more carefully to what Jesus is saying in the Gospel. He explains how prayer works and how prayer is heard.

Celine Goessl, SCSC

What would happen if we prayed persistently, perseveringly, and patiently for an end to the armaments race, the war in so many parts of our world, and the lack of real peace? Many people are praying, and the message given by Jesus is to continue that prayer because in his time, peace will return to our broken world. Let us take another look at the widow who wanted justice done as she returned many times to the judge. We sense how she filled the judge's mind with the injustice that she experienced. Every day she appeared to add a new reason for her request. She showed a new aspect of what she needed until the judge's mind was so saturated that he decided to give her what she wanted and deserved.

This does not mean that we consider God and the unjust judge on the same wavelength, but we hear this parable so that we can all look into our hearts and give an account of the three P's of prayer. The judge is finally motivated by his own convenience. How much more will our loving God be attentive to us? Then there is a final twist in the last sentence that makes sense: "When the Son of Man comes, will he find faith on earth?" That is a reflection for another day, but it reminds us that when we look at the quality of our prayer lives, without faith we cannot persevere, persist, or be patient.

Let perseverance, persistence, and patience
be part of our prayer lives.

Thirtieth Sunday in Ordinary Time

Luke 18:9–14

This is the final treatise in Jesus' triptych on prayer. We remember how he contrasted the nine insensitive men to the one foreigner who returned to thank him. Last week we thought about two contrasting figures—the widow and the unjust judge. This week we again meet two dissimilar figures—the religious leader, who kept all the laws perfectly, and the humble tax collector, who was thought to be an extortionist and a sinner.

Let us look at the Pharisee. He was a good, generous man, keeping the rules even beyond what the law required. His piety was outstanding, and his conduct was without fault. Somehow, he reminded me of Hyacinth on the TV show *Keeping Up Appearances* or even of myself when I become self-righteous. We can hardly do better than the Pharisee in self-conceit. Check the Gospel passage for today. He uses the word "I" five times in his prayer that contains only two sentences. He makes his prayer absurd with an exaggerated sense of his own worth.

On the other hand, we are attracted to the humility of the sinful tax collector. We immediately sense that his humble prayer touches the tender heart of God as he pronounces the few simple words, "Be merciful to me, a sinner!" His humility shows a beautiful attitude toward God, who gave the tax collector so many blessings. His prayer certainly touched God because of his honest conscience. This proves that our weaknesses more than our perfections bond us to God and to one another. People genuinely feel safe with those who can see themselves in a modest way, rather than those who send out the message that they are somewhat better than others.

This story today, my friends, is about us. It is about those who come to church faithfully every Sunday and perhaps also about those who do not come to church very often. We sometimes hear people say that they do not go to church because all the people there are hypocrites. So many go to church with pious faces, receive

Celine Goessl, SCSC

Communion devoutly, and then go out and live corrupt lives. The nonchurchgoers just do not want to join such phony imposters. This seems to imply that only very holy people should go to church—those who are good, fair, generous, and almost perfect in every way. Such people do not need God as much as sinners do. Some think the Pharisee definitely belonged in church because he lived up to the law. He could justly go right up to the altar and pray openly to God. But in the back of the church was a man who should not have gone to the church at all. He must have known where he belonged—way in the back, because he was not worthy to come to the altar.

Once again, Jesus' message today shocks us. He praises the sinner and condemns the saint. He exposes the bad heart beneath the perfect exterior that seemed to be directing his prayer to God but could not get beyond his exalted sense of self. On the other hand, we suspect that the tax collector never found religion easy to practice, but he met God in the honesty of his conscience and won approval from Jesus.

There is a bit of the Pharisee and the tax collector in each of us. How will we take this lesson to heart as we try to live this week, attempting to imitate the God who loves us unconditionally?

God, be merciful to us sinners.

Thirty-First Sunday in Ordinary Time

Luke 19:1–10

I usually take time for exegesis from several references, but this week I found a reflection from Joseph Donders that hit a nerve in my heart. I picked up this reflection from his notes and have taken his ideas and intertwined them with my experiences.

This story today makes me chuckle because like Zacchaeus, I am also small of stature, and I know how he must have felt. I can visualize him up in a tree, hidden away like a squirrel, watching everything going on down on the road as Jesus passed through the town. I believe he not only hid from view because he was small but primarily because he was not liked. He cheated the people in this Roman town by being their tax collector. He was a wealthy man, but money did not make him happy.

Zacchaeus heard that this stranger, Jesus, was coming through town, so he pulled out his ring of keys and began to lock up everything tightly—first his desk, then his safe. He closed the door of his office and locked it. Next he locked the front door of his house. By the time he left home, he had used a handful of keys because that was the only way he would feel secure. He was suspicious of any stranger. Money was the primary object of his life. As he walked down the street, he saw a tree that he could easily climb in order to observe this stranger, Jesus. He certainly didn't want to be among the crowd, jostled around by those who would try to touch Jesus. He didn't need some magical healing or conversion that others were seeking. He was just there to satisfy his curiosity.

How many of us resemble Zacchaeus, just sitting in church in order to observe, not wanting to be touched by Jesus because we feel safe just the way things are? Are we figuratively sitting in a tree, looking down but not really connected with the other people in church? If so, we might be one of those who looks down on others, thinking that church attendance should be more holy, thinking uncharitable thoughts about theologians who have said something that rubs us the wrong way, or wondering why bishops did not clamp down on their priests long ago. We might spend time in church thinking about what everyone else should or should not be doing. This is an attitude we might be tempted to take when we are not personally involved in ministry within our parish community. We can sit there and coldly observe, like Zacchaeus did in his tree. But it doesn't work!

We can imagine that Zacchaeus almost fell out of the tree when Jesus stopped and asked him to come down. His life had centered around money, so the first thing out of his mouth was to say he would give to the poor, restore anything he had stolen, and even give away half of his possessions. Jesus knew what Zacchaeus held in his heart, yet he simply asked him to come down and open himself up to new possibilities so he would no longer be tempted to restrict himself to being a mere observer.

That day, Zacchaeus and his family made a paradigm shift, and life took on new meaning and a different direction for his entire household. That is what we are called to do today. Let us be ready to follow the example of Zacchaeus by opening ourselves to new possibilities that will lead us deeper and deeper into the heart of Jesus.

Today we ask God to give our hearts a new direction.

Thirty-Second Sunday in Ordinary Time

Luke 20:27–38

Nature gives us the setting for our scripture reflection today. Daylight saving time has ended, and November darkness in our Northern Hemisphere draws our attention to the fact that another year is put to rest. It is also the end of the journey to Jerusalem for Jesus and an appropriate time to think about the end of earthly life for all of us some day. The main focus of the reading is to have us think about the meaning of life as we know it and the purpose of death as we believe it.

The Sadducees, a small but very wealthy group of arch-conservatives, are laughing up their broad sleeves, knowing that this time they will surely bring up a topic that will trap Jesus. They did not approach him with the "real" issue of not believing in the resurrection from the dead, but they went back to the book of Maccabees, using the law of Moses—that a woman whose husband died without producing children was passed on to the husband's brother. The question is about the absurdity of having seven brothers marry the woman and all of them dying. They asked which brother would be the woman's husband at the resurrection from the dead. They knew Jesus would never be able to answer that question, and indeed, he did not. He overlooked their absurdity by asking another question, using the ancestors that the Sadducees knew well—Abraham, Isaac, Jacob, and Moses. Did they think that God would overlook these good people and send them into oblivion at the end of their earthly lives or make them disappear into a cloud of nothingness?

Jesus answered their question in two ways:
1. He showed them how naïve they were in their understanding of resurrection. Eternal life is not a repeat of this life but a life that is transformed and does not include our earthly needs and wants.

Celine Goessl, SCSC

2. He shamed them because they were denying that God had the power to raise people from the dead. Our God is a God of the living, not of the dead. Death is the end of one journey and the beginning of another. We believe that dying is the only doorway into eternal life.

We proclaim our belief in resurrection in many instances in our Eucharist:
1. In the Creed
2. In the Eucharistic prayer, where numerous times there is mention of resurrection
3. In funeral liturgies having a strong emphasis on the fact that life is not ended but merely changed
4. In Christian scripture that so often speaks of resurrection

Two specific images appeal to us regarding life after death—the thought of being united with our relatives who have already died and the notion of returning to paradise. There has been enough research with those who have had near-death experiences that we have been able to sense a tiny glimpse of the beauty and peace that awaits us in eternity.

Let us spend some time this week reflecting on who we are and how we share God's life. We can put our trust in a beautiful life after death, where we will share God's life forever. Even here on earth, we can live each day, knowing that we already share a likeness to God.

Life will change, but it will never end.

Thirty-Third Sunday in Ordinary Time

Luke 21:5–19

Another year has slipped away, and we are asked today to set our thoughts on the end times. This is a perfect topic to accompany last week's reflection on life after death. The challenge this week is to put our lives in order because our readiness depends not on when the world will end for each of us individually or for all of us as we come to the final days of life on this earth, but on our readiness to meet God. This will depend on the way we have lived our lives day by day.

As Christians we cannot help but be affected by the times in which we live. Today's reading is difficult because it speaks so forcefully to our time. Today I will move from the television screen, where violence is so prevalent, to my computer screen, where I can reflect with you on the message Jesus brings us today. Every age has seen terror and ruin come and go, yet Jesus tells us the end is not yet here. So where do we look for some good news to support our faith? We cannot succumb to our throwaway culture, to fading relationships, or to a slithering market that necessitates the change of jobs three or four times over a lifetime. Even if this might not be an election year, the political climate often alternates and brings uncertainty. What about our beliefs that keep shifting with regard to what is important in life? A fundamentalist could look at all this chaos and proclaim the end times as an imminent reality. That is a futile reaction!

We turn to Jesus this week because he will teach us our true purpose in life. If we listen and follow him faithfully, whenever the end of time comes, we will be ready. Scripture says that there are three remaining things: "Faith, hope, and love, and the greatest of these is love." Whether it is the end of a year or of a lifetime, the only thing that we can assuredly take with us into eternity is the gift of love that we have been given so we can give it away.

People have always wanted to know about the events of the future. Is that not why so many place their hope in astrology? Jesus does not intend to give us a calendar of future events. His advice to us is to be constant in our faithfulness and live a life of grace each day as though it were the last day of our lives. It is far better for us to follow such a path than to keep searching for what the future might bring.

We need not fear, no matter how chaotic our times may seem to be. As long as we remain faithful to our baptismal covenants with God, we are on the right road to eternity. However, today it is time to take inventory of our lives. We will take time with God by doing the following:

1. Spend time in prayer.
2. Take leisure time with family and friends.
3. Be at ease and not overscheduled or overburdened.
4. Feed ourselves by breaking open God's word.

Today is the first day of the rest of our lives.

Feast of Christ the King

Luke 23:35–43

Contrary to Mel Gibson's *The Passion of the Christ* movie, Luke lessens the physical elements of the Crucifixion. It is evident from today's Gospel that he puts his emphasis on the reaction of the people who are gathered on Calvary. Let us look at four of these groups:

1. The people who stood by watching without becoming involved. Their hearts must have been crying out, but they remained silent.
2. The soldiers who mocked Jesus. As they offered him cheap wine, they taunted him by challenging him to come down and prove that he was a king.
3. The derision of the unfeeling criminal. He thinks only of himself and how he can gain release from the cruel death he is about to experience. He has no thought or concern for Jesus.
4. The other criminal. He certainly changes the mood on the hill as he chides his companion. Then he turns to Jesus with life-saving words, "Jesus, remember me when you come into your kingdom."

I must ask myself where I would be if I were standing on Calvary today. The contrast between Mel Gibson and Luke reminds me that faithfulness is not directed to symbols but to persons. At the end of another liturgical year, I need to ask myself what my relationship to Jesus entails. We are still fascinated with royalty. Children continue to read fairy tales; we give royal treatment to celebrities; we no longer have reigning kings and queens in our culture, but we still create them.

Jesus is our King, but his royalty comes at a tremendous price. He did not sit on a jeweled throne, but he hung on a cross. He did not wear a golden crown with gems but a crown of thorns. He had no armies at his command, but he was surrounded by a group of people

Celine Goessl, SCSC

who were powered by fear and who did not raise a voice to save him. Is this the summary of our faith?

Honoring Jesus as our King says we must make a commitment to work for a world where justice and peace will be given to all people. We need to roll up our sleeves and begin his work here on earth, knowing that he will be our guide. Next week we will enter the season of Advent, a season of waiting for this King to reign over us once again, but he cannot do this if we do not do our share of preparing for his reign. Every time we pray the Our Father this week, let us be especially mindful of the phrase, "Thy kingdom come, thy will be done," which calls us to do something in our personal lives that shows we mean what we pray.

Jesus, remember us when you come into your kingdom.

Special
Liturgical Celebrations
Cycles

A-B-C

I have chosen three special feast days as I reflect on my journey from life to death. Please take time to journey with me, bringing your own experiences of your faith life. Let this time of traveling through the church year be a rich experience for all of us who use *Breaking Open God's Word* to follow in the footsteps of Jesus and to prepare for eternity. Christmas speaks of the birth of Jesus. We can contemplate our own births as the beginning of our journeys through life with God. Ash Wednesday shows us steps we can take to redeem our sinful lives. The Feast of All Saints is the culmination of a journey when saints receive the reward of their earthly labors. We look forward to the day when God calls us home.

The Feast of Christmas

God quietly steals into the world
Wanting to share beauty and life
That was lost by the sins of our weakness
That turned creation back into chaos

Now is the time to re-sanctify creation
With the presence of God
Who stoops down to share love
Bringing a barren land back to its pristine beauty
By placing new life in our midst

Ash Wednesday

As we once more begin to replace life with death
God knew we needed another beginning
Relearning how we could become co-creators
By turning tarnished beauty into new life once more
We then walk for forty days with the baby, now grown.

A second chance to redeem ourselves
Time to ask for reconciliation
For the evils that we let creep into our hearts
We now need another re-sanctification

Celine Goessl, SCSC

Through prayer, almsgiving, and penance

Feast of All Saints

A lifetime spent asking for the gift of grace
To become like the Child given to us so long ago
So that we, like him, can come back to God
To enjoy the reward of our labors
Ready to return from whence we came

The final blessing of a grace-abundant life
God quietly stealing down to us once again
"Well done, good and faithful servant
Enter into the joy of eternal life"

The Feast of Christmas

John 1:1–18

Our Gospel today begins with a specific Semitic writing style as we read the genealogy of Jesus Christ, beginning with God the Father and continuing with John the precursor. Jesus was identified as the Son of God from the very beginning of the reading. God, faithful to the people living on earth, quietly came to the place where humans lived to bring a God-presence into the known world to the people who were lost through sin. This is the celebration of the event that brought God and humans together in a new relationship.

The people who should have been able to recognize Jesus had fallen away from grace, so God sent another human being to prepare the way and to show the women and men who belonged to the chosen flock how God's presence was still in their midst. Yet the chosen people did not acknowledge this man who grew up among them as one of their own. Yes, there were some who trusted Jesus and realized that he was the one who was to come as their Savior, but others, because of their blindness, let God's presence slip from their sight.

"The Word became flesh and dwelt among us." Light, once again, shone in our darkened world and angels, shepherds, and kings all followed the light that led them, in their simplicity or their royalty, to the humble barn where the Creator of light lay in a lowly manger. At the same time, renowned persons were blinded because of worldly concerns, so they did not recognize God in their midst.

Let us look into our own hearts to see if there is a reflection of Jesus to be found in us. Our gracious God has given us so many signs to show the life of the Father, the Son, and the Holy Spirit as the light that will bring us great joy and peace. Yet we seem to cling to the tinsel and worldly possessions so much that we do not have room in our hearts for the celebration of this special day. We need only to look at what is contained in our own family celebrations of Christmas. There will be the exchange of gifts and the affection shown to one

Celine Goessl, SCSC

another as we gather, but do not let these things be the core of why we gather. God came to earth thousands of years ago, but God comes again each year; in fact, each day! We are convinced of this because we have learned to see Jesus in one another as we enjoy special gifts, food, and entertainment today.

Turn back to the explanation of my life journey at the beginning of this section on Special Liturgical Celebrations, and read the two top stanzas of the poem. They were written in the spirit of Christmas, and they are meant to be a quiet reflection on the reason for this day. The world was dying but has come back to life because light has returned to the darkness. God has stooped down to share love with us in the form of a child. As you come to the end of this day, after all the guests have returned to their homes, sit down in the quietness of your home and let Jesus fill your heart with the greatest gifts that you could possibly receive. Pass those gifts on to your family, your neighbors, your acquaintances at work, or those you will meet this week. Continue to spread the joy of Christmas for the entire season, and remember—Christmas does not end tonight at midnight!

All the ends of the earth have seen the power of God.

Ash Wednesday

2 Corinthians 5:20–6:2

Let us return in spirit to the early days of the church when the Christian community was still filled with zeal and the innocence of fresh faith. It was a wonderful time in our history but unfortunately, it was short-lived. Already in the letter that Paul wrote to the community at Corinth, we read about conflicts, misunderstandings, and harsh judgments of the people. In such a short time, there was already a great need for reconciliation. It is strange to realize why people were not crying out for forgiveness and reconciliation, but it was God who pursued them with an appeal to be reconciled. God took the initiative to bring people back into the joy and peace of community life. In the scripture today, we read, "Now is the acceptable time; now is the day of salvation." Paul writes with a sense of urgency because it is time—or even past time—for people to give up their differences and become reconciled to God and one another.

The beginning of the season of Lent reminds us that we must focus on the need for prayer, fasting, and almsgiving. This has been a familiar Lenten practice for as long as we can remember. When we were young, it usually meant that we needed to give up something that we really wanted. However, there has been a paradigm shift in theology since that time, and now Lent has a new twist. Today we need to think about how we can change our hearts and become more Christ-like in our relationships with one another.

Prayer has always been part of our everyday faith life. We grew up learning a great number of rote prayers. Now there has been a shift to a more spontaneous prayer style. We can learn some fine habits from our Protestant friends, who seem to engage in spontaneous prayer with great ease. Rote prayer certainly has its place in our lives, but there are times when we must learn to have a conversation with God very much like what we would have with a good friend. We can tell Jesus what we hold in our hearts. He already knows, but it is necessary for us to deepen our familiarity with God by using new

Celine Goessl, SCSC

and enriching words that come from our hearts, filter through our minds, and come out of our mouths.

Fasting today has also taken a different form. We used to have strict laws of fasting, especially during Lent, when we spent forty days having only one full meal a day. There are other ways that we are encouraged to fast. It could be just as "holy" to watch less television, or to curb our tongues by not gossiping, or to speak only kind words about those whom we do not love as we ought. It is still good to curb our appetites in order to give more to the poor from the money that we save by not buying so much for ourselves.

Almsgiving is a good way of sharing our money, but if there are clothes in our closets that we haven't worn in many months, we might think of packing up some things to take to St. Vincent de Paul outlet stores. How about volunteering at a homeless shelter or a food pantry?

The text in today's liturgy seems to be more concerned with what is in our hearts than with what we might give up. Ash Wednesday is a good day to begin cleaning out what is not necessary in our homes and in our hearts. Scripture says, "Where your treasure is, there your heart will be." Time, talent, and treasure are core values that we are called to share.

God gives us the chance to make a paradigm shift.

The Solemnity of All Saints

Luke 6:30–31

Today we will reflect on the beatitudes according to Luke, who encourages us to become saints. He begins with four invitational beatitudes:
1. Give generously to the poor.
2. Share food with those who are starving.
3. Comfort those who are sad.
4. Remove any kind of hatred from your heart.

Jesus dealt directly with the contemporaries of his own time and teaches us to do the same. He reminds us that suffering in this life will gain us an eternal reward if we are patient and compassionate. Physical poverty teaches us to trust in God, who knows our needs and will be with us in our difficulties. When we are helping the hungry, let it remind us that we have spiritual hungers that the Holy Spirit can satisfy. When we encounter sadness, we know with certainty that Jesus will be there to comfort us. Hatred is always sinful, but we can use such an emotion to mellow our hearts and prepare ourselves for the joys of heaven. God is with us to share blessings when we think of others before we take care of our own needs and wants. We are not blessed because we experience difficulty in life. Blessings can lead us to follow Jesus more faithfully so we can anticipate the wonderful gifts of life with God in eternity.

We are reminded that the four statements of being blessed by God are followed by four woes that caution us—in particular, those who are rich, superficially happy, feasting sumptuously every day, and have many friends who think well of them primarily because of their position, beauty, and so forth. Woes should be able to teach us to accept what God asks of us as we are called to change our wayward lives. These verses of scripture tell us to become countercultural if we hope to be numbered with the saints for all eternity.

Celine Goessl, SCSC

Jesus was very radical in his preaching and his actions, especially when he showed that his mission was to the poor and downtrodden.

1. The rich who are not willing to share their wealth have already received their reward. Jesus told us that people who are truly wise are able to view hunger in more ways than merely feeling hunger pangs; they will be more concerned about their spiritual hunger.

2. Those who appear to be overjoyed in life might find sadness waiting for them beyond the grave.

3. Those who are accustomed to living from one worldly pleasure to the next will be blinded because of their lack of concern for other people during their lifetimes.

There might be moments in our lives when we feel a certain amount of sadness because of all the misery that enters our lives on earth. If that is our experience, we will be given grace to trust that God will show us unconditional love, right up to the moment we draw our last breath. Let us reflect on the demands of love that God asks of us this week. Remember the Golden Rule that we read at the end of today's scripture: "Treat others as you would like them to treat you."

Our reward will be great in the next life.

Conclusion

The liturgical church year is filled with the richness of grace, when we take time to contemplate the mysteries that lie hidden in the pages of scripture. May God be with you as you follow Jesus in the journey of faith by breaking open God's word. I pray that each of you will be a more faithful follower of Jesus as you create your own path in the depths of your heart. I hope you will be inspired to take time to write your own book, using all the gifts that God has given you.

Be ready for Jesus to change your heart and point out a more beautiful direction for your journey as you continue breaking open God's word, and let it cleanse your heart and wash over your being each week. You can tell Jesus what you hold in your heart and prepare to bring with you a fitting gift to give to God at the time of the presentation of gifts at each liturgical celebration. Let this spiritual gift take priority over any monetary gift you also might bring as your offering.

I promise to accompany you in prayer as you use this book of reflections to deepen your own spiritual life. Think about how your life's journey has enriched you as you walk through these pages and draw yourself closer to Jesus. Blessings on you! Walk steadfastly all the days of your life so you will deepen your love of God, who enables you to walk into eternal life, knowing that you already met God each week. This is my fervent prayer for you as together, we, the body of Christ, deepen our relationship with God and with one another.

Sister Celine Goessl, SCSC

CPSIA information can be obtained at www.ICGtesting.com
Printed in the USA
LVOW06s0747140815

450028LV00001B/1/P